With love and great appreciation to my wife Pamela for her support and countless hours of typing and proofreading of the manuscript. To my daughter Cheyenne, the greatest gift God could have ever given me. And to my parents for their unending love and support, which has kept my ship afloat during many a rough storm.

Lastly, to all the men interviewed for this book and their families, who have enriched my life far beyond the mere writing of words on paper.

THOSE PULLMAN BLUES

An Oral History of the African American Railroad Attendant

DAVID D. PERATA

THOSE PULLMAN BLUES

An Oral History of the African American Railroad Attendant

MADISON BOOKS
Lanham • New York • Oxford

MADISON BOOKS

Published in the United States of America
by Madison Books
4720 Boston Way, Lanham, Maryland 20706

12 Hid's Copse Road
Cumnor Hill, Oxford OX2 9JJ, England

**The Twayne Publishers edition of this book was previously catalogued by the
Library of Congress as follows:**

Perata, David A.
   Those Pullman blues : an oral history of the African-American railroad
attendant / David D. Perata.
      p.   cm. — (Twayne's oral history series; no. 22)
   Includes bibliographical references and index.
   1. Pullman porters—Interviews.   2. Afro-American train
attendants—Interviews.   3. Pullman Company—History.   I. Title.
II. Series.
   HD8039.R36P47   1996
   331.7'6138522'0973—dc20   96-11492
                                                            CIP

ISBN 1-56833-124-X (pbk.: alk. paper)

∞ ™ The paper used in this publication meets the minimum
requirements of American National Standard for Information
Sciences—Permanence of Paper for Printed Library Materials, ANSI/
NISO Z39.48–1992.

Printed in the United States of America

Contents

The crew of the Rexall Special including George Smock (left of engine, third from top; see chapter 1) and James Steele (front row, far left; see chapter 4).

Foreword

In both the romance and necessity of long-distance travel, the Pullman car holds a special place in our national memory and imagination. It was the mainstay of the American transportation system from the Civil War through the advent of jet airplanes. During those years the Pullman car porter and railroad attendant similarly became fixtures in American life. The Pullman Company hired African American men almost exclusively as porters and other service workers, seeing them as inexpensive, pliable labor. Yet labor conditions spurred Pullman workers to risk their jobs by organizing the Brotherhood of Sleeping Car Porters under the dynamic leadership of A. Philip Randolph. This oral history examines both the company and the union, but its true focus is the railroad porters and attendants. Through their interviews they offer observations about the changing conditions of their work, their mostly white passengers, and the racial stereotyping and prejudice that they endured throughout the "Golden Age" of rail transportation.

Oral history may well be the twentieth century's substitute for the written memoir. In exchange for the immediacy of diaries or correspondence, the retrospective interview offers a dialogue between the participant and the informed interviewer. Having prepared sufficient preliminary research, interviewers can direct the discussion into areas long since "forgotten," or no longer considered of consequence. "I haven't thought about that in years" is a common response, uttered just before an interviewee commences with a surprisingly detailed description of some past incident. The quality of the interview, its candidness and depth, generally will depend as much upon the interviewer as the interviewee, and the confidence and rapport between the two adds a special dimension to the spoken memoir.

Interviewers represent a variety of disciplines and work either as part of a collective effort or individually. Regardless of their different interests or the variety of their subjects, all interviewers share a common imperative: to collect memories while they are still available. Most oral historians feel an additional responsibility to make their interviews accessible for use beyond their own research needs. Still, important collections of vital, vibrant interviews lie scattered in archives throughout every state, undiscovered or simply not used.

Twayne's Oral History Series seeks to identify those resources and to publish selections of the best materials. The series lets people speak for themselves, from their own unique perspectives on people, places, and events. But to be more than a babble of voices, each volume organizes its interviews around particular situations and events and ties them together with interpretive essays that place individuals into a larger historical context. The styles and format of individual volumes vary with the material from which they are drawn, demonstrating again the diversity of oral history and its methodology.

Whenever oral historians gather in conference, they enjoy retelling experiences about the inspiring individuals they have met, the unexpected information they have elicited, and the unforgettable reminiscences that would otherwise have never been recorded. The result invariably reminds listeners of others who deserve to be interviewed, provides them with models of interviewing techniques, and inspires them to make their own contribution to the field. I trust that the oral historians in this series—as interviewers, editors, and interpreters—will have a similar effect on their readers.

DONALD A. RITCHIE
Series Editor, Senate Historical Office

Southern Pacific Lark skirting San Francisco Bay.

Preface

As a young boy in the late 1950s and early 1960s, I often had the opportunity to ride passenger trains of the Southern Pacific Railroad. There I met a group of individuals I'd never seen before in my predominantly white, middle-class environment. The Pullman and chair car porters, lounge bartenders, dining car chefs, and waiters all had one characteristic in common: they were black.

From the beginning, I sensed something unique about these gentlemen. It was an innocent attraction, no doubt greatly influenced by the television programming of that decade; old Shirley Temple movies with Bill "Bojangles" Robinson, vintage Abbott and Costello, Amos and Andy, along with many other shows that depicted black characters. All these shows perpetuated the stereotyped image of the black male as marginally intelligent and always singing or dancing. As a kid, I soaked it all up and filed it away.

When I later accompanied my parents on several train trips and saw that all the employees—with the exception of the conductors and dining car stewards—were black, I had already formed a mental image of African Americans. But the thought never really entered my mind that these railroad men were anything other than porters and waiters who just happened to be black. I accepted the situation for what it was, as kids are apt to do, but I had no inkling as to why it was so.

One idea, however, was for certain. Black people seemed to be sincerely warm and generous, and riding the train was the perfect place for a kid to get to know them firsthand. And I did. I still have an old telephone pocket book with the name and address of Fred Montgomery, a Southern Pacific lounge car attendant, entered in it in his own writing. From the chair car porter to the waiters in the dining car, the black railroad attendants seemed to appreciate the innocence of children who had yet to be influenced by the prejudices of their parents. Over the years, I gained a genuine affection and respect for these men and their craft. Jewel Brown, a former Pullman porter and Brotherhood of Sleeping Car Porters representative, perfectly summarized the experience: "This is what made those great trains and railroads

---

great—the type of service that was rendered by these Negro employees aboard. The train itself was just a cold piece of steel."[1]

As much as I loved watching those trains with my dad at track side, it was an altogether different experience on the inside. The railroad passenger car workers transformed these "cold pieces of steel" into a warm, inviting atmosphere and did more than simply provide a service: in their hands, passenger cars were a kind of theater, orchestrated by the railroads and sold to a willing audience. The car builders could decorate the trains to evoke any atmosphere they desired, but it was the African American men who worked these cars who brought them to life.

Many years later, while working for Amtrak as a porter on long-distance passenger trains in the early 1980s, I met up with these men once again as they rolled out their final miles before retirement. Some nights, when the hour was late and the dining car had been put away and cleared of passengers, they would sprawl out at the empty tables, swapping stories about the "good old days" and about what it once meant to take pride in their jobs. You could see in their faces the experience of every mile they ever traveled on the railroad. For the first time since my youth, I had that same feeling I used to get aboard those Southern Pacific trains.

My childhood curiosity about the African American passenger car workers was rekindled. I realized that once these men had retired and passed on, their story would go with them—a story, going back 100 years, of working on America's passenger trains amidst a climate of severe racial prejudice. I wondered what it had been like for them, how they had coped with discrimination, and how they felt about their jobs and white society.

The majority of railroad books have been romanticized treatments focusing on the physical equipment rather than on the people who worked them. The African American contribution to these trains is either totally ignored or mentioned in passing. The purpose of this oral history is to preserve the testimony of the rail attendants I interviewed about the difficult times and working environments of their lives. This is not a study of all African American train workers. The focus is on the individuals interviewed: African American men who were drawn to the railroad in different ways but who remained on the railroad in spite of hardships unique to their race. Their stories chronicle not only the elegance of rail travel during the "golden era" of passenger trains in the United States but also the stark realities of being an African American worker on white railroads.

Introduction

When Abraham Lincoln issued the Emancipation Proclamation Act in 1863, the United States had made little provision for the future employment of the freed slaves. As a result, former slaves who left the plantations found few opportunities other than those to which they had become accustomed: manual labor in the fields and factories or domestic positions as cleaners, cooks, and servants. The newfound wealth generated by the Industrial Revolution increased the availability of such jobs, but the choices available to the African American would remain unchanged for decades.

The railroad sleeping car was being developed at this same time and, within a few short years, would provide the free African American male—and to a lesser extent the free African American female—with new employment opportunities. The organization that pioneered this innovation and that would employ almost exclusively African Americans for nearly a century was the Pullman Sleeping Car Company.

George M. Pullman, the man who would change the course of railroad and labor history forever, was born in 1831. He began life as a poor farm boy whose only skill related to car building he had learned while employed at his brother's woodworking shop in New York State. Pullman acquired his first taste of wealth and prosperity at the age of 22, when he acquired a contractor's license and began moving houses for the Erie Canal Project, then under way in New York.[1] It was at this time that George Pullman had occasion to travel on what then passed for a sleeping car. His inability to sleep, (no sheets, blankets, or pillows were provided), fully clothed on a hard bunk sparked his idea of providing a better arrangement for the traveler.[2]

By 1858 he had made good on his plan, joining forces in New York with Benjamin C. Field, who held the patent rights to the Woodruff sleeping car. The Woodruff Company was one of a handful of eastern firms engaged in building and operating sleeping cars, a novel idea during a time when the function of the railroad was evolving beyond that of providing only simple locomotion and crude accommodations for passengers and freight. Pullman and Field began operating sleepers on the Chicago and Alton Railroad in 1858. These early cars amounted to no more than remodeled coaches outfitted with bunks. One of these cars was the now infamous Number 9, which made its maiden run in September 1859 and has been credited as George Pullman's first sleeping car.[3]

By 1863 Pullman could foresee the completion of a transcontinental railroad and the enormous potential for sleeping car routes it would represent. He began in earnest to acquire as many sleeping car contracts out of Chicago as possible, even buying up entire companies whenever the opportunity arose. But it did not take Pullman long to also figure out that if new markets were to be tapped on the scale he envisioned, sleeping cars would have to be refined to encourage general ridership. He decided to build his own cars from the ground up rather than relying on rebuilt day coaches or equipment manufactured by other firms. In 1864, using a small building on the Chicago and Alton property as his workshop, Pullman assembled the finest carpenters, pipefitters, varnishers, upholsterers, and other tradesmen the Chicago area had to offer. He then personally supervised the construction of his first major breakthrough in sleeping car design: the Pioneer.[4]

The Pioneer was constructed in 1865 for $20,000, at a time when the average coach sold for about $4,500.[5] The additional cost was largely due to its lavish interior decoration. Although previous sleepers were equally gaudy, the Pioneer rose to historical prominence in part because it was Pullman's first car built at his own plant.[6] In addition, railroads of this era had not yet set dimensional standards for passenger cars. George Pullman's Pioneer, built by his own standards, was taller and wider than the conventional car of the period.[7]

Had it not been for an uncanny stroke of fate, the Pioneer might have gone the way of a grand mechanical orphan, useless for interchange over rail lines with limited clearances. After the assassination of Abraham Lincoln on 14 April 1865, transportation was needed to carry his body and the funeral party from Washington, D.C., to Springfield, Illinois. It has been reported that the Pioneer was included in the Lincoln funeral train and that platforms and bridges all along the train's route had to be altered to accommodate its oversize dimensions. It is estimated that this single event, which gave George Pullman valuable publicity for the vast operational empire that would follow, shaved 50 years off the time it would otherwise have taken the railroads to make these changes.[8]

With the completion of the transcontinental railroad in 1869, the Pullman Palace Car Company—the new company name—extended its route miles into every major city and many small towns across America. By the end of 1881 the organization's earnings were estimated at nearly $3 million, and it had more than 800 cars in operation across the United States and Canada.[9]

For all the accolades and nostalgia that have surrounded George Pullman and the Pullman Company over the years, it must be recognized for what it really was: a finely tuned, big-money operation more interested in profits than in employees. The company's philosophy adhered to the strange dichotomy of values held by its founder. George Pullman was a deeply religious man who, on the one hand, was the morally forthright, benevolent patriarch who built a 3,600-acre Utopian-like town for his 12,000 employees at Lake Calumet, Illinois. Appropriately named Pullman, the town had its own churches, schools, mercantile stores, post office, library, and erecting shops for the building and maintenance of sleeping cars.[10] On the other hand, George Pullman was a shrewd businessman with an insatiable appetite for control and power: he paid his employees poor wages while controlling their income, rent, commercial trade, and social lives. His attitude toward the African American working class was no less parochial: keep the black man doing what he has always done, and pay him as little as possible to do it.

These practices eventually burst the idealistic bubble over the company town of Pullman. Workers often lived in poverty through the company's manipulation of both their income and living environment; the ensuing tension erupted into the Great Pullman Strike of 1894. Led by the labor activist Eugene V. Debs, this strike was the first attempt to organize all shop crafts associated with the railroads and the Pullman Palace Car Company. Pullman, however, refused to reorganize the newly formed American Railway Union, and in the end 12 people were killed as federal troops attempted to break up the strike.[11] The Pullman Palace Car Company's unwillingness to negotiate with its labor force would become the company's hallmark for years.

After George Pullman's death in 1897, the company was reorganized in 1900 under a new corporate title, the Pullman Company. Rail traffic between 1900 and 1910 tripled; the year 1913 saw rail profits of more than $19 million.[12] The Pullman Company reached its peak in the 1920s when 35 million passengers per year slept between Pullman sheets, and the company became the largest single U.S. employer of African Americans, with over 9,000 porters.[13]

Given George Pullman's attitude toward the African American and toward labor as a whole, it should come as no surprise that the labor pool from which he hired service personnel for the new Palace sleeping cars in 1870 was the ready-made work force of recently freed slaves.[14] There were no special job requirements beyond the domestic skills to which so many African Americans had been confined. For many, becoming a Pullman sleeping car attendant was simply a transfer from the plantation to the railroad. Indeed, whether Pullman fully realized the implications of his actions or not, he in effect sentenced thousands of African Americans to another 100 years of servility aboard the nation's railroad cars. The railroads not only had access to a constant supply of employees but conveniently retained the plantation racial infrastructure, redefined in a manner now acceptable to the general public.

The Pullman sleeping car brought African American "servants" into almost every American town through the vast system of railroad passenger trains. For the price of a Pullman ticket, even a common man could be waited upon and pampered in the grand manner of the privileged southern gentry. White America's willingness to preserve antebellum attitudes provided George Pullman with a ready market for his services. The rail's going public may not have consciously demanded white tablecloths, fine china, sparkling silver, and black servants, but they easily became accustomed to such amenities through Pullman's adaptation of plantation hospitality.

In 1924 the Ku Klux Klan boasted nearly four and a half million members; over 1,000 Negro lynchings had taken place since 1900. "By being raised up in a segregated environment," recalled Julius Payne, a longtime Pullman employee, "you knew [racial discrimination] was going on. You resented it, but you could not change it individually. All you could do is get yourself in a lot of problems. The easy way to deal with it was to stand your ground to a certain level and gracefully get away from it."[15]

Like Julius Payne, successful black employees developed certain psychological skills to help them handle abusive passengers so as to diffuse explosive situations before they escalated into threats of violence. In doing so, however, they were forced to swallow their pride for the sake of their job. Those who reacted emotionally were usually fired.

Norman Bookman, another seasoned Pullman veteran who worked every class of service from sleepers to private cars, offered an example of such restraint:

> One time a man was riding with us on the Lark. He was talking and they were discussing politics, and they were saying, "Well, there's so many niggers in San Francisco and so many niggers in L.A.," and so on. The woman with him looked up at me—I didn't say anything. I'd fixed them a little hors d'oeuvres, you know. So I didn't say anything till the next morning.
>
> [The train] came in, and she was with him. They were not together. And I said, "Pardon me, I'd like to ask a question if I may. What did I do wrong last night? I've been up all night wondering what was done wrong. I thought I was giving fair service."
>
> Then he started apologizing for having made the mistake in saying those words, and he wanted to give me a little piece of change for it. I said, "Oh, no, you don't owe me nothing."
>
> But now, you see, I could have put it another way or jumped in that night. They're all drinking, and it could have been an embarrassing thing, or he could have gotten angry, or maybe I got angry and cussed him out, or something else. So you learn how to handle these things this way.[16]

Even though the Pullman porter was a national figure and entrusted with generations of young and old alike, the unenlightened traveling public still regarded the Negro as having his proper place both on and off the trains. He was socially acceptable in his working environment, owing to his servant status, but that acceptance did not often carry over into civilian life once he stepped down from the steel vestibule. For example, many women thought nothing of undressing in front of the porter, almost as if he were invisible. It is doubtful that a white woman would have ever undressed with a white hotel bellboy present. Thousands of mothers entrusted their children to the porter's care while they went off to socialize in the club car or eat in the diner. How many mothers today would do the same? By contrast, relations between black porters and male passengers were sometimes not so trusting. Most of the confrontations between black train personnel and white male passengers were fueled by the latter's excess liquor consumption in the club car. In Pullman Company advertising of the era, the body English between the porter and his white male passenger always suggested dominance by the passenger.

The Pullman Company capitalized on the folkloric images of the maternal Negro mammy and the docile black servant to establish the porter as an extension of the notorious plantation hospitality of an earlier era.

The African Americans who worked on passenger trains were employed by either the Pullman Company or the individual railroads. According to a report by the Department of Labor in 1926—in what is generally regarded as the peak decade for the railroads—20,224 African Americans worked as Pullman and train porters, the largest category of black labor on U.S. railroads. The Pullman Company had sole control of the thousands of its employees who provided the sleeping and café/buffet car service offered on every railroad in the nation, whereas each railroad handled a much smaller personnel roster confined to commissary points along its own lines.

Railroad on-board service employees who did not work for the Pullman Company included coach and parlor porters, cooks, chefs, bartenders, and dining car waiters. Only the chefs and cooks, who were fairly well insulated from the traveling public because the kitchen was off-limits to all but the dining car crew, seldom experienced racial discrimination while working aboard the trains. But as one black chef observed, passengers ate food prepared by black hands, who would have otherwise refused to shake that same black hand off the train.

The coaches did not require the porters to experience as much intimacy with passengers as did the sleepers, which by their very nature exposed porters to most every facet of the human condition, good and bad. Although a coach full of children or complaining adults could prove challenging, for some porters the chair cars were far less stressful than the sleepers.

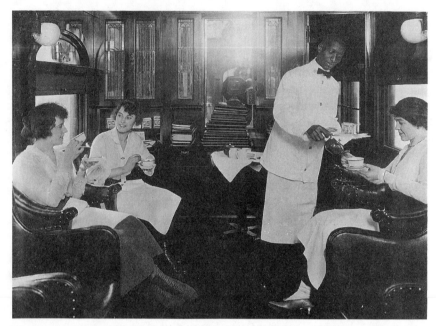

Women being served tea in the Great Northern Oriental Limited observation-lounge car prior to the 1924 re-equipping of train. St. Croix Historical Review.

A railroad dining car on the crack trains was like a restaurant open all day, serving breakfast, lunch, and dinner; on a train with 500 people aboard, each meal often ran right into the next. Southern Pacific waiter Alex Ashley describes the dining car crew's life on the railroad's new streamliner, the Shasta Daylight, in the early fifties. After departing from Oakland's 16th Street station at 8:22 A.M., the train arrived in Portland, Oregon, nearly 16 hours later:

> We started seating in 16th [Street] Station—train loaded—and you know, I didn't sit down till I got to Portland? That's facts. *Didn't sit down!* We pulled into Portland that night—people still at the tables eatin'. Didn't have time to eat, just grab us something and started walkin'. You get into Portland around eleven o'clock at night. You get over to the hotel around twelve o'clock. You get to bed—look like before you get to sleep good, they're waking you up five o'clock in the morning to get back on this train, see. No, you could never get a good full night's sleep.[17]

The Pullman porter was undoubtedly the most universally recognized of the African American employees who worked aboard America's passenger trains. The quintessence of the Pullman Company's vast operation, he repre-

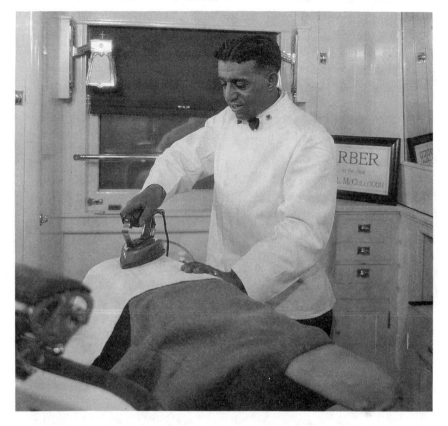

Pressing suits provided extra income for porters and attendants. St. Croix Historical Review.

sented the basic building block around which the entire premise of first-class accommodations revolved. On the thousands of rolling hotels that operated each day for the company, the porter served as innkeeper, maid, waiter, bellman, electrician, and entertainer, all embodied behind one compulsorily smiling face.

There were four classifications for Pullman onboard personnel: busboy, sleeping car porter, café/food service attendant, and private car porter. All four types of positions required bed-making skills, an ability to handle the public, and a working knowledge of the assortment of air-conditioning systems and car types that Pullman operated. Cooking classes were mandatory for those entering food service.

The Pullman busboy worked on the buffet and café cars that ran either as a supplement to railroad-owned and -staffed dining cars or as the sole source

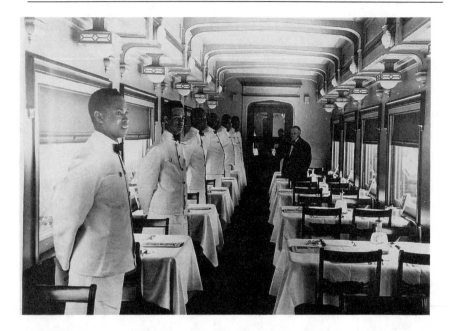

Waiters at attention with steward in Baltimore & Ohio dining car in the 1920s.
B & O Historical Society

Bar attendant mixes a cocktail aboard Art Deco Missouri Pacific lounge car.
Union Pacific Railroad

A 1940s Pullman ad featuring Kate Smith.

of meals on smaller runs. He was given the basic sleeping car porter training in addition to training in food handling. The title "busboy" is somewhat of a misnomer, for he also waited on tables and reset them.

The sleeping-car porter attended only to the sleeping car and associated duties. He set up the car while in the yards, greeted passengers, and settled them into their rooms, making sure that their every need was taken care of while they were on board. He was also responsible for monitoring the cars' air-conditioning and heating systems, making the beds and cleaning the rooms, shining shoes, pressing suits, mailing letters and telegrams, and bringing meals into rooms on request. Of all the employees on the train, his psychological skills were perhaps the most highly developed, owing to the extreme intimacy of the Pullman car.

The café/food service attendant was instructed in very much the same manner as the busboy but was also taught to prepare meals. He often doubled as the porter in those cars that contained rooms as well as a buffet section.

The private car porter, the cream of the Pullman men, worked on special cars and assignments, such as serving presidents, visiting dignitaries, entertainers, charter groups, and the like. The Pullman Company handpicked private car porters, usually veterans with years of service, for their exceptional expertise in all phases of Pullman operations.

Rendering service, reinforced by proper etiquette and decorum, was at the core of the Pullman philosophy. It is this dedication to service, with pomp and circumstance, for which the Pullman porter is still remembered. The cars themselves were designed with service in mind. Each room contained porter call buttons, individual room temperature controls, electric fans, shoe lockers for the porter's traditional nightly task, and numerous other amenities. It was the porter, of course, who was expected to make sure all these systems ran smoothly.

To ensure that porters adhered to a uniform standard of service, the Pullman Company devised a mind-boggling array of rules and regulations on everything from how many inches to fold back a bedsheet to the proper way to pour a bottle of beer. Norman Bookman underscored Pullman's strict adherence to its 127-page manual: "They wanted you to do it like they wanted it, and they didn't force it on you. Whatever was done—whatever instruction was given—they would go over it again and again. And when you said, 'Okay, I understand it,' you signed that you understood certain things. There was no way you could go and say, 'I didn't understand that.' You signed it!"[18]

The making of a Pullman porter was a gradual process; few young black men came off the street with sufficient polish and poise to work on the Pullman cars. Young men of good stature and with a clean-cut appearance were picked for the extensive training program. Each man's background was thoroughly checked, even to the extent of asking questions about him in his community, such as, "Does he have any bad habits?" or "Is he a big drinker?"

Once the applicant passed the initial test, he underwent a 14-day instruction period in the yards that covered all the fundamentals of the Pullman operation. Then, he received further training, depending on the job category to which he was assigned.

Norman Bookman recalled his advanced classes:

> If you were an attendant, you had to take cooking and bar courses. Now, we used to have a head chef out of Chicago. He would take a steak, and this is all he would do the whole period of time—he would determine which is the best place to puncture a steak, where not to puncture a steak, and so on. And he would give you reasons after it was over. He could take your pastry and crumble it like that and tell you where you've done wrong. But we'd go through whole classes without anybody saying one word until it was over. Then we'd say, "The waiter leaned in too close, his coat would probably drag in his soup," or something else, and all of the operations were really thorough.[19]

After such classes were completed, the new porter was sent on a student trip with at least two veteran porters. These were most often short overnight runs to put theory into practice with actual passengers. During his first six months, the new porter was on probation, and only after that time was a decision made as to his suitability. Once fully hired, the new porter was sent out on the road on his own, largely left alone to acclimate himself to the job.

The relationship between the Pullman conductor and the porters was similar to the old plantation relationship between the overseer and the slaves: a white man was a sole authority figure over a predominantly black crew. In fact, some white conductors openly referred to the porters as "their boys" and could be extremely possessive of and protective toward them when confronted by outsiders.[20]

There were actually two conductors on most passenger trains: the railroad conductor and the Pullman conductor. The railroad conductor, the supreme authority on the train, controlled all train movements, oversaw ticket collecting in railroad-owned cars, and handled problems with passengers. Directly under him was the Pullman conductor, who was in charge of all Pullman employees and the passengers in the buffet, café, and sleeping cars. The Pullman conductor's jurisdiction was limited to Pullman-operated equipment. The Pullman conductor on his own had the power to bring the terminal superintendent into any disciplinary actions against Pullman employees. Such power over mostly black employees invited discrimination and trouble. Although the conductors were a benevolent lot as long as the black crews towed the line, the fact remained that authority was always white, resulting in many abuses of power.

For instance, "The trainman could say he didn't like who the porter was, and he would be called in about that," according to Jewel Brown. "The conductor said, 'I don't want him in my crew. He's a little darker than the rest of 'em. I want another one a little lighter than him.' The superintendent's wife, I've known her to do such things as that. 'Why don't you get him out and put another one in there and make 'em all the same color?' Those were the types of things that were perpetrated on the employees because they had no redress."[21]

Inspectors and spotters were the other nemeses of all-black train crews. Arriving on trains unannounced, it was impossible to tell who they were unless a particular inspector was widely known to the train crews. The inspector was a company official who boarded the train at any point along the line to ensure that standards and rules were being observed. Inspectors had a great deal of power over employees, and like some conductors, some inspectors certainly used their position to vent personal prejudices. The spotters were paid civilians who spied on the train crew and reported on their behavior. Pullman Company spotters were allowed to set up situations to trap a porter. Many were of a sexual nature: female spotters, for example, would attempt to lure unsuspecting porters into their drawing room. Other traps were designed to catch an employee suspected of stealing money or supplies.

Pullman porters were subject to a merit/demerit system, with marks going on their permanent record. Merits could be issued for passenger letters of praise, good manners, or cleanliness. Demerits were issued for acts as inconsequential as stepping on a seat cushion to make an upper berth. Whether or not such violations were officially noted largely depended on the personality of the inspector.

The 1920s were banner years for the Pullman Company, and it was no coincidence that its black employees were tired of the tyrannical working environment and ready to organize. C. L. Dellums, a Pullman porter and Fourth International vice president of the Brotherhood of Sleeping Car Porters, recalled that,

> When I went to work for the Pullman Company in January 1924, they paid $60 a month. If you worked all the calendar month, you might get $60, but the odds were 10 to 1 that you'd never get $60 while you were a young porter. Now, once you were there long enough to have enough seniority to hold a regular run, as long as you didn't miss a trip during that calendar month, you'd get your $60. But the runs were not regulated. The company set up their runs the way they wanted to set them up. Let's say one porter might have a regular run from Oakland to Seattle. You'd total up the number

of hours that he was actually on duty in an ordinary 30-day month, and he might work 300 hours. Then there might be another porter working right out of the same place, let's say running to Chicago, and he might work 350 hours. Both of them would get the same $60.[22]

Those porters without enough seniority to hold a regular run were on the "extra board": being on call at any time of the day or night to report for a run. The older men with years of service were at the top of the seniority roster and therefore commanded the best runs, with a few days off in between. But if the sign-out man, who issued porters their assignments, didn't like a particular porter, he could keep him doubling out for as long as he wished, with little or no time between.

The Pullman Company avoided paying additional hours to the extra-board porters by establishing the "P.M. time" rule: the company would not begin the porter's pay on P.M. time. For example, a porter would normally have to report at least two to three hours ahead of his train's scheduled departure to ready the car and receive passengers. If the train was to leave at midnight, no matter how many hours before midnight he had reported, his time card did not start until 12:01 A.M. Later the rule was modified somewhat so that time cards started when the train actually moved. But again, the hours of preparation before departure and after arrival amounted to thousands of gratis hours received from porters each month.[23]

Overtime pay was practically nonexistent. The porters were required to put in 400 hours or 11,000 miles each month, whichever occurred first, before overtime kicked in. Then a porter would be paid an additional 60¢ per 100 miles. The catch was that most porters spent the better part of the month trying to accumulate those 400 hours—leaving little time for days off, let alone overtime.[24]

Porters were also frequently mistreated by district superintendents, who ran them on the road for long periods of time and doubled them back out with no time to clean up or rest. Reportedly, even office boys harassed porters. And conductors and platform agents were notorious for using their power to coerce porters. In a letter to C. L. Dellums dated 27 May 1941, Brotherhood First International Vice President Milton P. Webster cited the case of a Pullman platform man who habitually accused porters of drinking on the job—even some individuals who did not drink. "It seems, so the story goes, that he comes into the car and makes some inquiry about the work, and if the porter says anything in defense of himself this fellow yells at him, 'You must be drunk.' "[25] Similar stories are legion among porters. Certainly there were decent supervisors, but the overwhelming majority of white Pullman managers still regarded the Negro as his subordinate. By the early 1920s the porters were fed up with such abuse.

* * *

Black porters had been trying to organize themselves since the early part of the century, but their political impotence and low social standing had undermined their efforts to unionize against the powerful Pullman Company.

The first national attempt at organization was made in 1912, when the porters circulated petitions amounting to little more than a plea to the company for whatever they could get in the way of a raise. The Pullman Company obliged with a token $2.50 per month raise, bringing the porters' salary to $27.50 per month.

Pullman did voluntarily double the porters' salary in 1917 to $45 per month, but solely to offset the keen wartime competition for manpower. Shortly thereafter, the Pullman Company was put under the jurisdiction of the U.S. Railroad Administration, and the $45 per month salary was raised to $47.50, the same rate paid to office boys. Subsequently, the monthly rate was raised again to $60, but even that was a poor income for a long, tiring, back-breaking job. The Department of Labor announced in 1926 that $2,000 per year was necessary to maintain the average American family "in a decent living." With a base salary of $720 a year (excluding tips), the Pullman porter was paid far below that sum.[27]

Passenger tips provided the only real means by which a porter could earn a respectable living on the Pullman cars. Tipping was a time-honored tradition that served not only the porter's interests but his employers as well. The Pullman Company counted on the passenger to pay the balance of their porters' salary through tips. Without tips, a porter would never have been able to support a family. Naturally, with so much at stake, porters devised innumerable ways to get money out of passengers' pockets.

The art of soliciting generous tips, however, was a source of controversy. Referred to as "Uncle Tomming," kowtowing, hustling, and an assortment of other degrading terms, the tipping tradition was more than a matter of rewarding an employee for good service. Because the porter depended on tips for a living wage, he was forced to solicit gratuities any way he could—hence the reputation of the cunning, sly, sharp Pullman porter. In the eyes of many porters, they became beggars to their white clientele. Malcolm X, the black nationalist spokesman and dissident, worked briefly for the New Haven railroad as a dishwasher and later as a sandwich man, selling food in the coaches of the Yankee Clipper, which ran from Boston to New York. In his book *The Autobiography of Malcolm X*, he speaks of the relationship between black train employees and white passengers: "We were in that world of Negroes who are both servants and psychologists, aware that white people are so obsessed with their own importance that they will pay liberally, even dearly, for the impression of being catered to and entertained."[28]

Eventually, however, the additional money made in tips by African American train employees was too great to overlook. When a Pullman porter revealed to the *Saturday Evening Post* how much he received in tips on his runs, the Internal Revenue Service immediately made all porters report their tip income and set a minimum that every porter had to claim on his return.

The year 1918, however, held considerable promise for what was thought to be a new era in freedom of speech for the Pullman porters. The War Labor Board mandate giving porters the right to engage in collective bargaining through representation of their own choosing boosted morale among the men.[29] In July 1919 two small groups of porters from New York and Chicago joined forces to form the Brotherhood of Sleeping Car Porters Protective Union.[30]

The Pullman Company watched this development with keen interest. The company was uneasy about the numerous wildcat groups that had been springing up across the country; unchecked, these could have proved to be a great source of trouble for Pullman. Taking advantage of the confusion caused when too many organizations claimed to represent the porters, Pullman formed its own in-house union to satisfy the requirements of the War Labor Board's mandate and offset future organizing attempts. This new union was called the Pullman Plan of Employee Representation; its officers were handpicked for their loyalty to the company.[31] The Pullman Porters Beneficial Association was a sister organization. Its function was to gain further control over the porters through crude sickness and death benefits while keeping the porters amused with extracurricular activities to distract them from pursuing more meaningful issues. Benefits were actually drawn from the porters' yearly dues. In effect, the porters were paying out sick benefits to themselves.[32]

The two organizations served Pullman well for a number of years until the porters recognized the subterfuge. They wanted a bona-fide labor union, separate from the company, through which they could effectively bargain. Pullman once again rose to the occasion by calling the Wage Conference of 1924.[33] It was the first joint conference held under the Pullman Plan of Employee Representation. The porters chose representatives from around the country who they felt would best convey their needs to the company. The major issues were paring down the 400-hour work month to 240 hours and restructuring overtime regulations. But the Pullman Company had been hard at work intimidating porters by threatening to dismiss anyone who voted for the 240-hour month. The majority of porters might have welcomed the idea, but few were willing to risk their jobs fighting for it.[34]

Ashley Totten, secretary-treasurer of the Brotherhood and a Pullman porter before his dismissal on company-fabricated charges, reported that one porter-delegate told the convention: "I hope that these delegates who are asking for the 240-hour work month realize they are playing with fire. I am going to do what the management wants me to do, and I think if everyone would follow this advice, we would do well." The majority of the delegates followed this misguided porter's advice, and the conference amounted to no more

A. Philip Randolph

than a well-orchestrated smoke screen by Pullman, which threw the porters another $7.50 per month bone.[35]

The dismal outcome of the 1924 Wage Conference was a turning point for the handful of porters who were trying to organize a union. They realized that the power to fight the Pullman Company would not come from the rank and file. A leader would have to be found, someone who was forceful, had strong convictions, and remained unmoved by threats of dismissal. The search led to a Harlem soapbox orator by the name of Asa Philip Randolph.

A. Philip Randolph had gained a reputation as a radical and a troublemaker. His newspaper, *The Messenger*, began publication in 1917 and lasted 11 years. *The Messenger*—and *The Black Worker*, its successor—was Randolph's pulpit from which he reached thousands of black workers and citizens throughout the country regarding all the controversial issues of the day.[36] Randolph was subsequently branded "one of the most dangerous Negroes in America" by then-acting U.S. Attorney General A. Mitchell Palmer.[37]

The Brotherhood of Sleeping Car Porters was officially launched on 25 August 1925. Five hundred porters gathered together in New York City to hear Randolph lay the groundwork for the organization.[38] Response to the meeting was immediate: the next day over 200 porters applied for membership. Soon New York City claimed a strong Brotherhood affiliation, but

Cartoons from the *Black Worker*

success there would have to be repeated throughout the country before the Brotherhood could make any attempt to claim official representation of the Pullman porters. In October, Randolph embarked on a national barnstorming tour to reach porters in every corner of the Pullman system. He later recalled: "Hundreds of meetings were held. Porters were button-holed on streets, in barber shops, on the cars, in the yards—everywhere porters could be found by determined men in the service—and given the message of trade unionism."[39]

But reaching thousands of porters in this manner was not without obstacles. The Pullman Company began spreading rumors that Randolph was a Communist and that his interest in the porters was purely financial. Milton Webster spoke about those early days at a meeting of the Brotherhood in Detroit in 1948: "Everybody told us that we were doing the wrong thing. They told us, 'If you don't watch your step you're going to lose your monopoly'. . . . They said that Randolph was a crackpot, and that he had an insane idea if he had the slightest idea of trying to organize the Pullman porters."[40]

African Americans had been struggling hard to gain equality within white America; many felt that white leaders would grant more concessions to complacent blacks than to demanding ones. A backlash ensued against Randolph and the Brotherhood, which many feared was too radical to benefit the Negro. "Opposition to the Brotherhood did not only come from the Pullman Company," explained Randolph in November 1936. "Opposition also came from the Negro church, press and leaders. . . . From some churches the Brotherhood was barred; maligned and condemned, or damaged by left-handed praise by practically the entire Negro press, with even bishops joining the pack against our movement."[41]

From the inception of the Brotherhood, the Pullman Company put pressure on those porters who also acted as key officials within the Brotherhood. Employees were beaten, threatened, and intimidated in an effort to smash the union in major cities.[42] In 1928 alone, Pullman dismissed 45 men in Oakland and suspended 45 others. The roster grew so thin that cars out of Oakland that were normally staffed with porters from that division had to be staffed from cities at the other end of the run. Such realignments created a need to quickly hire and train new porters. The quality of service aboard the affected trains took a dramatic nosedive.

The porters became so fearful for their jobs that all union activities had to be carried out clandestinely; company stool pigeons were reporting on their fellow Brothers. The Randolph biographer Jervis Anderson stated, "In many cities the Brotherhood was forced to operate like a secret society . . . and there were dues paying members who crossed to the other side of the street to avoid being seen sharing the same sidewalk with Randolph or his organizers."[43]

The Pullman Company also attempted to play one ethnic group against another. As far back as 1925, Pullman had warned that as porters joined the

Brotherhood, Filipino men would be hired to take over their jobs. "It is not because the company loves Filipinos any more than it does Negroes," wrote Randolph in a 1930 editorial, "but because it found it convenient to use the Filipinos as a whip of intimidation over the porters to scare them away from a bona fide organization."[44] A few Filipinos were put on the club cars in 1925; over time more were hired, specifically in food service capacities. But their numbers were few in comparison with the thousands of black porters on the roster. A group of Chinese attendants was hired in 1930 to operate cars in Union Pacific trains nos. 11 and 12 out of Portland, Oregon. Paid $90 a month and granted working conditions more liberal than those of the black porters, they were soon withdrawn from service, owing chiefly to passenger complaints.

In 1926 the Railway Labor Act, apparently the long-awaited salvation for the Brotherhood, was passed. It allowed railway workers the right to organize and bargain collectively. Randolph immediately wrote to Pullman Company President E. G. Carry, informing him that under the conditions of the new bill the Brotherhood was now the officially recognized spokesman for the porters and requesting a conference with Pullman.

One of the major questions confronting the Brotherhood had been, who represented the Pullman porters at the bargaining table? The Pullman Company maintained that the porters' loyalty lay with them. The International Hotel and Restaurant Employees' Alliance and the International Bartenders' League both claimed representation of the Pullman porters. The Pullman Company was not too concerned with the Hotel Alliance or Bartenders' League because the porters held no clout within those organizations. The Brotherhood, however, was another matter.

Pullman did not reply to Randolph's letter. A lengthy dispute followed, with both sides claiming representation of the porters. In a vote taken among the porters, the Brotherhood received 53 percent. But Pullman ultimately pulled in 85 percent by waving a dismissal slip in the face of every porter who had voted for the Brotherhood.

The Brotherhood was at least able to break away from the Hotel Alliance when it was accepted into the powerful American Federation of Labor in 1928. Although the Brotherhood's weak financial situation and low membership disqualified it for an international charter, it was set up as 13 locals governed by AFL President William Green and his council. This move was very important because it began to establish the porters as railroad workers; in the hotel unions they had been classified as restaurant employees. Indeed, this classification would be a key issue against Pullman a few years later.

The election of Franklin D. Roosevelt to the presidency in 1933 gave the Brotherhood new hope. Two amendments to the Railway Labor Act of 1926 were immediately passed into law and appeared to give the Brotherhood the legal power it needed to fight the Pullman Company. The National Industrial

Recovery Act provided for the right of workers to organize and bargain collectively through their own representatives, and the Emergency Railroad Transportation Act outlawed company unions like the Pullman Plan of Employee Representation. The two bills gave the railway unions a strong position in labor negotiations. The Pullman Company, however, maintained that as a common carrier, not a railroad, Pullman and the porters were outside the jurisdiction of the new railway bills.

Randolph therefore began to lobby for another amendment to include the Pullman Company. After he wrote to FDR and other Brotherhood sympathizers, the Railway Labor Act and the Emergency Railroad Transportation Act were revised in 1934 to include sleeping car and express companies. Passage of the amendment marked the beginning of the end of Pullman's domination of the porters. "As a result of this signal victory," Randolph would later write, "a very definite upturn of the movement began and the porters, heretofore hesitant, uncertain and afraid, took new courage and rallied to the Brotherhood, from coast-to-coast, by the thousands."[45]

Pullman retaliated by laying off hundreds of porters. It also claimed once again that the Brotherhood did not legally represent the porters. This charge prompted the National Mediation Board to hold a national election between 27 May and 27 June 1935. The Brotherhood clinched the victory, 8,316 to 1,422. On 1 July the Mediation Board recognized the Brotherhood of Sleeping Car Porters as the official representative of the Pullman porters.

After the election victory, Randolph attempted to begin talks with Pullman, but the matter went into mediation almost immediately. Pullman was not willing to concede that it had lost a ten-year battle. The Railway Labor Act was also being challenged in the courts as unconstitutional. Pullman stalled for time.

In the meantime, the Brotherhood achieved an international charter within the AFL in June 1936. Full union status meant stronger support within the AFL. AFL President Green recognized the importance of the charter in an open letter to the porters: "The Pullman porters are the first group of Negro workers to battle their way to organization for the advancement of their interests and the assurance of their rights."[46]

Finally, on 1 April 1937, just three days after the Railway Labor Act had been upheld in the courts, the Pullman Company begrudgingly agreed to sit down with the Brotherhood. Ironically, 25 August would mark the signing of an agreement between the Brotherhood and the Pullman Company. That date, 12 long years before, had marked the start of the Brotherhood in New York City.

The Pullman Company agreed to reduce the work month from 400 hours to 240 and granted a wage increase of $12 per month, plus back pay for several months. Providing renewed job security were new grievance rules pertaining to issues such as doubling out without rest, P.M. time, and racial discrimination by supervisory personnel. The Brotherhood was especially pleased by the outlawing of spotters' reports as evidence to convict a porter of misconduct.

The Brotherhood negotiated further wage increases in increments of $24 in 1941 and 1943, and $44 in 1946. A. Philip Randolph continued to lead the Brotherhood of Sleeping Car Porters until his retirement in 1968, although by that time the organization contained only 2,000 members; the Pullman Company closed its doors the same year. Not even dwindling membership, however, could erase the Brotherhood's important place in American labor history. The Pullman porters' fight for industrial and social reform for the African American lent inspiration and set precedent for the civil rights activists of future generations.

George Henry Smock

I

─────────

GEORGE HENRY SMOCK
Pullman Porter and Buffet Car Attendant
1935–1939

George Henry Smock is the eldest of three brothers, the third generation of Pullman Company employees in their family. The first to sign on, in 1902, was George Anderson Smock. He had gone to Pullman from a job as a knocker (the person who kills the steer) in the stockyards. Working out of the Chicago district, Grandfather Smock labored 27 years on the road. He died around 1929, while making a bed aboard Santa Fe's California Limited. His son, Garrard Sr., joined the ranks in 1915 and was active in Pullman's in-house union. Garrard taught his sons the culinary arts at home with training that prepared them for work with the Pullman Company. He worked 35 years for Pullman, until his tragic death in an automobile accident in 1950.

Garrard had introduced his son, George Henry Smock, to Pullman in 1935. Of all the Smock men, George was the least attracted to the Pullman way of life and left the company after just four years.

In direct opposition to George, his brother Virgil Orite Smock loved railroading. By the time Pullman management finally hired Virgil in 1936, he already knew the mechanics of the job from helping his father, brother, and other porters in the yards and aboard the cars. Virgil worked 24 years out of Los Angeles, until buffet cars in California were discontinued in 1960.

Garrard Wilson Smock, nicknamed "Babe" by his family, is the youngest of the three brothers. His Pullman service began in 1937, when he joined his father and brothers on the Southern Pacific Lark train running between Los Angeles and San Francisco. Like Virgil, Babe enjoyed railroading and retired in 1960 after a 23-year career at Pullman.

For a brief period in the late thirties, Garrard Sr. and his three sons all worked on the overnight Lark, prompting Ripley's Believe It or Not to publish the fact in its weekly newspaper series. Pullman officials, however, were not as enthusiastic as Ripley's and ultimately prohibited that many Smocks from working concur-

(Left) Grandfather George Anderson Smock holding his son Garrard Henry Smock, 1915.   (Right) Garrard Henry Smock, about 1941.

rently on the same train. Even so, the three brothers would continue to work together many times on the Lark.

The Lark became two trains at San Jose, California; the main train went on to the end terminals of San Francisco and Los Angeles, and the rear buffet-observation, a sleeper, and a baggage car ran as the Oakland Lark serving Oakland, California. The Smocks all worked the rear buffet car, which provided light meal service and limited sleeping accommodations on the Oakland portion of the run.

Born on 10 December 1914 in Los Angeles, George Smock worked in nightclubs and as a railroad station redcap before starting work for Pullman in 1935. With

2

a good word put in from his father, George began working the buffet car on the overnight Lark. George soon found out that his personality did not fit Pullman's strict regimentation and atmosphere of racial prejudice. He was fired a couple of times for losing his temper. George, as he put it, was "in consistent warnings from the Pullman Company."

On 19 September 1939, George traded his Pullman blues for olive drab, beginning a long and successful career in the army that lasted until December 1969.

When I was seven years of age, I would catch the streetcar and go down and meet my granddad when he would come in through the Santa Fe station. I was taught then how to pick up the linen and how to stack the linen. I was later taught how to break the beds down. In other words, to put the seats back together and to put them down so that a bed could be made. And he would go back and forth till I got the knack of it.

And later it was a part of going to meet my dad in his endeavors. Because of the fact that we were in school at the time, we didn't get the chance to go as frequently with my dad as we did with my granddad. My granddad worked out of the Chicago district and never—in 1929 when he was deciding to retire—he never changed his district. My grandmother brought her family west on a pass from the railroad to Los Angeles, and the body of them went back to Chicago to stay. But my dad, who was the youngest, stayed with my grandmother here in Los Angeles.

I was 13 or 14 years old before I found out what was meant by discrimination. I didn't know anything about difference in the race of people. I was born and raised in an Italian neighborhood, and there were Jews on the west of us, blacks on the south of us, Mexicans on the east of us, and Italians on the north of us. All of us went to the same school. We played and screwed and everything else. It was just one of them things. But when I got to where I started into junior high school, you seemed to feel a pulling apart. You could do this, you couldn't do that. And it wasn't among the teachers. It was just a feeling of withdrawal that was being practiced or being taught at home.

Josephine Solomon [a white girl] and I used to be regular mates. We'd go to the show and so forth together. But when we started high school, my mother said, "If you hadn't noticed it, you should have." There was a black and white couple, the Streets, down on 28th and Hooper. My mother'd say—at that time they used the term "colored"—"Colored people don't want her, and white folks don't want him. And if you and Josie are gonna look at things toward it being a closer relationship, you gotta look at the Streets." And that kind of did [come] between us. It told us a little different. Both are ostracized among both races.

When I went to Jacob Riis High School, I had a teacher by the name of

Downs. Miss Downs was one of the only woman teachers. She was our English teacher. And from time to time she would take one of the athletes home with her after school and have you do some work around the house and so forth. And she would tell you, "George, you have to be careful. Such and such a teacher is very prejudiced. Whatever you do, don't do anything around him that will agitate, because they can get you put out of school."

So you were being taught. And you went cross-town to play football, and they called you a nigger here, and you went to play baseball and so forth, and "You dirty niggers," and, "Go home, we don't want you to play here," and those kind of things. And then you were getting the emphasis of what was actually going on in the other part of life.

There used to be a statement made by my grandfather: "Lincoln freed the slaves, and the Pullman Company hired 'em." And it was a statement that was true in a form, because it really was the only job. You had to have no formal education to perform the job. We were taught that at that time for a black person to gain any type of profession or trade, that the Pullman Company was one of three or four of the highest paid at that time: a doctor, a teacher, a postman, and then the Pullman porter. And with that we were told that when you are old enough, you'll be able to come to work for the Pullman Company.

And of course, being married and with the opportunity for making money immediately, it settled it in to a part whereby that had been the money maker and the monies that took care of their family prior to me, and I accepted the same thing. And each of us thereafter accepted the same thing, with no feeling that the Pullman Company or that railroading would ever disappear.

I started with the Pullman Company in 1935. I was 21 years of age. Prior to that, I was a redcap at the Santa Fe station, and as a young man I hustled dishes and later became a busboy at Earl Carrol's nightclub on Sunset Boulevard. My dad operated car 71 on the Lark. Virgil, Babe, and I operated car 70. Now, car 70 is a buffet car. It has five bedrooms and one drawing room on it. The porter takes care of those bedrooms and the drawing rooms and all the upstairs orders that were ordered. "Upstairs" means that you go from one car to another making a delivery of drinks or food—whatever the case might be—from the buffet car. Many times the two or three men that were on the buffet car on the end of the San Francisco train would have too much for them, and they would require having assistance, so the porter would go up there and assist them.

When Virg and Babe came to work, they were placed on the Oakland Lark. At that time I was steward-in-charge on the Oakland Lark. Virgil was the person who prepared the food and the drinks. Babe was our waiter. But after a couple of trips, we traded off so that anybody could be the cook. Virg in the kitchen or Babe in the kitchen would trade jobs, vice versa. Didn't make any difference what was going on. It was just a beautiful working thing

4

Typical Pullman 16-section tourist sleeper similar to the one George Smock grappled with in 1935. Santa Fe Railway.

with us, and that's how we happened to be known as a family operating a train.

The Pullman Company, when my granddad went to work, he made—when he told us about the Pullman Company as a Pullman porter—he received $12 a month, and he had to pay for any lost linen. My dad, when he went to work, he received $25 a month. Of course, you say, "Well, $12? How did he get along with $12?" It was $12 and whatever tips he received was what made up his family salary. Now, I went to work far later than any of them; in fact, some 58 years later than my granddad, and I went to work for $60 a month. Now, the one thing about my work, and that was, it entitled the Pullman Company to get from me 288 hours of work for that $60. Now, when you break that down into dollars and cents, you can say I was working for pennies. Now, it's true that in many instances a porter made that $12 and over on a trip that he made, and it was how well he had treated his passengers and how well they thought of him as to how much he got in tips.

It was nothing for a person to get off and give you a dime, and it was nothing for a person to get off and give you twenty, thirty, or fifty dollars even.

The Pullman Company took advantage of the employee. Everybody made more money than the Pullman porter. You could go to some people in the yards and find that they made more money than the actual pay from the Pullman Company because they took advantage of the passenger—the passenger would take care of and give them or pay them the salary that they should have been paying. The Pullman porter would have been one hell of a person if he had been making a decent salary and receiving sometimes those good train tips.

You bid for various runs because of the type of passenger that was transported back and forth on these various long trips or business trips and so forth. And in doing so, all-room trains like the Century [20th Century Limited] and the Lark brought a porter good tips. Many of them, it made a difference in life or death for his family because of illness and so forth. Many of them, it made them wealthy. Many of them, it made them foolish in that they made so much money—more than any other person in his surroundings or in his caliber of life—that they became gamblers or they became alcoholics.

Running on the Coaster [Los Angeles–San Francisco coach train] was a situation wherein very little tips. You could go to San Francisco and back and come back with $2.70. And that was a case of leaving on Monday and coming back on Wednesday morning—and have $2.70 to show for it. In order to beat that, you'd get you a dozen oranges—took two oranges to get you a 14-ounce glass. The glass sold for a dollar, and you got all of yours out first, and then you sold the Pullman Company's. Now, made sandwiches: take a pound of bacon and a couple of tomatoes—never the amount that was so noticeable that they find out what's going on—but you could figure fifteen to eighteen dollars for a trip for your sandwiches and so forth. That took care of your expenses on the opposite end. It's another form of stealing, but then that's another way of making life pleasant for yourself.

Pullman porters have been known to have taken a family member across the country. They would ship them into the railroad chair car during the daytime hours and put 'em in a bed at night. If he had a bed that was open, he may be able to sleep for five hours and then they were going to pick up somebody at a station, and it was a case of rousting them out and making that bed over so that the passenger that was gonna have that space would be able to have that space.

The Pullman Company had a way of trying to trick its attendants and porters about something of which they were doing. Pullman would have inspectors get on, and you'd go out and serve the passenger, which was the inspector, and not knowing that he was the inspector, you would write one item down on the check and not the other item. In other words, you might have three items: he might have a sandwich and coffee and a little wafer or something of the kind, or sometimes when we were on the kitchen car we had ice cream. Okay, the sandwich and the wafer might be on there, but the ice cream wasn't on. Or the ice cream and the wafer's on, but the sandwich wasn't on. And you would write it down, and you would lay it there, but when it come time for the passenger to know how much it was they paid, you would pick the check up and tell him what his check was. Then you take it on to the kitchen, and you'd put down whatever you wanted. Either you put it on or you did not.

At one time I come outta Sacramento. I was then on the West Coast Limited, and the Pullman Company made you account for everything that was on their car. A lemon was worth 30¢ to the Pullman Company. If you had lost a lemon, you owed them 30¢. It took a half a lemon to make a lemonade. They had nice, big, juicy lemons, and it had lots of juice on it, so you'd take a slice out of that lemon to be a part of the decoration. You'd put a cherry and a slice of the orange, and you'd charge 30¢ for the lemonade.

I went into the buffet—well, I was making my car down—this fella comes through, goes and sits in the lounge. It's extremely warm while waiting, and they don't put the cars on stand-by refrigeration when we were in Sacramento at the time. So I'm sweatin' like the dickens tryin' to make my car down, and this guy rings the bell. I go back and ask him what he wants. He wanted a lemonade. Well, it takes so much to go through for all of that. So I make up the lemonade, and I take it out there to him, and he asks how much he owed me, and I told him—I think it was 31¢—and he gave me 40¢ and said "Thank you," which was 9¢ for all the work I was doing. And I picked it up, and I went by the buffet. I sailed the doggone tray—the little stainless steel tray—sailed the tray into the kitchen, and you know that all the kitchen is metal anyway, and you could hear that sucker ring from now on end!

But he wrote me up. And he wrote me up because of my anger and that we were not supposed to expect tips from passengers. I was written up for my anger, for expressing my anger. And he did everything he could. He wrote me up because I stood on the arm of the chair of the berth in order to hang a curtain that the hook had fallen off. I walked by and I hooked it, but in hooking it, it didn't stay, so I stepped on the doggone arm and hooked it. And he wrote that up, and he stated that I was discourteous to my passengers and so forth. So he in turn had wired this into the Los Angeles district before I arrived, so that when I got there, the platform man met me and asked me to come up to the office. And I went up and they gave me a reaming, and I wasn't gonna take it, so I told 'em where to go to. I left and went back down to the yards.

Now I had come off of the car before I got a chance to completely put my car away, so I had to then catch a streetcar and go out to the yards and complete puttin' my car away. And I went out there, and I didn't completely check my car, and again, as I say, they talked about firing me and everything.

And I—Virgil and Babe can tell you—I really told the son of a bitch where to go hang his hat [*laughs*]. Now, my father's mother's mother was Irish, and he always told us, "It's that Irish temper that gets you in trouble all the time."

My dad would talk about the passengers from time to time, and as I said previously, he learned very fast. He would tell stories about how easy it could have been that we as blacks could have been conductors as opposed to having had Pullman conductors. Black men could not become conductors, but he operated a car and was the porter-in-charge, and there was no conductor on it. Two cars went into Prescott and Williams, Arizona, and between Phoenix and then going to Prescott and to Williams, he was the conductor. He'd manage the tickets; he'd collect tickets and so forth.

Many Pullman conductors were slave drivers, in a sense. They always had a hard-on for you. They'd write you up. They'd talk about you. They would make it hard for you insofar as the Pullman Company was concerned and with the passengers. We had a young porter, Sylvester Brice, who, one of the passengers, she wouldn't lay off of him. She practically threw him into the bed. And the Pullman conductor—name was McCloud—almost had him thrown off the train by the train conductor. Sylvester was not the agitator—the instigator—in that instance; it was the passenger. But McCloud made it look like he was the one who actually was doing all this.

A Pullman porter was taken as a person in one's own home would take a nanny who would be taking care of the house, or the doctor who came to the house, or the neighbor, who was administering to the sick. If a woman was ill, regardless to whether it was her period or whether they had children, they always asked the porter as though he was able to do something insofar as comfort was concerned. He either had some pills in his bag or he would go hustle some type of medication from another porter that would assist the passenger.

On one particular occasion that's most outstanding in my railroading, a passenger rang the bell in his car and asked the porter if he had anything that could take care of hemorrhoids. His wife was down with hemorrhoids. And he came up and asked us if we had any bacon grease. And yeah, we have plenty of bacon grease. We saved the bacon grease and then put it in the refrigerator, and then when it gets hard, we take that home with us when we get off of the car. He said, "I need a little bit. I gotta lady up here with hemorrhoids." Needless to say, we did not know what the outcome was with that passenger, but I had a passenger who was suffering from hemorrhoids one time on the Lark, and he asked me, "Porter, could you help me? I don't have a medication, and my hemorrhoids are down," or something of the kind. And I said, "Well, let me go back and get you some bacon grease, and I'm sure that will take care of it, until you get to a doctor." The next morning he gave me a $50 tip! Now, what it did—I don't have hemorrhoids, so I don't know what the situation was—but for some reason or another, it actually assisted the passenger in whatever was wrong with it.

From time to time, women who were in a family way that needed assistance and so forth, Pullman porters they looked to without any feeling that he was nothing other than a doctor taking care of them. Other times children were ill, and the porter would take it from its mother and walk it the length of the car, take it to the vestibule and so forth. Those are the things that hardly ever are known to the public so far as what their job and career called for.

As a Pullman porter, many times people'd get up and sit in the smoking room and give you a long line of what he did and so forth and mention something. And your asking of questions gave you an opportunity to learn things that you wouldn't have learned otherwise. We lived just five miles from Cucamunga, and Grandpa Smock on his way from Chicago on the Super Chief was told by a passenger where to go to buy some land that he considered "gold land." Now the term "gold land" didn't enter Grandpa's mind other than you would find gold there. But it is a sandy area, mountainous, and with this, Grandpa Smock couldn't see anything that resembled making money off of it. Now he bought it for 90¢ an acre. He bought 170 acres. And one year later [his wife] sold it, because she thought that he had done something wrong. Today you can go over that acreage, and it's worth fifteen to forty thousand dollars an acre [laughs]. But those are things— information that was given to Pullman porters.

Each of my two brothers, my dad and my granddad, actually got a universal education in the acts of working in employment for the Pullman Company. Regardless of all the hardships, there was something to be gained, and it took care of our families and brought our families to a start that we were able to take care of them.

The Pullman Company fired me a couple of times. One was for striking a passenger. A passenger called me "Gawge," and I tried to explain to him that the name was spelled G-e-o-r-g-e, and not G-a-w-g, or however he might want to spell it in his pronunciation. And being told he'd call me what he wanted to, I laid one on him [laughs]. That was on the Lark. Oh, I was ready to go to battle very readily and very quickly, and sometimes it didn't take more than two or three words to be exchanged before the fire rose and had to be extinguished by actually expelling my fury upon someone. Well, I didn't take it, let me say it that way.

The 16-section tourist car was a mainstay of the Pullman Company for many years, owing to its high capacity and lower fare; many a chair car passenger who could not otherwise afford a Pullman room could purchase a bed for the night. Hundreds were in use all over the country, requiring the attention of new porters who did not have the seniority to work room cars. For the porter, a tourist car was a never-ending nightmare of beds to be made down or put up, and they involved the equally taxing task of pleasing the varied assortment of passengers this class of travel attracted. The cars eventually lost favor with the public after World War II; GIs who had traveled thousands of miles in these cramped cars did not care to ride them again in peacetime.

I at one time kicked a platform man. I was called upon to jump off of the train that I was on. I was going out as a waiter on a train, and the platform man came over and told me to get my bag. He had to put me on a tourist car, and the car was all made down and everything. I went to Fort Worth, Texas, on it and got off that morning very, very tired because it was hard work.

The average 16-section car can be made down—all 32 beds—in less than two hours' time. That's walking on the car, puttin' your towels out in both the ladies' room and the men's room, puttin' your soap out, puttin' your toilet paper out, throwing your linen, making your beds, hanging your curtains, gettin' your baggage put away—then gettin' you some rest and then taking care of your shoes and gettin' ready for 'em in the morning.

But you can vouch for it that on a tourist car they're carrying a lot of damn cardboard boxes and straw bags and all that kind of fool stuff. That's what makes it so hard is shifting around and getting the passenger, when their section is made down, to be able to either go to bed or get lost someplace. Some of the baggage is going underneath; some piece of baggage is gonna go up into the upper because they're gonna have to use that to undress by, and they'll have to ring for you later on to get that bag down for 'em and so forth. When you start out with no beds made, with all this baggage here, you ask your passengers to sit with one another long enough for you to move all the baggage out. And once you get one made, then you take your baggage there and the bags from another section and put 'em in there, and get another one made. Then you keep trading back and forth down the line. Or you start and you move everything—just start to going from one side to the other—and move everything to one side: passengers here, bags standing, some of them in the vestibule, and you make your car down that way.

But it takes you a good five hours to make a car down like that. Oh, God, man! Ooohh! You see, especially when you're starting out and the train is gonna leave at seven o'clock in the evening, you should have one side made down. Or if the train leaves at five o'clock in the evening, see, you don't have any chance to make any down. Some porters get ahead of the game, and they make one section down. And then the passenger—because these are tourist cars, and it's the cheaper passenger—he isn't treated any different than anybody else, but he doesn't get all the service that he would have ordinarily on the room cars and the higher priced Pullmans, in other words.

Now, if you was runnin' a tourist car on the Gold Coast—not the Gold Coast, the "Coaster"—and that car was goin' from Los Angeles to San Francisco, San Francisco back to Los Angeles, it's a hard deal because the train doesn't leave until six-thirty in the evening. So you've only got one or two beds made down, and then you're fightin' that sucker up till about ten o'clock at night—ten, sometimes eleven o'clock, according to how your passengers are and so forth.

But anyway, I reported in the afternoon having gotten some rest, and I was placed on another tourist car coming back to Los Angeles. I went to the yards not knowing that I was not supposed to make the car down. I jumped in and made down one side: 16 beds. I was sitting in the smoking room smoking a cigarette—undressed—and this platform man came through and brushed the curtain back in the smoking room and then stepped into the other part of the car. And when he looked in there, he came back and he says, "You nigger son of a bitch! Who told you to make . . ." and he didn't need to get the rest of it out because I was on my feet. He knew what was about to happen.

I ran—there's a locker at the end of the vestibule there—I grabbed the window jack out and started after him, but he was making tracks so fast that I couldn't strike him with it. As he turned the door, all I could do was get my foot in the air, and I kicked him off the platform [vestibule].

People who heard the commotion—the porters—they put me up in the front car in one of the small toilet areas. I stayed there until such time as we got to El Paso, Texas, wherein I went up into the chair car and stayed there until we got into Los Angeles.

Now my dad, again in his fieriness, told the Pullman Company and a man by the name of Thatcher, "I told you never to send one of my kids down South. He has never had to go through that foolishness, and with that he's gonna fight, and with that he will get put in jail or he'll have something happen to him. So don't ever send one of 'em down there." Needless to say, the Pullman Company was about to get rid of me, but through the actions of my dad, why, they kept me working.

The Pullman Company had its own union. Of course, most all industry has their own union to keep unionism, really organized unionism, out of their particular plants and/or industry itself. My father from time to time was fired by the Pullman Company for his association with the union. He was a member. He joined the Pullman Porters Beneficial Association back in the early twenties and from time to time they did things that were against the Pullman Company's wishes. And, of course, they turned the porters loose.

Dad, being a fiery young man that associated himself with right, was doing everything he could in order to raise the scale not only of pay but status insofar as employment was concerned: speaking up for another porter for something that may have happened that the Pullman Company was against. It might have been talking back to a passenger or something of the kind.

And speaking for one another caused the Pullman Company to not want to listen to what was being said and dismiss the individual. It was the puppet union for the company.

He was a fervent worker in the union itself here on the West Coast. Now, he ran from Los Angeles to Chicago and, from time to time while deadheading as a porter, would be sent all over the country before he gained enough seniority to hold a regular job. But in between, regardless to whether it was a regular job or not, he—in his fieriness with the union—caused the Pullman Company such fear that they fired him.

He went to work for Portland Cement and one time used to drive and deliver. And they did their own swamping: 24,000-pound trucks. That's truck and trailer. Swamping means a person who is the assistant to the driver insofar as loading and unloading the truck. As a child, I've seen him load and unload a truck himself.

My dad, well, he was a person quick to learn, and he'd go do odd jobs insofar as cooking, and from others he would learn the use of various knives: French knife to carving knife to a prune knife and grapefruit knife and all those kind of things. And he in turn, while we did not have that type of knifeware, would draw a picture and show us what it was, and we would laugh about there being a long prong and a curved prong and etcetera. And he taught us basically the use of knives, which made it very easy when we started doing any cooking.

Now my dad, because of his light skin, used to play in pictures whenever he would come in and they would have a call for extras for Indian parts. He had a wig and a leather thong that went around, and a tomahawk, and he would go out to the studios and play in these multi-scenes and so forth.

Yeah, in fact, he had an old rifle that he had been given, and he brought that rifle and tomahawk and his wig home. We're all comics. We were always doing things around the house, comical things to do. We were sitting at the table. Dad was eating, and all of a sudden he got up—he walked out—and we just thought maybe he'd gone to the kitchen or gone to the bathroom. All of a sudden, he come at us—"Whoooooooooo! Whoooooooooo! Whoooooooo!!!" He had put this wig on and had taken off his shirt, and he had on these kinda half-long drawers with this damn thong around him and this hatchet. We never did get through laughing over that. Everything was just too quiet for him.

The Pullman Company occasionally assembled an entire train especially for a specific group or company, painting the train in whatever colors the customer desired and outfitting the interiors with appropriate motifs or displays. The Rexall Special of 1936 was one such train.

Of the known named cars to have operated in the train were the Adrienne, Ad-Vantage, Bisma-Rex, Cara Nome, Puretest (the rear-end observation-plat-

form car), Research, and Symphony. Rounding out this group were two lounge cars, a diner, and two head end cars used for food storage, linens, liquor, and, unofficially, "gambling." The rear-end private car, the Puretest, was used by Mr. Liggett, president of the Rexall Company.

I joined the Rexall Special on the 14th of April. James T. Steele and I were two attendants in Los Angeles, and they had asked for attendants from the L.A. area to represent our district. We were selected because we were just good, fast, hard workers, and consequently that was the way we got on there. And it had some 16 or 18 porters and waiters.

The men were made up from different areas. We had some from Texas; we had some from Louisiana, North Carolina, California, Michigan, and Illinois. And to combine this entire crew without there being any animosity practiced among them was terrific.

We had one, he'd drink up everything you could see. And yet when it come time to go into that dining room—he was a pantryman—he was just . . . [*sits up alertly*].

That fellow right there [*pointing to the group photograph*] didn't know what the bottom of the bottle looked like because after he got so far down in he was looking for your bottle, because he didn't want to finish his out. He had to have something to keep on going!

There was a rotten man that caused me more trouble than anything. He was ill, and he had $2,000 on him that he turned over to me. I went back to the private car to work while he was incapacitated, and went up to the baggage car early that morning. They had started a crap game!

The baggage men and one of those engineers had started it, and they had their money all on the floor. And two guys—it had finally gotten down to two of 'em finishing the game off—they were shootin' between one another. And a few of 'em were standing around there.

And I looked down, I said, "All that money?"

"Shooting it all, shootin' it all!"

I said, "Covered!"

And this is the other man's money: $1,600 down there!

The guy threw a crap, I reached down to pick it up, he said, "Show me the money, show me the money."

So I pulled this money out, and I picked all the money up. And this other guy started to send me home because they found out what I had done with it. I didn't have any business gamblin' with his money. I wasn't even in the game. I just passed there, and the money was laying down there. I was not that type of gambler. I just happened to win. What if I'd lost? [*laughs*].

On a train like that, you had no feeling insofar as the passengers were concerned. You were just doing a job and getting it out of the way. You were getting paid, and it didn't make any difference whether the passenger gave you anything or not. A lot of tips were made on a trip like that because there was no money coming out of the people's pocket you were serving; they were being treated.

I made an average of $100 a week in tips, and in 1936 that was like striking a gold mine! They gave you a carton of cigarettes, a quart of whiskey, and it could be either scotch, bourbon, gin, or vodka. Or you could exchange and take a box of cigars in place of cigarettes. That was just a gift! We had one car, baggage car, that was loaded with nothing but beverages and liquor, and we continued to replenish that at various stations throughout the trip.

Now the two cars that were known as lounge cars is where they held their convention, and they had these seminars and so forth. The dining car served the crew, and people who were invited. The three chefs on there were chefs from Illinois Central, New York Central, and . . . damn, where'd he come from? There were three chefs off of various railroads.

The [people] who acted in charge of the train in place of a Pullman conductor [were] Spencer and Allen. They traded off insofar as the dining car to act as stewards, though there was no charge. They would go in and see to it that the passengers were taken care of and all.

There were some people who actually rode on the train that were part of it—the pharmacists—and they had a nurse, and they had two women who worked in the pharmacy car that gave out boxes of Whitman's candy and things like that. Then you had two electricians, four Pullman porters, three chefs, two inspectors, two traveling engineers, and one porter-in-charge.

We set here one night talking about the Rexall Special and everything they did. Pheasant on toast was nothing. Lobster in all forms, whether it be humidor or broiled or what'd be the case. All kinds of fish, all kinds of French foods, all kind of Louisiana foods!! The three chefs were outstanding cooks, and whatever you could ask for, one of them knew how it was to be prepared!

And many times, rather than have a regular menu, you would be asked what your needs were for the day or what would you like to have—come up with some idiotic thing—and bingo, it would be right out there for ya. Oh, it was an experience out of this world.

Working on a passenger train day after day can become pretty routine. Although the passengers are generally new each trip, the scenarios are similar. To break up the monotony, porters were famous for playing tricks and practical jokes on one another.

Ooooh, man!! All kind of tricks! Go crawl in the passenger's bed, you know, and pull this trick on so-and-so. We'll call him Jackson, and you're supposed to put his passenger off during the night for him. The curtains are pulled closed, and somebody's in this bed, and you go through and say, "Say, weren't you supposed to put a passenger off at so-and-so?"

"Yeah. Well, so-and-so put him off."

"Did he?" and keep on going.

And he goes there and sees this doggone [*laughing through the story*] curtain pulled, and the first thing you know—if you go peep and you see this body turn over in this bed—you know that they hadn't put that passenger off, and he'd gone past his stop. A porter'll just about go out of his shoes because it was his responsibility to get the person off, not the person that you'd left on duty or on watch.

And he'd go to wake up the passenger, and there'd probably be a guy standing on each end of there laughing like hell. And, of course, you who had played the trick was laying there in the bed. When you turned over, he saw you! Sometimes they got punched, sometimes they got kicked, and sometimes they would get to laughing about it. Sometimes the passengers didn't know what the hell was going on, three or four porters there and they would be laughing to beat the band. Man! Oh, yes!

And switch bags. That's a bad trick to pull on anybody. Or switch shoes. Now some young porter might be on, and these old porters didn't like for the youngsters to even be given a chance to run on the Lark and the Sunset and so forth with 'em. You know people used to put their shoes under their bed at night? The porter came along and picked up their shoes or put 'em in the little shoe locker. Some guy come along and just switch two or three pairs of shoes. That's the worst thing in the world that can happen to ya. Your passenger is up and trying to get dressed, and you have got the wrong shoes there. [*laughs hysterically*].

Let me switch from there a second and give you this. A passenger is sitting at the table, and you are coming to wait on them, and one of the guys has said, "Man, be sure to take good care of her. That's Miss Ready-money." This woman was the owner of horses at Calumet Farms. She was a very wealthy woman. Now, he didn't get all of it, but he thinks you said, "Reddimoni." So he goes and—say he's taking her something—"Good evening, Miss Readymoney."

"Miss what???"

Needless to say [*laughing*], you've ruined his trip, because man, he's all flustered and so forth, and when he finds out he's made a mistake or you played a trick, he comes back and then he goes into what we call "up a tree," because nothing he does is right.

He's supposed to take water out and set it on a table and put something else on the table. He probably is taking some coffee out there, and then he's got a passenger over here that's got bacon and eggs and another one over here that's got sausage and eggs. And this one gets the bacon and eggs and this one gets . . . nothing is right. He's up a tree.

Now the only way to get out of the tree is stop doing everything you're doing, take a lull. Walk through the vestibule and stand and look out there for something and come back and try to get yourself together. Sometimes the passengers are irate by that time, that the waiter has just left and nothing is out there. He comes back and makes the switch here and gets back to where he actually should be.

Just before I went to work for the Pullman Company in 1935, Franchot Tone and Joan Crawford got married, and they were staying at the Ambassador Hotel located over on Wilshire. Oh, man, that was big time! That was big time!!! I was a redcap then at the Santa Fe station, and I was one of five redcaps on duty at the time. Now, no redcap wants to be tied down; he wants to be moving. A guy by the name of Buster Brookens was the redcap-in-charge. There were twenty-one redcaps for that station, but there was only five on duty at that time. The chauffeur comes up, and Franchot Tone and Joan Crawford get out, and they go on through, and the redcap, he goes and talks to this fellow, and they send him over to Buster Brookens. Buster Brookens comes over and gets me. He says, "Go along with him to get some baggage."

It turned out to be 21 damn pieces of baggage! We had to go back to—now I got my uniform on—and we had to go back to the Ambassador Hotel and get baggage and bring it and go back again. Now, the train didn't leave until twelve o'clock midnight, but this was just a little before nine.

Now, I'm not gonna make a damn thing. I got one person I'm taking care of, is all. And when I come back, he comes up to me, and he says, "Did they leave an envelope for ya?"

I said, "No, they didn't." I thought I'd been burned, see?

He said, "Come on, go with me."

So I walked on with them, walked on in. They got this whole room car. They only got one drawing room, and the rest of the car is theirs. 'Course, they had baggage and stuff spilled all over the car and everything by that time. And Franchot Tone reaches in his pocket and gives the chauffeur the envelope. He says, "I intended to give it to you. There's something in there for you, too!"

A $100 bill! I had never seen a $100 bill in my life! I got a $100 bill, and the chauffeur had any number. But there was a little envelope there with mine. That's the best tip I ever had carrying a bag or any baggage.

That was another one of the highlights of my life, because I had seen all kinds of movie stars. I saw the Valentino funeral. Our dad used to work in the movies, but to be that close to Franchot Tone and Joan Crawford, man, I was all ogle-eyed! Man! You didn't ask for signatures and so forth then. But man, I couldn't keep my eyes off of her. And she would look up and kind of smile. Just a short time I was with 'em, but it was a real goodie-goodie for me at that time.

W. R. Richardson was the architect and builder of Port Hueneme, and he

16

was a hell of a drinker. And of the Smock brothers, [I] was a hell of a drinker and could stand up with the best of them! When Mr. Richardson would get on, he would—well, this is the time when the three of us were together—he would ask them if George was on. They'd say yes.

"Tell him to bring a case."

Now what he meant by case was 12 bottles per each little case of individuals (miniatures). That's 1.7 ounces of liquor in it. I would go ahead and get myself squared away, whatever I had going, and leave them to take care of the lounge and whatever cooking and any upstairs work. And I would go sit with Mr. Richardson and talk with him and drink with him and go get another case!

Sometimes we drank as much as two cases. Needless to say, I was incapacitated to the extent I wasn't able to help 'em much in the morning. But then, that may've meant fifty, sixty, or a hundred dollars, and that was far more than we would've made in our tips any other way. So I punished myself talking with Richardson half the night—getting drunk with him—and then being able to collect that which we broke down, we three brothers.

We split evenly. Now my brother Virgil, Babe, Steele, Bookman, Brown, King, the Davis brothers—any of us that got on the car—once we got on the car, we got a tall glass, and everything that went to the glass come in as tips, regardless if it was up the train or anything of the kind. If somebody gave you a $50 tip out in the dining car because of something that you had done, or you had done something up the train or had assisted a passenger and they thought to compensate you, it went right to the glass. And when we got off the car, we split it three ways. When we got to town, we either went our ways going home or we'd go over and have something to drink and get some food and go out on the town or go to the races if we were in San Francisco—Bay Meadows or Golden Gate.

But there's only been two men that I ever run with after awhile I did not split my tips with. There was an individual who would steal from himself, and with that everything that he made he had to keep, because we would never split with him. And you find that in everyday life. There's always some fool in the bunch!

But as Pullman porters, they respected one another. At night when they were on watch—one would be on watch and the other would be asleep—if he had a passenger to put off, he put that passenger off and collected the tip from him. He put it in the linen locker so when you got up, you go to the linen locker, and there was your money.

We used to have Bing Crosby. That's one of the best passengers a man ever wanted to have. Be up in San Francisco, he'd come down; now he's got a small bag and his golf clubs. Maybe he'd have two or three other bags, but the redcap porters are taking care of that. Here he comes with his golf bag and this little bag, and you are the first car; you're either on car 72 or you're on car 70. And when he gets down there, you just reach out there and take it away from him anyway. He laughin' and, ah, "Get me a scotch and soda."

So you go take his golf bag, and you set it in the corner; you go in and order a scotch and soda. When he comes in, soon as he walks in there, they see who it is, and they hand it to him, and he goes and sits in the lounge, or he sits at one of the tables. It's good for a $20 bill! Every time! Not one time, but every time! One of the best tippers, and one of the nicest guys I ever wanted to meet.

Tell ya a little story. C. A. Brown used to be vice president of Universal Studios. He was the big man. We had a guy by the name of Harold Carr who was the cook at the time. I was the upstairs waiter (working cars up the train) and the porter-in-charge. It was one of those busy nights and everybody was working. All of us was going out and working in the buffet and so forth. The car was full. In fact, there were people standing in the back. There were different movie stars and so forth that were going on location. You ever see an observation? Okay, so you know the enclosed observation lounge [heavyweight car with rear platform]. People were standing round in the back there. That's where the drinks were going.

And Brown had ordered some food and he asked for wheat toast. And in the helter skelter, Carr put toast down there and it was white toast.

Brown called him, told him, "I ordered wheat toast." And Carr took it back but for some reason or another he got white toast and brought it back out. And Brown says, "Goddamn, you dumb sonofabitch, I told you I wanted wheat toast. Now go back and get me some whole wheat toast."

I'm standing in the back when this man started to shouting like that. And old Carr, he's a great big tall man. Carr looked at the toast—we covered it with a napkin—he looked at it, looked back at him. He walked real slow back, and he put the toast down. And he goes back out.

Now, Carr weighed about 200 pounds, but only stood about five-seven. He put his hands on his hips. And man, everything got quiet as hell. They thought he was going to strike him.

He said, "Mr. Brown? Can you bake a cake?"

Brown looked up at him, you know, and he says, "No, I can't bake a cake!"

Carr said, "You dumb son of a bitch," and he walked on back in the kitchen.

And everybody laughed, and Mr. Brown started laughing, and he started clapping his hands like that [applauding slowly]. He reached back in his wallet, and he pulled out four $10 bills, and he said, "Come here, Carr. Thank you very much."

Another time Joan Davis, who was a comedienne, she was riding the train. She had been up on location in Portland or Seattle somewhere, and they came in on the West Coast [train]. She came back into our car and was having a drink, and she wanted to know if we were gamblers, and if so, bring some dice. She wanted to roll some dice on the table.

Now, you couldn't do anything like that! But she went up to her car and come back and produced a pair of dice. She rolled it out there on the floor, and she fell over! I reached and picked her up and set her back up and told her I thought it was best that she go back to her car because she was becoming inebriated. So she wanted to take me back to her car.

I took her back to her car, went in the drawing room, closed the door, took her clothes off, put her into bed. But when I opened the door to come out, there was the Pullman conductor and the train conductor standing trying to see through that thick glass as to what I was doing in there. Oh, they wanted to know what I was doing in there, and they couldn't see why I didn't leave the door open and all that bullshit. And you know me, told 'em where to kiss and kept on going. She was the least of my thoughts insofar as having anything to do with her.

And that was not the first passenger the Pullman porter has ever had to strip down and put into bed or take their clothes off and put 'em into bed or something of the kind. But that's just the way they reacted during those days.

Virg and Babe will tell you right now, "We liked the railroad. He didn't." I didn't want any part of it. I got to the point I just despised even looking at a train. I didn't wanna get on that train to have to go. I've gone down and made my car down and so forth, trying to make over my mind to come up with a story not to be able to go out. It just wasn't me, that's all. They [Virgil and Babe] stayed beautifully. I possibly would have stayed if I hadn't gotten into the trouble, and then maybe again I wouldn't either too, because in time it would have caught up with me.

There's good and bad in everything. There was more good in the Pullman porter and more good stated by passengers and people alike about the Pullman porter than there's been any other profession the black man's had. I don't care whether he was a doctor, a postman, a preacher—none of those: a Pullman porter, it stands out.

Virgil Orite Smock

2

VIRGIL ORITE SMOCK
Pullman Buffet and Lounge Car Attendant
1936–1960

Virgil Orite Smock was born in January 1916 in the Boyle Heights district of East Los Angeles. Because of the strain of the Depression and the fact that his father, Garrard Sr., was on the road most of the time, Virgil's mother was unable to attend to the children by herself. Virgil therefore lived with his Grandmother Wilson for much of his childhood, later moving near the railroad yards with his parents.

As part of a railroad family, Virgil began his Pullman career unofficially as a youngster by helping the older porters set up their cars in the Los Angeles Pullman yard. By 1936, after being chased off the Southern Pacific Lark numerous times while helping the buffet men, the local Pullman superintendent relented and gave him a job on that train.

Virgil gradually rose in rank to become employee-in-charge on the Lark's buffet-observation car, often working alongside his brothers Babe and George during the late thirties. He also worked the Southern Pacific/Rock Island Golden State train from Los Angeles to Chicago and Union Pacific's City of Los Angeles, as well as numerous other trains that used Pullman-operated equipment.

Unlike his brother George, Virgil thoroughly enjoyed his years with the Pullman Company. Upon his retirement from the buffet cars in 1960, he continued to go out on the road for Findley's Fun Time Tours, a charter railroad car company operating excursions out of Los Angeles. He was head of on-board services for Findley until poor health forced him to retire from railroading in 1991.

The best job you could get would be in the post office, work for Pullman, or for the county. See, the prejudice was the fact where the county would hire ya, but you'd be janitors and whatnot, you know. Some work up to maybe clerks, like in water and power. The best jobs were Pullman. Anybody [African American] that had money would be Pullman.

21

Virgil, George, and Babe Smock, October 1938.

I used to go down to the yards and pull beds down and put up the headboards, put up the deflectors. They had deflectors before they had air-conditioned cars. And the old man would give me 50¢. I'd be doing two or three cars in the evening and had a couple Italian kids—friends of mine—we'd all go down together, and maybe if there's three of us we make about two bits apiece. We'd work those cars, and when they'd pull out to go to the station, we'd get on our bikes and go home.

Actually, I didn't apply with Pullman. My brother George worked on the Lark, and I used to meet the Lark in the mornings and help the fellows on the buffet car make out their supply report, and I got to learn that pretty good. I got to know the job so well that I would ride the red car [streetcar] out to Glendale and board the train and sit there and work the book coming in so they could get off early when they got into Los Angeles.

Well, this superintendent, Mr. Greer, got on one morning, and he asked me, "You work for us?"

I said, "No, I don't."

He said, "What's your name?"

I said, "Smock."

He said, "Well, you work for us!"

"No," I said, "my dad and my brother work for ya."

He says, "Well, you can't ride. You have an accident or something, and you sue the company."

So I told him okay. Then I would sneak on at Glendale, 'cause he would get on the front end of the train, and I'd go into a room and work the supply report. Well, the platform man, Mr. Schulte, told Mr. Greer that he didn't want to see me on these cars no time, even with the train coming to the station to ride to the yards.

So another particular morning he caught me, and he drug me up to the superintendent's office, and he says, "This is the Smock I was telling ya about. Just can't keep him off our cars."

He says, "Does he know the work?"

"Sure he knows the work. He's been working with his dad all his life out there."

He said, "Well, we need a man tonight, so send him out."

I went that particular night. I was due to work at noontime chauffeuring Mrs. Gratzner. I chauffeured for Alice Calhoun—silent movie star—for about a year in Beverly Hills. I was livin' at 76 Benedict Canyon Drive, and after that job, I went to work for Mrs. Gratzner. So I called her and told her I was—I don't remember now, it's been so long—I give her a long story. It was okay.

The Santa Fe doctor at the hospital couldn't examine me that particular day, but they sent me out anyway, as a busboy. So I went out that night and come in town and went to see the Santa Fe doctor, got a layover, and went out again.

I went out on the train they called the Coaster. That particular train, we had a kitchen with two men and three men in the diner with the porter, and I worked in the kitchen, see.

Then from there I built up a little seniority, and I went over to the Sunset, and that's the time the Sunset ran between New Orleans and San Francisco. I worked that until the union had separated the commissary department from the sleeping car department. I really wanted to go into the sleeping car department, but Mr. Leach talked to me and said that he didn't think my health would carry in the sleeping car department. I was small and slender, you know.

They started me out at $59.75 a month, went to $77, then one hundred and a few dollars, and I think when I retired, I was makin' about $400 a month—when I retired in '60. And every two or three years the union would go in for a raise. But then, you really didn't feel the raise in a way, because Pullman would slick you out of your money one way or the other, you know. You had a time sheet, and they'd prorate your time to next month into the next month. They claimed it was hard to pay you because you'd make one and a half trips a month to Chicago, one and a third trips to New York— you know, pay us on the first and fifteenth flat rate.

I know one time I had a porter named Mike Day. He was a type who liked sporty cars and sporty clothes, you know, and all. This fella named Diebert—he was a time clerk—and he was always taking your time, and then he'd try to change it. So Day was a big dark fella. He says, "Don't change my time, Mr. Diebert." And Diebert changed it. Day snatched his time book away from him so when he jumped up—he was a German fella—he jumped up and Mike Day hit him and knocked him flat on his ass. Bam! He Sunday'd Mr. Diebert! Those days, the office is full of clerks, so this lady jumped and says, "You fellas gonna let this big black man knock Mr. Diebert down?" Well, she called him a nigger, and Mr. Leach [superintendent] came right out of his office. He walked out and he says, "Get up, Diebert," and he says, "You fellas go into my office there. Miss Hughes, your service is no longer required at the Pullman Company."

Just like that! Then Leach talked to 'em. I don't know what he told him. Day was defending himself, you know, 'cause when Diebert jumped up, he thought he was gonna hit him so he hit him first, knocked him flat. But he didn't fire him, got it straightened and brought him back out, see. Jim Leach was a straight, straight fella.

We'd come in town, and the cashiers would be countin' money, and the porters were trying to get their check to go home, and they'd look at him and just keep workin'. A Pullman conductor could come in with his money—they'd take him right away, you know. So Leach come up the stairs one morning, and a guy was grumblin', and [Leach] says, "What are you porters sittin' in here for?"

I says, "Well, he don't want to pay us our money. He keeps takin' care of the conductors and countin' money."

[Leach] tips to the cashier, he says, "Come here. When these porters come in here, you give 'em that check. If it's here, you give it to 'em. If this conductor comes up here, you let him wait. These fellas got a home to go to. They been out on the road workin'. These fellas want to go home. If I see more than two porters in here from now on, somebody's gonna lose their job."

Straight, straight shooter!

My tips overrode my salary. Tips were pretty good, according to who you'd catch, you know. On the Lark were good tippers. You'd catch people like Bethlehem Steel, Hammond Lumber, American Can—people who worked outta that particular company. Buyers for Capwell's buyers from Macy's, or Mr. Ritchie—guy that built Port Hueneme—all those fellas down there. Those big contractors. We knew those fellas, you know. Those were good tippers. That's the reason we hustled, you know.

We had all kinda ways to hustle. You could be standin' receivin', and I ask, "How you doin', Mr. Dave? Oh, hi gentlemen." They used to go by, give me five dollars! They weren't even in your car!

Tips were good, but you had to be a senior porter to ride the Lark. You had to have at least 30 years to be on there. But see, by us being in the commissary, they took all the old men off the commissary cars and put young men on there. So I'd be workin' next to you, you'd maybe have 35–40 years, and I only have but three years, see.

But the old men schooled us, you know, they kept us in line, taught us how to do our work and how to keep our cars clean, make sure we had our towels folded. I had to guard his car at night when he went off duty. If you're due off duty at ten o'clock, I'd go out at your car between ten o'clock and two o'clock. If anybody wanted anything—if anybody hadn't gone to bed or wanted some water or anything—to ring the bell. I had charge of your car, see. At two o'clock, I'd call you. You'd get up, shine your shoes, and I'd go to bed. Four hours down time.

But usually the attendants didn't get that much time. If you had a big party drinkin', you cut 'em off at two o'clock. We couldn't sell no more liquor. What you would do, you say, "We have to close up at two o'clock. We can give you three or four boxes of scotch or bourbon or whatever you're drinkin', and you can keep on partyin', and then we can open 'em for you." We'd be busy cleaning up and feedin' 'em, or they'd leave at four-thirty or five o'clock. Then it's time to start breakfast, so you didn't go to bed. But the company wouldn't pay you for that though, see, 'cause you're supposed to close down. But if the tips were good, oh, say your guys had an eight-dollar check. He'd give ya three dollars, something like that, see. But you had to split. We had three of us on a car. We split our tips.

And then again, we'd raise it more. Say you're leaving town tonight, and we'd say, "Well, look here, we ain't gonna close up till we get $100 in the kitty." See, if you can catch the same crew all the time—when I catch certain waiters and cooks, we'd work close together. Then you'd start hustling, you know. They would hustle until a point where when you'd get on—we know you're a good tipper. We'd take a 35¢ cheese sandwich on a crew check— 75¢ for the passengers, 35¢ for the crew—write on a crew check, make some hors d'oeuvres, put some olives and set 'em out there, and say, "This is on the house for you fellas." [Passengers:] "Ah, no, no."

[Virgil slaps his hand.] Ten bucks!

So they'd be drinking a while, and maybe you'd take a box of Black & White or whatever they're drinkin'—ten in a box—set it on the table and say, "Now, you fellas have been real nice to us. We wanna buy this round." [Passengers:] "Oh, hell no." That guy'd get out $20. "C'mon you fellas, get back now. Let us finish playing our poker."

Man, we got $100. Let's close up.

We had to press suits! On the buffet car, there was on the menu—it says on the bottom "Valet Service," you know, pressing and blah-blah-blah. Dollar and a quarter to press a suit, and I think it was a dollar and a half for overcoats. Maybe you'd get on a car, and the porters hustle for themselves. But you'd always tip the porter a quarter for bringin' the suit back, and you'd start pressin' suits at ten o'clock. You'd press maybe to four or five o'clock the next morning. You'd have a dozen suits hangin' up there. I'd press awhile, maybe Handy Moore'd press awhile. The cook didn't press. He'd tell you he'd go to bed. He could press, but he didn't press. But that was a hustle, ten or twelve suits.

Pullman Company required you to shine shoes every night. They issued you a whisk broom, a hat brush, and your keys. You had to buy your own polish, your own rags, and everything. Everybody had to have their own shoe kit. And we carried our pencil, so when you picked up shoes, we just mark in there "8" or "B" or whatever room it was. Then you take 'em in the smoking room, you shine 'em, and you put 'em back. Now that was required whether you got any tips or not. You could only shine the shoes in your car. No, see, you didn't go in the other car. You stayed in your car. That porter catch you hustling in his cars, like to jump on you and fight you.

I know the time the Lark would come outta there, not a passenger on the car. With a porter on there, the railroad had to pay the Pullman Company for hauling that car, regardless if there's anybody on it. See what I mean? When Christmastime come and the holiday, there'd be just a train with maybe twelve, fourteen people on it. Maybe five people on it. Say you leave Christmas Eve, and there's nobody on this car—that car's blank. They'd just send the car anyway with the porter on it 'cause he had to go and bring it back. In later years, when the railroad took over, if there wasn't nobody in that car, they'd cut that car out.

Christmas Eve or Christmas night, if a certain car didn't have nobody and according to who the conductor was, we'd have a good time. We'd be sitting there, we were working my car, drink eggnog and everything else, you know. If an inspector got on, we looked at every stop, and the porter on the front end would say, "The inspector's on, and everybody be in your car."

But like on New Year's during that holiday, there'd be people going back both ways. I've come out in the yards, and we're looking for my train; I said, "Where's my car?" "You're on the second section." And there'd be maybe three sections of the Lark—all heavyweights. That was in the late thirties. We didn't get streamlined on the Lark until '42. So they'd run three sections—first 75, second 75, and third 75. The regular train would be a ten- or twelve-car train. The next section would have eight cars, all of 'em going to San Francisco. There'd be three cars on the back end of one of those trains would go to Oakland. One rear-end car went to Oakland, and one went into San Francisco. I'd go to Oakland.

On the regular section would be the Meadow Lark, the Oakland car, and the Family Club. The Family Club'd be the next buffet car. But when you got to San Jose, they'd cut off the Meadow Lark and the Oakland car. As soon as we'd pull into San Jose, the switch engine'd pick us off, put us on, and hook us on the back of the Oakland section—about ten minutes. The big train'd sit there a few minutes, and they'd sail right on out. As soon as they got that mail transferred, they'd be gone.

The war came along, and they called us in and asked if would we ask the union would they mind dropping the porter [on the Lark buffet/observation car]. See, the war effort, you know.

They said no, so we dropped the waiter [busboy] and keep the cook and the porter. I think the union told them you can drop one, and they dropped the busboy. That left the cook and the attendant on the car, both of us getting the same pay. The busboy got less than the cook and the porter did. So then we worked—we stretched out. That means I had to work the beds and wait tables, and the cook would cook and run out and wait tables.

As soon as the war was over, we asked for the man back. They said, "Well, you worked it four years without him, why should we put him back?"

So I left the job.

I went on the [Union Pacific] City of L.A. 'cause it was good over there. I was there when we'd carry—during the football season—we'd carry USC to Pennsylvania. We'd carry 'em to Notre Dame. That was a good train, see. We held that car not quite a year—the Russian Hill—the rear car.

I know one time we come outta there, and we had two cars with USC alumni. There was Bob Hope, Bing Crosby, all that bunch of guys. We started to work at two o'clock that afternoon—we got to report in at noon. The train left at two something that afternoon, and we didn't stop serving until we got to Chicago. Then when they take us to the game, see, the next morning, we backed down to South Bend. That's where they park the cars. Went to the game and brought 'em back—put us on the back of no. 103 [City of Los Angeles] and brought us back to Los Angeles. Them guys was eating and drinkin' all the way. Bing was up in the other car.

Our car, we had Bob Hope and another fella, some big shot with the alumni. They had suites in that car. Then they'd run tabs. I think Mr. Bing Crosby's check was nine hundred something dollars. Yeah, they just drinking and put it on his check. Bob Hope had a tab, a running tab. And when we'd get back to Los Angeles, whatever your check was, that's what your tip was. That's right. They give you a thousand dollars. Bing Crosby was a good tipper. That guy'd see your check—he start countin' you out. Well, when we got through—was three of us on the car—we made about $1,200 apiece for a week's work, you know. We didn't make that much hardly in a year. But they were good tippers!

We carried Bing Crosby lots of times. We used to catch Bing Crosby going up to Klamath Falls to hunt birds on the West Coast [the Southern Pacific train that ran from Los Angeles to Seattle via Sacramento]. Yeah. Oh, they'd go up and shoot ducks. We'd carry 'em up, and we'd pick 'em up again coming back. We'd put them ducks in a linen sack and load 'em with ice at

Klamath Falls, and I'd load ice on there at Sacramento. They'd be in a room car, in the Seattle car. And I'd keep 'em on ice for them.

Had one star on there—now there was a sport. Pullman Company put a car on the back of the City [of Los Angeles], and he and another fella had about four girls on there with just brassieres and panties. Told me to keep that door locked. They had bagels and all kind of cream cheese, and I was taking care of the bar. Cut off at Las Vegas, spend the day in Las Vegas, and came back and had a bunch of new girls; take 'em to Chicago. He was a nice-looking dude, though.

And this fella, what's the singer here? Blue Eyes? Sinatra! He's a nice man. Oh, I had that bunch several times. Sinatra's good. Had him on the City going east. Had him on the Lark a number of times. Yeah, he gave me a hat. We had him outta San Francisco going to Chicago, he and Peter Lawford, and I tried Blue Eyes' hat on, and I liked it.

I told him, "I sure like that hat. It fits me good."

He said, "Does it? Yeah, you can have it."

Yeah, I kept it. Nice hat. Expensive hat. It was just another hat for a while. I wore it in Chicago.

Then I had this fella—who's the big fella that made that radio show, and it frightened everybody? Orson Welles! We had him one trip. The guy in the car next to me, we was going to Portland on to Seattle, and this new porter's name was Sessions. He's a friend of my wife's. So Orson Welles asked him for a table, you know, they give you a table in the drawing room.

So he asked Mr. Welles, he said, "You want the 25¢ table or the 50¢ table?"

He said, "I'll take the 50¢ table."

So he got one and hooked the table up. Okay, so he gave him 50¢. He didn't say too much.

So the next day he says, "You know, I didn't particularly like that 50¢ table. How about a 25¢ table?"

So he went and got a 25¢ table—put it back up.

That evening he called the conductor in, and Orson says, "Conductor, I want you to talk to this porter. I imagine he hasn't been working too long. I asked for a table, and he asked me if I wanted the 50¢ table or the 25¢ table, and I told him. Now he brings me another table here, it's the 25¢ table, and it's the same table. Now I know the difference. I know the Pullman Company wouldn't charge for tables. Can you get him straight?"

So when the conductor found it was Orson Welles, he said, "Well, I take care of it with the company. . . ."

"No, I don't want the company to know a thing about this. It's between you and I and the porter. If anything else comes up, I'm gonna deny it . . . but you talk to him."

So he went back there and shook Sessions up. But you know how guys do, young porters!

We had one lady would get on in Los Angeles. We knew her well, pretty woman. She always wore a black dress with a little fringe on it. As soon as she'd come on, when she walked or sit down, we'd give her half a drink. Well, the conductor knew her, the Pullman conductor anyway. He'd go on through. And she'd sit there, and she'd pick out her man. The guys were flirting anyway, in the Pullman lounge.

Say a drink is $2.50—guy'd give you $5. She'd say, "Give this man his change." And she'd slide you a dollar, she threw out a tip. Then pretty soon they would go off to bed. She don't have a room. You take her to your room. I've never been on there when they didn't make a hit. They probably know when they're on the train who they're gonna pick out. That's the way they worked it.

Then she'd come back outta San Francisco. Now, she could come through the side gate at San Francisco, come out on our car, and we pour a scotch and water, half a drink. And she'd be sitting down next to some man and start talking. When the conductor come through and says, "Tickets, get your tickets," the conductor, he would say, "Got you at the gate," and come on through.

Naw, she didn't pay. She'd sit there and drink with that guy—or whoever she was drinking with—from say nine-thirty to about twelve-thirty or one o'clock. So you may pick up fifteen, twenty dollars out of it. They'd go and stay in a room till next morning. The conductor'd get a fat tip. Everybody got part of the action. Sometimes she'd come back the next morning and have breakfast and give you a tip. They'd see you got that tip. The guys from these big companies knew them. They knew 'em.

If I was to open a restaurant, I could make money, because Pullman educated every man that worked for them how to handle food. We got a long loaf of Pullman bread that was seven or eight orders to the loaf. But it was about four or five slices over. Now when that tally comes up, you have to have seven orders of toast or a sandwich or something to tally for that bread. They put five lemons on there. You had to get forty orders outta that five lemons. Eight slices to the lemon. I think you got one whole one for lemonade, and if you put down tea with lemon, and you're an eighth of a lemon short, you had to pay.

Then once a month they'd come down—you'd pay the shortage. You paid for a spoon that was lost. They'd give you a bushel of peas, and they expected so many orders outta that. And if they figured you were short a couple orders, you had to pay unless something happened, and the cook burned some toast or he ruined a steak. You tell the conductor, "Here. Condemn this steak." Conductor'd look at it, he would sign it. If he didn't sign it, you paid—everything on that car that Pullman Company got their money for.

29

On the kitchen car, they'd throw a ham on there and some beans for the crew. Anything else, you wrote a check for. Sugar—they could tell you how much sugar you're throwing away. Cream—how much cream you're throwing away. Milk—everything was checked. On prunes, we used to have an order of prunes, and we'd take one or two prunes out. But we all skimmed. You make up the hotcake batter that morning, and end of the trip you'd have hotcake batter left over, so the crew would eat hotcakes. But if we thought we ate too much butter, we'd go to the store and get a quarter pound of Challenge butter and bring it back on the car. Everything on that car was checked. And there wasn't a month you didn't have some kind of shortage.

When my dad was working years ago, he had to count all the towels. If his towel's short, he had to pay. Same with napkins, but then after the union got pretty solid and got in there they broke that up, 'cause people would take things. Why, I've known people to take a sugar bowl at night, and I'd tell the conductor, "When he's puttin' away the bed, I wanna go back and take it."

He said, "No, you can't do that, Smock."

"But, oh, yes sir, that's the man that took it."

But you're afraid to approach the passenger. If you say you don't have it, the Pullman Company's in jeopardy of a suit.

And they take the silver. I know the time when we'd have our silver at night, go in the next morning to serve breakfast and count silver before you get off the car. Can't find it. Somebody took it. Had to get the garbage chute out and go through piece by piece trying to find it. Like we go to town, and I don't count the silver, and the guy come along and say you were a knife and a bullion spoon short, you had to pay.

At the end of every trip, we polish silver going into Los Angeles. See, we'd have silver creamers, crumbers, shrimp cocktails. Everything was silver. We polished all that stuff, whether we used it or not. We had a couple of chemists, one fella come on and told us we take a granite pan and take a half of a 15¢ box of epsom salts, pour in this boiling hot water, and stir the silverware around in there and bring it up and dry it. It would be polished pretty. But in 12 or 15 hours, it'd be just as black as it started out. It's just a quick fix, you know.

Introduced along with the streamlined train in the thirties was the concept of the "unit train": an entire train would remain joined together trip after trip, uncoupling only for equipment changes or shop work. In the heavyweight era, it had been common practice to pick up or set out dining and lounge cars at selected points along the way. It was thought that the wages saved in reduced hours for labor, plus lower car mileage, would result in a significant savings to the railroad. Once the new trains arrived, however, it became impractical to continue this practice. Schedules were tightened wherever possible, and the extra time cutting cars in and out added precious minutes to the timecard.

The Lark's triple-unit diner was permanently coupled together, making such maneuvers impossible. As a result, this practice was for the most part discontinued not only by Southern Pacific but by the majority of railroads. Virgil Smock remembers the prestreamlined Lark and recalls how they managed this operation.

We didn't have no dining car on the train till morning on the Lark or the Sunset. Yeah, see, the dining car'd go out on the back of the Coaster at night—two diners—and they cut 'em off at Santa Barbara [when the Sunset ran from San Francisco to New Orleans]. And the next morning, when the Sunset came through, a switch engine'd pull us out, set the diner in the train, shove us back in, and they'd feed breakfast along with us [the buffet car]. The Lark would do the same thing.

Now, say, for instance, we would get four or five hours late, the switch engine would bring that car pretty near halfway to San Luis Obispo up to Surf or Guadalupe and wait. Say at Guadalupe the Lark is late. Well, they pull that diner up to Guadalupe and set it in the siding. When the Lark would come in, it'd go down past the cut [where the cars waited to be coupled into the main train]. The switch engine would come in, get the back of the Lark, pull it down, go in the hole [in the siding], pick up the diner, come back out, slap it on, couple it up, have an air test, and away you go. Out right away. You're on the road. So until we got the lightweight equipment, that's what we done, see.

On the Lark we done all the feeding at night, and they would come back there early—8:15—getting dinner. All we served [on the buffet car] was steaks, cold plates, and sandwiches at dinner leaving L.A. We had fellas come back there and wanna look at a steak. We'd have nice fresh steaks. They said, "I don't want that. You got any old steaks?" Up in the front car we had some old steaks. All the new steaks go in the back car. A guy'd tell ya, "Hey, wash that off and give me that medium." Be real whiskers on the meat! Aged steak.

Now we had a smart cook on there, you're talking big fat steaks? He'd slice it right down the center. Now a lady gets on who orders a steak dinner, see, and her steak's kinda thin. The other half's for the crew! End of the night, we'd have maybe four or five steaks. The crew would have steak leaving San Luis Obispo for dinner, see? And then we would take and cut the end off the steak and throw it in a pot when they had the big kitchen. End of the night, when the crew would get on at San Luis Obispo or getting off at San Luis Obispo, we'd give 'em what you call Mulligan stew.

Anytime [Pullman employees] ate on a dining car, you paid. Some dining cars wanted a third, some wanted half. I had a buffet car—it wasn't actually a buffet car—on the Golden State. I served sandwiches and liquor. That was on the Golden Divan and the La Mirada—can't remember the other [Golden Vista]. There was three cars [rear-end lounge/observation cars that rotated trips] on the Golden State, but I just served liquor, and I'd always go up in the diner to eat.

I'd go in the kitchen and get a tray and maybe clean off several tables. I'd do that maybe two or three times a night. Well, around eight-thirty the waiter'd come in: "Hey, had your dinner, kid?" I said no. "Come on up, man, get your dinner." Get a free dinner, see. Next morning he'd come out, say, "Hey boy, come in here and get your breakfast." I got so I didn't pay for a meal.

If the waiter brought a meal back to one of the cars, I'd take them dishes up to the dining car. When the summertime passenger load be light, I'd go up there in the kitchen in the afternoon and wash a few dishes, you know. Just foolin' around, hustlin', didn't pay for a meal.

At one time the Pullman Company had dining cars on trains, and they hauled prisoner specials or Kiwanis specials or the old Shriners. You've always got a few that has a rowdy bunch. The Shriners, they had a few off-the-wall guys. A lot of those guys were doctors and lawyers, and their personality was different. But you take the veterans of wars, the veteran specials? They'd take those big cherry bombs—and like, your shoe boxes [shoe lockers for passengers] there? You'd go to bed at night, and two o'clock in the morning, they say, "Well, we gonna wake old Dave up." They'd take a cherry bomb and put it in there and blow the doors off the box. A guy thought the world had come to an end!

The porters were nice, and I got along with them. When I made attendant, I couldn't understand why the porters would come in in the morning, and there'd be four or eight, and they'd sit at a certain spot, sit in my buffet and drink their coffee and toast. Then the conductor and the brakeman'd sit on the other side.

So after I got my foot in the door, when they come in, I told the brakeman, "You sit over here."

He said, "Well, we sit over here."

I said, "Over here. You sit over here now." Porters right along with them. Set 'em all right in there together as they came in. They didn't like that. The porters sort of resented it. Some of the old porters would see I was right. Sometimes the brakeman would lay around late, to come in late. But if he came in too late, he had to stand up and drink his coffee.

I said, "You gotta stand up in the corner and drink your coffee, 'cause the fellas have changed the tablecloths already."

The conductor turned me in to the superintendent, and Mr. Leach called me, and he says, "What's the problem out there?"

I said, "There's no problem out there, Mr. Leach. Every time they sit down and drink coffee, we had to change tablecloths. You know, tablecloths cost the company money. We seat 'em, and if the conductor don't wanna sit with the porters and the brakeman don't wanna sit with the porters, well, I don't know what's gonna rub off on 'em."

He said, "Okay, it's all settled." He didn't tell me whether I was right or wrong, just that it was all settled. Didn't have any more problems.

My dad always told me to see that the porters got fed. When a porter comes in your car, feed him. See, the porters had sort of a bad time when they'd go to the dining car. The stewards were sort of snotty, some of them were, and some of the waiters seemed to think that they were better than the porters. So what happened is that the porters treated me real nice. They knew me. They'd say, "Well, that's Smock's boy." They was always a help. I knew the work. I was treated real nice by all the porters.

The old porters were a little different. We didn't take the chance that these younger porters did. See, the younger porters would just speak up and talk back. And they done everything wild, you know. They were just a wild bunch. When you talk to my brother, you ask him about some of the things that happened on the train, on the Rexall Special. They had some wild bunch of fellows on there, and this fellow that run it gave 'em a fifth of whiskey every night and told Mr. Allen, the Pullman inspector, to leave 'em alone. They worked all day, let 'em have some fun, let 'em blow off steam. So as I say, George, Babe, Elliott, Leonard, Handy Moore, and Payne—all those fellows, about a dozen of 'em—Mr. Hatch named 'em the Dalton Boys 'cause he'd say, "You fellas all gonna get fired, the whole bunch at one time." But we were just a bunch of young fellows.

We had a guy on the Lark with us. He'd say [*whining voice*], "You know, I didn't make but eight dollars, all them people." But he may have made twelve, fourteen, fifteen. He put eight in the kitty. We knew he was stealing, but nothing you could do about it. Well, he wasn't stealing, he just wasn't playing fair.

I understand—my dad was tellin' me, if I can remember right—when the porters were trying to get a union up and they went in to strike, they hired a lot of Filipinos. They done the cooking. I had two Filipinos I was working with, and these guys told me, they said, "Look, all you make you keep, and if anything goes up the train, whatever that tip is, we'll give it to you. We'll keep what's in the diner." That's okay with me, but I'm still the boss. I'm in charge. Well, I'd go back there and see if dinner's all right. If they have a check, I'd punch the check. I'd go back and do my work. I wouldn't bother them.

So I came in town one morning, and the commissary called me and wanted to see me, said, "They want you out at the yards." So I went out there with Mr. Drake from Chicago, and I thought he was having some kind of meeting. He told me to sit down, got me all relaxed. He said, "Look through these checks."

And I looked through 'em. "See anything wrong with them?"

"No."

"Whose signature?"

I said, "My signature."

"Who's in charge?"

I said, "I am."

He said, "You see any orange juice on those checks?"

"Some of 'em."

He said, "So-and-so told me there's four orange juice went up the train, and there's no checks made for them."

I said, "Those fellas they want to work the diner together, and I go out and see the checks are priced, and everything is on the check, you know."

He said, "Here's some with no tomato juice on it, and the tomato juice tallies with the supply report."

I said, "Okay."

So he got all that stuff together and said, "We're gonna have a hearing." He got the cooks in.

They said, "I don't know." Waiters said, "I don't know."

So they went just about down to the end of the wire. Then Mr. Leach said, "Now, Virgil, you know what's going on out there. If you don't, you should know. Now, you can get fired, because you're in charge. You're responsible."

I went to the cook and told him, "Look, I don't know what it is, but I'm not gonna be fired. I don't care about the job itself, 'cause I can go to work, but my granddad and my dad and my big brother all got good reputations out there, and you're not gonna put no mark on the Smock name."

Finally he said, "Well, all right."

So they walked in there and confessed to what it was. They were charged with several pots of coffee they served without a check and these orange juice. Now the orange juice went to spotters up the train—four large orange juices. That's what got 'em, see.

On Mr. Roosevelt's car, we had a black cook. I saw a black cook and a Filipino waiter and a black attendant in charge. I never worked his car. I went into Chicago one time, and Mr. Cartwright told me that they was cutting my car out and he wanted to see me down at the office. They wanted to send me to Washington on a special. That's the way they'd get me home. I said it didn't make any difference. I remember they questioned me there, and I went out to the yards, and he told me I couldn't leave the train. Mr. Roosevelt's car was on the rear of the train. Anyway, I cleared the questions they asked me, you know. I guess it was the Secret Service. They were at the Pullman office down there at the yards—what was that—Pennsylvania yards. So we came out of there, and I went to San Francisco. That's the way they got me home.

I got a chance to see Mr. Roosevelt several times. We could go into the train, but in his private car these Secret Service men sit there all the time, so we talked back and forth, and we couldn't transfer food back and forth. The only thing we transferred was water. We had Pullman water by the case. See, they didn't use the tap water off the reservoir, just Pullman water by the case.

I had car Chieftan [a heavyweight car containing six single bedrooms and a dining lounge]. We had a couple cars of Secret Service men, couple cars of press, then had a hospitality car for senators and dignitaries. That was the car that I guess dignitaries come down and you serve hors d'oeuvres and stuff like that. That was about a ten-car train. On the front they had three cars with all kind of electrical equipment, radios and stuff like that. But the army was in charge of the train. We didn't make too many stops. Stopped at Kansas City, we were on the UP [Union Pacific]. I think we stopped at Ogden, Omaha, Cheyenne. [President Roosevelt] boarded a destroyer, I guess, in San Francisco.

We had a job and we did the job, that's what it was, see. We didn't look at it like we do today, you know. We didn't look at it as black over white, or white over black, or being kicked around. For instance, before they had a lot of dining cars on the train, we used to stop at La Juanta, and we'd stop at Albuquerque—the Harvey Houses. Well, then the porters would go in the back part and eat. So there was no feeling. Even on the SP at El Paso, we'd jump off. Then we'd get on the diner and have hotcakes, 'cause it's cheaper, see. We didn't feel any different then. Certain places in the South we could put our boxes, but we couldn't go in the station. We just felt that was the trend, and that was it.

I had a fella working with me named Handy Moore, and sharp. He went two years out to UCLA and was very smart. People would come and say [does the "Here dog" whistle], calling Moore. So Moore would come out looking under the chairs and table. Somebody'd say, "You lose something?" He said, "No, this man be calling for a dog." All that kind of stuff, you know.

These guys in the Chevrolet Motor Car Company'd come down in groups. And we had a fella, he was smart, too. He always had a smart answer. So this businessman says, "Hey, come here. What's your name?"

He says, "Harold."

"Harold, now, we want to go in Los Angeles, and we heard about the

Alabam [a nightclub]. Can you tell us where we can get a couple nice black girls to take us and show us around?"

So [Harold] Carr thought a few minutes, and he say, "Well, I tell ya. I just can't put my finger on it. You see, my wife is white, and all my friends are white."

That tipped it right there. They walked off. One of the guys called him a smart SOB, and they went on to bed. But see, you had guys that play that kind of stuff, you know. But you overlooked it.

Like Mr. Leach said, "If it disturbs you, don't say nothing at all, just walk on off." Now I could tell you when a passenger comes down the platform at night or in the daytime, the way they approached you, that he was either gonna have hell with him or he's gonna be a gentleman clerk of the county. He'd come down there, and you could tell the looks of him the way he approached you.

There was quite a bit of dissension because the conductors were white and all the officials were white. They looked down on the porters like they had a hoof over them—the coloreds, you know what I mean? We had some decent conductors. There's an old man named George. He was from Mississippi, a southerner. I don't know whether he owned a plantation or not, but he looked on his porters as his boys, and nobody jumped on him.

I don't care if the superintendent got on there, if you started harassing, he said [*with a deep southern drawl*], "Now, wait a minute. That's my boy. Now, ah, if you have anything to say to him, you talk to him when he ain't on these cars. When he's on here, he belongs to me, and I don't want nobody running over him."

See, I was born and raised in Los Angeles, and I never felt that part of the society [racism], because I was on trains that went from Los Angeles to Chicago and New York. I never got south until the fifties on the train.

I had porters tell me what they come against. That's before Martin Luther King started his crusade. My way of life wasn't patronizing to that, you know, but in my later years it sort of disturbed me. It disturbs me now more than it did then because I sort of feel it in some ways now. I know the time that really struck us, before the war, was San Francisco. San Francisco was San Francisco! People dressed! They—well, you know, people *dressed* in San Francisco.

We used to go to the top of the Mark Hopkins [Hotel] in the late thirties and the forties and have cocktails on Sunday. We were just young bucks, but we wanted to be with the elite, you know. We'd go up there and call ourselves doing something big on Sunday afternoon before we'd come to work. But then the war came along and that. Well, it didn't change at the Mark Hopkins, but it changed down at Market Street, you know.

We'd go down to Kress's [drugstore] to have our lunch at the counter— until the war came along. Then we went to eat at the counter, and the woman refused to serve us because she come from Oklahoma or Kansas or down south, and that's what they didn't do. Things began to change. That's when people came out to work in the war effort, you know, and then San Francisco started going to the dogs. It hit me more so, as I say, in the fifties, when I would get off the railroad and chauffeur around the country, and I was turned down several times for a place to sleep.

Even with tips added on to their base salary, the Pullman porter earned barely enough to raise a family. Many porters were forced to moonlight on their off days or vacations. Virgil Smock describes his experiences in the Deep South while chauffeuring for a dentist and his wife.

He called me and told me, "I understand you're a cross-country chauffeur." I said, "No, I'm a Pullman attendant with the Pullman Company. I just drove Mrs. Brown several times across the country." He said, "I want you to drive me to Florida. I'm going to the ADA [American Dental Association] convention." So I finally go to Mr. Schulte [Pullman supervisor] and told him that my family got property down south, and I have to go down and take care of it. I'd lose a trip plus my vacation.

When I went with Dr. Sharpe—when I got to Grand Saline, Texas—I put 'em to bed, and I went in, told this lady, "I'd like to know where you'd like me to sleep tonight."

She says, "Well, you can't sleep here, son."

"If I can't sleep here, where will I sleep?"

She said, "Well, there's a colored motel"—see, it was "colored" in those days—she said, ". . . a colored motel about 12 or 18 miles just right down the 180."

So I went back and knocked on the door. I says, "Dr. Sharpe, I'm going to have to borrow your car tonight." And I never took his car other than when we were working.

He said, "You found you a girlfriend already?"

I said, "No, there's no place for me to sleep in this town, and I can't sleep in this Lincoln."

"What do you mean no place to sleep?"

I said, "There's no colored people in this town."

"What's that have to do with your sleeping?"

I said, "Doctor, they don't sleep colored people here. Now, where am I gonna sleep?"

He got just mad—he was about five foot five, you know—he started running around and told his wife Agnes, he said, "Aggie, get your clothes on. Go back and get my money. You help Agnes get dressed here and pack my bags. We're leaving." It's about eight-thirty at night; he's ready to go to bed. He went around and jumped on this lady. I felt sorry for her. He didn't swear, he just gave her the business.

So we went down the road, and he stopped another man, and this fella says, "Well, what can I do for ya, uncle?"

He says, "I'm not your uncle. I'm Dr. George C. Sharpe, and what you can do for me is have a decent, respectable place for my driver to sleep."

He said, "We can take care of that."

"All right, put Mrs. Sharpe to bed first."

So he got her signed in.

"Now, you take me and Virgil to where he's gonna sleep, 'cause I want to see it."

So he called some house and went around a big magnolia tree in the yard. I went in, come back, I said, "Very nice, Dr. Sharpe."

And every place we stopped, he said first, "Where can Virgil sleep?"

Things went along good until we got to Silver Springs, Texas. Beautiful hotel. Pulled in there, and the lady said, yeah, had a single and a double. So she was signing us up, and I come out to get the stuff outta the car, and this fella was shaking his finger.

She says, "What harm can it do?"

Dr. Sharpe says, "What's the matter, Virgil?"

I said, "I think I'm in question here. She said it's okay, and he says it's not okay."

He said, "Drive on."

We'd made a reservation, but he hadn't paid. Just drove on out. Went to another motel, and the guy says, "Yeah, all I have is a room with two beds in it."

Dr. Sharpe said, "He look like a half a man to you? He can't sleep but one bed at one time." This owner was shocked.

He says, "Well, I can put him up."

So then, "Where can he eat?"

I ate at the counter, you know, sit there and ate, and people come in, and they look at me. It didn't bother me, 'cause I heard about it. The only time I got excited was in Baltimore. Now, I just knew Baltimore would be okay. Pulled in this Hotel Baltimore, and he says, "I need a single and a double."

"What'd you mean you want a single and a double?"

He say, "That's what I said. I want a single for my driver and a double for my wife."

"I got a double, but I ain't got no single for him 'cause he ain't gonna stay here 'cause we don't sleep 'em. And I'll close up before I sleep 'em."

By that time the old man [Dr. Sharpe] got to arguing, and the guy put his hand on the door. I got my pistol, 'cause I thought he was gonna hit the old man. The old man was raising sand with him.

So he said, "Now, you get your car and this boy outta here, 'cause he ain't gonna sleep here. We don't want him to sleep here."

Dr. Sharpe told this guy, "I'll tell you one thing. You get ready to close up, 'cause they're coming. And they'll be here sooner than you think."

But in New York, no problem. You'd maybe go to some big fine restaurant, then I would put Dr. Sharpe out, and he said, "What about the man . . . well, bring out his food."

The waiter'd come out and said, "Look, you don't have to eat in the car. Come on round the back." So I'd go in the back and eat on the meat block. The kitchen guy'd put a new cloth on the meat block, and I'd eat there.

But I prefer those days to the days of today. I think the era up to the fifties—we carried a different class of people. We took people outta Chicago and started putting them off at Tuscon, put 'em at Chandler, Phoenix, Palm Springs. Those were a different type of people, you know. They made their children respect you. People that 80 percent of them were more classier people. They knew how to speak to you. They knew how to approach you. They got the service, and they dressed to the occasion. I like that. We still call it the "good old days."

I would like to see an old train leave here once a week with the 1934 equipment when they first started, air-conditioned heavyweight cars and the steam engine—just to show people.

Garrard Wilson "Babe" Smock Jr.

3

GARRARD WILSON "BABE" SMOCK JR.
Pullman Buffet and Lounge Car Attendant
1937–1960

Garrard Wilson Smock Jr., the youngest of the three brothers, was born in Los Angeles on 14 May 1918. He lived with his parents until 1928, when he moved in with his grandmother, Anna Virginia Smock, with whom he lived until 1932. Although christened "Garrard," he has gone by the family nickname "Babe" since childhood.

Had he been born four decades later, Babe might have become a professional musician. His love of music, nurtured by his grandmother, led him as a youth to the violin and one of four seats in the Los Angeles Unified School District Orchestra. But classical music opportunities were extremely rare for a black child of that era, and the Pullman Company would offer him the safest and quickest avenue of employment in the 1930s.

Babe's attitude on railroading fell somewhere between his two brothers. He was not drawn to the life, as Virgil had been, yet he did not find it distasteful, as George did. Babe found himself out of work when Pullman pulled off the buffet cars in 1960. After working a number of years doing day work for a family in Los Angeles, he eventually went back to railroading with Findley's Fun Time Tours and once again worked side by side with Virgil, traveling across the United States and into Mexico. After Virgil left Findley's, Babe worked a while longer, until the rigors of the road became too demanding on his health.

After coming out of school in 1937, I went to work for a private family, a Mrs. Gratzner in Westwood, and I worked as a chauffeur-butler. I worked for her from probably June to October, when this opening came to come up on the railroad, and my father asked me did I want to come to the company, and I told him yes. And so they took me down to see Mr. Leach, which was the superintendent. He was reluctant to hire me, due to my age of 18, but having a past history of a grandfather, father, and two other brothers, he accepted me.

41

I only was supposed to go to work for the railroad for a period of about, well, I would say two or three years, 'cause I wanted to pursue music. But after going down south in 1936, I found that I was further advanced than they were, and the field of music was not open to blacks at that particular time.

Let's say they would bar it in a way of speaking, that "at the present time we have no openings—the classes are filled." That's an easy way of going around it, their putting it to you that way. See, during them times, whenever you signed an application for anything, it would put down there "white," "Negro"—all different languages and nationalities was differentiated. And especially when you crossed out "Negro," that automatically told them that you were black. Nothing was open towards us, so there was no field for us to go into. And that's one reason why I just took the easy way out and stayed on the railroad.

I don't think we as a generation at that time paid any attention to it. A lot of 'em never paid any attention to it. They just went ahead and accepted it. And I would say today that if it hadn't been for Martin Luther King, a lot of the standards would still be the same. When I was coming along and when I went to school, if somebody call me black, we had to fight. Now, if you *don't* call him black, you gonna have to fight him because he wants to be called black.

I today would rather work for a southern person than I would for a northern person out here on the West Coast. The South, you know where he's coming from. You know his policies. You know where he stands, so in Rome you do as the Romans do. He's subject to call you "boy" and think nothin' of it. The guy out here in the North, he says, "You know one thing? I want you to know that I'm on your side 100 percent," and pat you on the back [*pats his shoulder*]. That's while he's talkin' to you, but when he gets out there in Beverly Hills, it's altogether different. See what I mean? His feelings is altogether different: "Ah, them goddamn niggers, so and so, blah-blah. . . ." But you know where that southerner comes from.

If you was a black person and you were ridin' Pullman to New Orleans, you could only come up into the dining car when the dining car was just about empty, because they would pull the curtains and you sit and ate in this area. You could not eat in this dining car area. That is correct! When you left here from Los Angeles to go to New Orleans on the coaches, they put all of the blacks in the first coach forward. And when you went through such towns as Sweetwater and them places down there, you pull the shades down. You don't, they'll throw rocks through the windows. You had to be up front. The same way it was with the engineers and firemen; they were strictly white. You got black engineers out there now. You got black firemen; you got black switchmen. You got black airline pilots. But who would have ever thought of it during that time? But the trend has changed, and God knows what this next generation is gonna go through. Yeah!

The Pullman Company hired anybody who applied who could fulfill the job, but they didn't have to be necessarily young blacks. The majority of the porters stayed on there until they was ready to drop. They were ready, actually, to drop. The majority of the porters when I was coming along there, Uncle Billy McCormick and all of 'em, they all of 'em was 70 years of age then, until the Pullman Company just got so that they forced 'em out. But now the new law is you cannot force a man out at 70 years of age. You can continue to work.

I started to work—made my first trip on 18 October 1937 on the Lark to San Francisco. Now, the Lark buffet-observation had a drawing room, compartment, and two bedrooms, and that was the biggest joke there was because if you bought this drawing room, you're right next to the kitchen. And when we start shoveling coal at five o'clock in the morning, you in that room could hear everything. It was just a sin and a shame for anybody to have that particular room.

Many people would get on the Lark, I don't see what they bought rooms for. They never go to bed. No, they never go to bed! And, 'course, there was a two o'clock law as far as sellin' whiskey is concerned, but as long as the train is runnin' and the train conductor is on your side, you don't have to worry about nothin'. You can just buy whiskey all night long. Yeah! [laughs].

We'd catch passengers, presidents of Western Union, Bell Telephone, and various banks. They would come up—say, a businessman, he would leave Los Angeles with me tonight, and he'll say, "Babe, you're doubling right back tonight, aren't you?"

You say, "Yes, sir."

He says, "Well, it looks like it's gonna be a good day in San Francisco. Would you keep my coat for me tonight?" Well, they'd leave half their belongings on the train because they were coming right back with us. And we made 11 trips a month, and some of 'em make half as many with us. They would go up and come right back.

See, us on the train were just like one of the passengers—knew everybody. They knew me, knew Steele, knew Virgil and George. And some passengers would call us and say, "Who's going out on the rear car tonight?"

"Well, let's see—Dago."

Well, that's it. They won't go that night. They don't like to go with Dago. No, but like you go up to Sam Tibbs. Sam Tibbs knew everybody on that Lark that come in the lounge. They knew Sam and Broussard and Little Shorty and all the rest of 'em because they were there every night. There was no such thing as going out here and catching PSA [Pacific Southwest Airlines] or United or Western [airlines] or somethin' like that—everybody rode the train. Oh, yeah. And during that time we had the Lark, which left out at nine o'clock at night, the Sunset left out at six something in the evening, and then there was 69/70, which was the local train. It left out later on at night. So there was three trains going, and then they started the Daylight. People was always train-conscious.

Now, I could say going back to when I lived with my grandmother back in '28, '29, where there was a train leaving outta Los Angeles every hour going to Chicago. Every hour there was one going. If it wasn't the Southern Pacific, it was the Santa Fe, it was the Union Pacific. The Santa Fe had all kinds of trains: the Navajo, the Scout, the Missionary, and they were going every hour, and those trains were filled to a certain capacity every hour.

Then all of a sudden, when the railroads started petering off, and everybody started flying the airplanes. Why not? Forty-eight minutes to San Francisco. Then they started cutting back on the various trains, and they—well, I think during that time there were freeloaders, which was pass riders, that only ride a certain train. Then they limited the passes to certain families and things like that.

We, as a Pullman porter, never received a free pass. No. We had to ask. If I wanted to send my wife down to Mississippi to visit her father, I had to put in a request for a pass, and they have to turn around and notify the Southern Pacific, and the Southern Pacific asks, "How long has he been working?" and blah-blah this, and finally they'd send me a pass and I'd give it to her, then she'd catch a train and go down to New Orleans, and then go on up to see her father in Mississippi. But railroad fellas after so many years got a free pass. They kept their pass in their pocket; he can ride whenever he got ready. But not with the Pullman Company.

The Pullman porters were—well, let's say there was a line between the dining car service and the Pullman service. We did not feel that we were better than the dining car waiters, but sometimes they felt that they were better than us, and it was just a conflict. We were friends and talk and everything like that, but when it came down to working on the train, it was an altogether different situation. Yeah, there was a friction there, a little jealousy. We were paid a little bit better than the dining car waiters were.

We served the best very reasonable. The Pullman Company was economical down to the very last. If they put two dozen potatoes on, I'm supposed to get so many orders out of them potatoes. I'm supposed to get so many glasses of orange juice out of the oranges. The tomato juice was put on in individual cans. You had to count for everything, and when you got back in town and turned your money over to the conductor, you fill out your book what you have left on the car; then it would go to the commissary, then they would check it. Then they would go over your meal checks. They were so stinkin' tight that they could tell me that, "G. W., you're using an excessive amount of sugar this time." Potatoes: we knew the potatoes had to be served one potato per customer. Orange juice: every orange don't give the same amount of juice out of it. Just because it's a bigger orange—one of 'em may be larger than the other one. But if it's that way, then you make a notation, "An extra orange was used," and they were very tight.

When my grandfather come along, the company stayed on them—just as you make an expression—"like white on rice." They stayed tight on them. Say you had so many towels that you went out with, and you used so many towels, and when they'd count your linen and count what's used and what's left, if you were one towel short, they'd charge you for a towel. That was during his regime, but the younger generation began to change, and the old diehards began to move out, and the younger generation came in. Their theory was a little bit different than maybe Dick Shore was. Dick Shore was assistant superintendent, and he believed in knucklin' right down to the line. When they moved him out and Schulte come in, Schulte was more the congenial fella that walk up and pat you on the back and "Hi, G. W., how's everything? How was your trip? No problems?" Okay, and he's gone.

But the others would stay right on ya, like Schelmeyer. Schelmeyer was a superintendent. Schelmeyer would get on the car, and he'd look for things. He'd move this to see what was behind it. The mop couldn't be behind the toilet, the mop had to be here. Or your runners [cloth runners to protect aisleways in terminals] for your car had to be rolled up correctly, 'cause when you come in town, you roll your runners down. But Schelmeyer was just that way: "Why isn't this rolled up better than this?" The rest of 'em didn't pay no attention to them runners. If I folded a runner up and put it in the cupboard, long as it's put away, it was all right. But not with Schelmeyer and Dick Shore and Major . . . oh, what was his name? He was a major in the army. I can't think of his name now. He was another strict one.

Now, Conners tried to go underneath that same theory, and Lucy, but the younger generation was different. They'd get on the car there, and they'd look around, but Schelmeyer would look for things [moves ashtray]. "What's that doin' there?" Damn, if you hadn't raised it, you'd never saw it. But see, you couldn't talk to him like that. "I don't know, Mr. Schelmeyer." "Well, I don't wanna find it that way again." You had to, in other words, kiss his ass to get along with him. But the rest of the generation, no. No!

Once every thirty-some-odd days, we would rotate around where George was the cook, Virgil was the porter, and I was the waiter: three of us working on one car together, until old man Armstrong come down one night, and he looked up there, he says, "This can't be. This can't be! The whole Smock family on one car?" Well, that's the way it rotated. He said, "Well, it won't rotate that way no more," and he didn't want that. He didn't want no three of the same family on one car. But we got along fine.

We get along fine as brothers and always have been that way, because my father got killed in 1950. Well, I was at the bowling alley, and see, my name is Garrard, but I've went underneath Babe. Everybody knows me as Babe. And one day I was at the bowling alley in the afternoon on 49th and Central, and the telephone rang. I don't know what the conversation was, but the guy hung up the phone. We went on back to laughin' and talkin' and bowling. Pretty soon the person called back again and still no so-and-so.

So finally, third time, he says, "Hey, anybody in here named Garrard?"

I said, "Yeah, that's me, why?"

"No, Babe's your name."

I said, "No, Babe is just a nickname."

"Well, there's some lady on the phone here."

So it was my mother. Said, "Babe, you promised to take me to church. I'm ready to go." So I said I'll be there in a few minutes.

Now, you know when you're bowling, you don't wanna stop in the middle of the game, see. So I finished that game and jumped in my little old Ford and headed down Central Avenue, and just as I rode over to Hooper Avenue, my father was making a right turn at the corner, taking her to church. So I went upstairs to a dentist's office, a doctor I hung around with upstairs, and he's always got a bottle. And I was upstairs I guess about a half an hour when somebody hollered, "Babe, your mother and father were in an automobile accident."

Well, as he was crossin' Naomi and Washington, the people in the first and second lane had stopped 'cause the signal said green for them, and this guy was comin' down the outside lane, the center lane, and hit him broadside and knocked him out the car, and he fell on his head and had a brain concussion. They rushed him over to Queen of Angels [Hospital], but he died the next day.

That was one of the setbacks as far as the family was concerned, 'cause my father was like, well, my mother and my father were just like our older brother and older sister to us. My father was strict to a certain extent, but yet lenient in another way. Now, if he tell you to do something, you do it. Then if he scolds you and he'll give you a whippin', he may give you a whippin', but five minutes later you're down there on the floor wrastlin' with ya, playin' with ya. He's forgotten all about it. He never harbored nothin'. What is done is done. It's over with.

Yeah, but we all got along fine, and we stayed that way. Then after he died, then we all took to taking care of our mother, and she was just like a baby sister to us. She was an arthritic rheumatoid, where her knees were swollen up with arthritis, her fingers were all gnarled so that she couldn't pick up this thing here without it being pain in her hands and stuff like that.

My grandfather never transferred out of Chicago. His home base was Chicago east, which came over the Santa Fe. Now, he would come out to Los Angeles, say he'd get in Los Angeles on a Monday. He'd stay Monday,

Tuesday, then he'd leave and go back Wednesday. Then he'd spend the rest of his time in Chicago. We only saw him about every 11 days when he'd come out. But meanwhile, my father and him never ran in conjunction with each other, only if they met when he was here in Los Angeles. And I don't ever recall it from 19——let's see, he died in '29. He was making a bed going to Chicago, going into Albuquerque, and this passenger walked beside him and touched him—now, this is the conversation that was related back to my grandmother—and he says, "George, you make my bed down when you finish this." And he said he never recalled hearing an answer. But coming back from the dining car, as he passed, my grandfather was still in the same position leaned over. And he reached to touch him, he said, "George, is there something wrong?" and he just keeled over. He was probably dead, he says, when the man talked to him the first time. He died going into Albuquerque. I would say grandfather was in his sixties.

There was more prejudice within the company than there was out on the road. Not, I would say, the company as a whole, but certain individuals who worked in the offices. Well, I don't know why, it was just a. . . . It makes me so mad—sometime you'd go up to the office and sit there, say I'm gonna go see Mr. Schubert, and I'd go in there and sit down there, and they'd look all over the top of ya, till finally somebody would say, "What do you want?"

I'd say, "Mr. Schubert."

"Well, he's busy right now. He'll be with you in a minute."

They'd make you wait, and that's something I never did like to do. If I come to see you, if you sent for me—"G. W., I want you up to the office at eleven o'clock today"—okay, fine. If I walk in there at eleven o'clock, I want to be seen at eleven o'clock. Don't let me sit there for 15 minutes and cool my heels until finally somebody decides to do it. But I don't know why that I've always felt that way. I guess because I saw it, specially down in the southern area. The people in the office—the Pullman porter wasn't nothin', but yet he was the backbone of the service. Without him, you can just forget railroading. 'Course, they gotta put some women out there, some Chinese or whichever you wanna do, but the Pullman porter was the backbone of the service. Just like you gettin' somebody that works for you. As long as you got somebody out there workin' good, you don't have to worry about the business.

'Course, it was the old adage of . . . they tried to . . . well, they considered they're paying you a decent salary, then they turn around and pay somebody to slip around in the middle of the night to catch you doin' something wrong. Oh, yeah. They'd trick you. Do anything—send women out on the train to trick ya, try to get you to go to bed with 'em. Yet there's some other guy that's along with her, waitin' for the move to be made. All kind of things like that.

I don't know. I said and I still say there was more prejudice within the company than there was out on the road. I never found it out on the road. I found some of the most best customers. And they just were friendly people. Didn't know you, but it was like the old, let's say, southern of the mammy, down there where she raised the children. They never worried about the children long as Mammy had her—they forgot all about it. That's the same thing it was on the train—as long as the Pullman porter's there, they never worried.

'Course, there was a lot of Pullman porters who abused it, and they got their comeuppance, they got fired, and no better for them. Lettin' somebody trick 'em into—some woman trickin' 'em into going to bed with 'em or stealin' and doing stuff like that. See, you were screened to a certain extent. Ah, they had a fella on there—he's dead now—I don't know why they hired him. He was fired from Kress's, he was fired from the Bank of America, he was fired from Security Pacific Bank, but yet the Pullman Company hired him. Biggest thief there was.

As far as me is concerned, they accepted me on family. Now, some of the rest of 'em, they may have went back on 'em, say five years at the most, but there were so many lies.

The majority of the dining car waiters originated out of Texas. They used to work at the big hotels back there. When they started lookin' for dining car waiters, a lot of 'em left the hotels and came out west here to get jobs on the trains. But Pullman porters, lot of 'em were hired off the streets. A guy would apply for a job, and he was recommended by Mr. Smock. 'Course, I don't know how they went about it, 'cause it didn't affect me. Like they say, something that don't affect you, you never look into it.

But other than that, that was just about the way that it was. Like I still say, I've traveled extensively where I've had to go into offices in Boston, Massachusetts—Boston was very good, very good. I walked into the office in Boston, and I was broke. I wanted to get their $10 time check. That means an advance on his salary. So when I walked in the door, the lady said, "May I help you?"

I said, "Yes, I'm Attendant G. W. Smock transferred from Los Angeles, and I was supposed to pick up a group today, but they're not going out until tomorrow. I want a $10 time check."

She said, "Where are you staying?"

I said, "I'm staying on the car."

"Will $10 be enough?"

I said, "Yes."

"You got the time on your books?" I showed her my books.

"Oh yes, you've got plenty of time. Well, let's make it out for 15."

But you go down south there, New Orleans: "What do you want it for?" Chicago: "What do you want it for?" "Well, I'm broke. . . ." Or, "How come you didn't leave home with money?" All that kind of jive. It's my money. If you don't want me to have it, then you should never said you could issue time checks. But you can't get hostile with 'em, 'cause the minute you get hostile, then they do make you wait.

Now we had a very good superintendent in Los Angeles, before he transferred east as assistant president. His name was J. P. Leach, and he was strictly a Pullman porter's superintendent. He came to you first if there was any controversy between you and the conductor. You go to the office and— you come into the office—and Mr. Conners is sittin' there. Mr. Conners says, "Oh, yes, Mr. Leach. . . ."

And so Mr. Leach says, "I wanna hear G. W.'s story, then I'll hear you." That incident happened in Redding, California. I had a bunch of schoolteachers, they were getting off in Redding. I was working the West Coast. And I notified these teachers at Red Bluff that their next stop would be Redding. No, it wasn't Redding. Where did they get off at? Red Bluff? Yeah, Red Bluff, but I notified them before we got to Red Bluff that they would be ready.

So they got up and went to the ladies' restroom, and they started washing up. And I started gettin' their bags together and put it out on the platform. And as I got there—the train pulled in—there's this inspector standing there. His name is Lucy, "the devil" [*laughs*]. So while I'm standing there waitin' for the train to holler "all aboard," he and Conners goes into the car. I had put my step box up, I was on the rear of the train. They come back: "Come here" [*in gruff voice*]. So they went right up to the ladies' washroom and pushed the door open. "Look at this. This place hasn't been cleaned up since we left Sacramento."

I said, "Yes, it. . . ."

"Aw, you can't tell us that. You get in there and clean this place up right away."

Then he rode me from there on to Portland. He stayed in my car. I wasn't doing this right, I wasn't doing that right. So when we got to Portland, he made the trip back with me again, and Kinsey told him, said, "Mr. Lucy, lay off the boy. This is his first trip out [on this type of car]. Now he may've done something wrong which I don't know, buy lay off of him."

So anyway, when I get back to Los Angeles about two trips later, I come in, and Mr. Schulte told me, "G. W., are you gonna get off in the station?"

I said, "Yes, I am."

So he said, "Well, go up to the office. Mr. Leach wants to see you."

So I walked in there, sit down. He and Chuck Conners was sittin' in there, Conners with his legs crossed. I walked in. "Hi, Mr. Leach" [*indicates with gestures that Conners tried to talk first*]. "Hi, G. W." (They called each other by their first initials.) "Have a seat."

He read this letter to him about the washroom and everything like that.

So I says, "Mr. Leach, I had these six or seven ladies to put off. While coming into Red Bluff, I notified them that they will be getting off and I was going to get their luggage, and they went to the ladies' room to clean up, and I put 'em off on the ground. When I arrived there, Mr. Lucy was standing on the ground, and while I was waiting for us to get started, he and Mr. Conners went into the car. As I put my step box up, they accosted me and took me to the ladies' room."

So then he said, "Did you pick up any ladies there at Red Bluff?"

I said, "No, sir."

He says, "Did you have any more ladies on your car?"

"No, sir."

He says, "Did you go to the ladies' room with them?"

I said, "No, sir."

Then he asked Mr. Conners, "What right did you have going to that ladies' room when he had nobody to pick up, to go in there without him being in your presence?"

"Well . . .," he says.

"I don't care to hear no more about it. G. W., you can go. I'll take care of you, Mr. Conners."

I said, "Well, Mr. Leach, Mr. Conners and Mr. Lucy rode me all the way to Portland and back. They just kept me on edge every minute. Now, I'd never worked a fan car before, and they stood over the top of me."

He said, "For what? They're not Pullman porters."

I said, "Well, they did."

He said, "Well, I'll handle that, too."

I guess it was about six months later I ran across Mr. Lucy. "Ah, so you're the fella who made the big stink?"

I said, "No, you made it."

But now, the fellas in there told me, don't back off from him. Go at him as he goes at you. And so we was up in Banff, up in the Canadian Rockies, and he needed some money to pay off some Pullman porters. Now, I'm the only one that had money, 'cause I had a buffet car, and I tell him, "I'm not gonna give you a penny. I'm not authorized to give you no money."

"Well I'm Mr. Lucy. . . ."

I said, "I don't give a goddamn who you are. I'm not giving you a penny" [laughs].

So finally he left, and he come back with a telegram from the superintendent in Seattle authorizing Mr. Lucy to draw some money from me. But I never did have no problems with him. Never! Never, never!

So like I say, it was not the company itself, it was some of the individuals who were with the company. Many Pullman porters had confrontations with conductors, and like Mr. Leach would say, "If you can have eight porters and one conductor and seven others can get along with that conductor, why can't this one?" So the fault lies in you, not in them. Oh, yeah. But that's the way it was. My grandmother told me a long time ago, "You'll gag gnats and swallow camels before you die!" Yes, sir!!

I only remember one time in the history of my railroadin' that we ever had to put a passenger off. He got so drunk one night, he began to break up the stuff in the rooms and everything like that, and the Pullman conductor, Mr. Hatch, told me to fix him some coffee.

I said, "Mr. Hatch, I don't want to go in that room with that man. He's raisin' hell now. People are wanting to move out of the car and everything."

So finally I made some coffee and had a little silver tray and a pot, and he had on a pair of silk pajamas. And just as I set this tray down on the side of the bed, he sit down and that coffeepot hit him right here [points to groin area]. And you thought he'd fell off the Empire State Building!

One man wanted tea at the tunnel and tea at Palo Alto, which means at 7:58 if the Lark was on time. We hit the first tunnel up on top of the hill coming into Los Angeles. You have that tea and everything ready, and you ring that buzzer and knock on that door. He says, "Okay," and he opens the door, and you give him tea.

Now, you're in the tunnel. He's got tea at the tunnel. And the same thing for tea at Palo Alto. And if you missed? "What's the matter? You don't have no watch or nothing? You can't do as people say?"

I said, "Well, I'm awful sorry. I got busy in the lounge."

Well, that was that. They had to chew you out something, but I never paid attention to it. No!

I remember one morning I got ready to put the people off and everything, and something came to me. I said, "Wait a minute! We're on our way to the yard." So I knocked on the door. She said, "Yes?" I said [laughing, barely able to talk], "Oh, my God, I forgot to call this lady!" I'd put everybody off in the station, and we're taking her to the yards. So she says, "I'm getting dressed."

I said, "You better do it in a hurry, because I forgot to call you. We're on our way out of the station."

"Oh, my God," she says. "Some people were supposed to meet me."

So when we got to the yards, I jumped off and went on over to the office there and told somebody to get me a cab. So they got a cab to come, and I took her bags to the street on Mission Road and put her on. She still tipped me a dollar. But I forgot this lady. I knew there was something wrong. No, I forgot to call 'em many times.

One time we was on our way to the big game, Cal and Stanford, and we was on the section going up the coast. Going up the hill leaving San Luis Obispo, the guy [train] coming down the hill ran through the whatchacallit, and I'm in the rear car, and it [locomotive] hit the car in front of us and sliced right into it. It hit it on the side where the hallway was. And you talk about a bunch of sick chickens! Here we're stuck on top of this hill up in San Luis Obispo, and these people all goin' to the big game, and got their tickets and everything, and God!!

Finally, when daylight came, they got us and brought us back down. They eased us down because one car—it wasn't knocked off the track, but it just gouged it. So anyway, they put us on buses and gonna drop us off in Palo Alto. They put us on buses that had no toilets, and every gas station there was we had to stop. They got to the game. What we did, we stopped at San Jose, and all the people that was goin' to the game, they put 'em in certain buses, then all those who's goin' to San Francisco, they transferred over to another bus.

Next to the rear car, that was Bonnie Daniel's car. Bonnie, they tried to settle with Bonnie. Bonnie said, "No, I'm allright. I'm allright." They offered Bonnie some money, and Bonnie didn't take it. Bonnie wanted to stay, wanted to go on back to work. I think he was dead inside of a year. I don't know what it was from. And see, the Pullman Company had one of those insurance policies which, a lot of porters, they didn't know anything about, because they know they got an insurance policy, but it was a decreasing policy. The older you got, the less money there was. Heck, yeah! If your insurance policy when you started out was two-thousand-some-odd dollars, and you worked up till you were about 70 years of age, it's down to about 300. It decreased. That was the way the policy was set up.

And like they said about the union. Unions are fine, but I hate a union. The union can be two things to ya: beneficial or detrimental to ya. I would say sometimes that the damn Brotherhood of Sleeping Car Porters was in conjunction with whatchacallit. You take, for instance, like today. Now, if I reported today to work to go out on the Lark at six o'clock—the train leaves at nine—you know they take them six hours and prorate 'em over the next month? I don't get those six hours. No, it's carried over, and then at the end of the next month they'll prorate something else over. So those six hours are gonna just keep jumpin' and jumpin' and jumpin' and jumpin'. You'll actually never see it. Shoot, yeah, they did it. A guy'll report to work at six o'clock in the evening, and his time don't start till midnight. No. Heck, no.

In June 1939 they pulled a car off Los Angeles, and you know, seniority prevails, and then I had to get bumped. Virgil bumped me. So that put me out of a job. I was home about two weeks, and I got a telephone call from Mr. Leach to come down to the office. I went down there, and he said, "G. W., how would you like to transfer temporarily to Chicago? They need some fellows to work back there."

I said, "Fine." And I went back there, and I worked on, well, all the roads that led outta Chicago that had buffet service. The majority of times it was

New York on the 20th Century—finest overnight train in the world. Lark was no comparison to it. The Lark was fine, but when you walked into the 20th Century Limited, it was just something—the nostalgia, you know—the 20th Century Limited known the world over!

I practiced and I rehearsed, and when I made my first trip on there, I got down in the yards—I was due in the yards I think at 10:20 in the morning—I was down there at eight o'clock. I was so happy to be on the 20th Century. Oh, yeah! Set my bar up and everything and had my little cash register for my change. It was a buffet lounge with a barbershop and stenographer.

I didn't have to receive no passengers because I didn't have no rooms. And no sooner they started receiving for passengers—I think we started at 1:10 and left out at 1:40—them people would hit you with both feet. Drink—ready to drink—and you're on your toes! Then I had to make sandwiches. I made cheese sandwiches and potted-ham sandwiches and made coffee and still tryin' to serve drinks, too! Right next to you is the barbershop. People are taking reservations for the barbershop. Then right next door to that was the stenographers there with the typewriters and everything. Then the guy from the barbershop would come there and tell me, "Would you call Mr. Sloan to the barbershop?"

"Mr. Sloan, the barber wishes to see you," or something like that. Or, "Mr. Malcolm, the secretary is now ready for you."

They would get up and go, "Bring me a drink while I'm in there."

Oh God, the 20th Century Limited. Mmm, mmm, mmm!!!

And that's when I began to run wild. See, I would come in this morning at eight o'clock from New York on the 20th Century and be right back out. You get it in New York at 8:10 in the morning—you double right back. You had to clean up your car and everything and get your own ice. If you needed any supplies, you had to go over to the commissary. And then you count your money. You got about a hundred and fifty, two hundred dollars' worth of tips just on an overnight ride. Oh, boy, that was . . . shoot! I'd make a trip on the 20th Century, get back into Chicago, Mr. Edison said, "How you feel?"

I say, "Well, I'm a little tired."

He said, "Okay, I'll lay you over today. Tomorrow you will report to the yards. I'm gonna send you up to Detroit. From Detroit, you're going to Baltimore, Maryland. You'll be on a tour." Then maybe I wouldn't get back to the 20th Century for another two or three weeks or so.

From Baltimore they put me on a separate train and sent me to Hyde Park. That's when we picked up Roosevelt and his entourage. Oh, he was a grand person. Naturally, you know, you can't get to him, 'cause he's in the private car, the Marco Polo, but my car was right next to him, and I happened to talk to one of the gentlemen. He was a Secret Service agent.

So he was standin' in the door; they were always standin' in the door talkin' to him and everything like that. So I says, "What's old prez doing?"

He said, "He's sitting. Wait a minute. You can see him from here."

And naturally, he's sittin' there with that cigar holder like that. So when I peeped, he looked and did like that [gestures to come in]. I walked in, and I said, "How are ya, sir?"

He said, "Just fine, and your name is?"

"Garrard."

He said, "Last name?"

"Smock, Garrard Smock."

"Oh, glad to know you. You have that car there?"

I said, "Yes, sir."

He said, "Okay, fine," and I went on back out.

Oh man, I'm happy. Shit, I was walkin' that high off the ground.

But '39 was all of my travels throughout the East, like this "running wild," as you would call it, on the extra board. I like it better on the extra board than I did the fellas that was runnin' regular 'cause I was there as a single person in Chicago, living with some relatives, till I decided to move out to a hotel by myself. But I could go when I want to. I'd come in today and go out tomorrow. If I didn't want to go out tomorrow, I'd tell Mr. Edison I'm tired, could I stay home a day. They had the Lou Gehrig Special when they gave him honor in 1939. I was on the eleventh special outta Chicago. Eleven sections going to New York!

Then there was cars that was going, oh, every hour to Detroit. Strictly buffet cars then. See, the Pennsylvania and then a lot of New York Central's [trains] didn't have dining cars, so they used the buffet cars because the dining car would leave here at 1:20 in the afternoon going to New York. But after dinner was served, we'd get to Lima around about nine o'clock at night, and the dining car crew would get off. They would go someplace and stay until the train come in the next morning, and they would get on the train and then come back into Chicago. That way we had the Pullman buffet service where people could get served at all times.

We did have some buffet cars that were half baggage, and then the rest of it was buffet-lounge. I had a buffet-lounge car with a half baggage like that when we made the Banner Tour [a charter tour group]. My car was all the linen for the trip. And see, we were a 14-day trip on there, so the porters would come up and draw linen from me. When we'd pull to a stop, I'd get a little wheel cart, and they'd run up there and say, "Well, Babe, I need 50 sheets." Well, I give 'em 50 sheets. Then I'd keep the dirty linen on the car. I had a baggage-buffet car going to Boston in '39. I picked up a bunch of girls. There was nine or eleven, and they all had bicycles. We went all the way to Washington, D.C., from Boston, and we spent two days down there, and every stop we would make where we'd lay over any length of time, they would pull me off, and the girls would go skeetin' off on the bicycles. I kept the bicycles up front. They had another sleeping car that they were in, and they used the lounge. Those girls didn't think no more about me. They'd run through that car with no clothes on and everything else.

"Jesus Christ, will you all get dressed."

"Shut up!" [*laughs*].

All college students. I don't think they's more than 21, 22 years old. I stayed on the car, and then they flitted all off on the bicycles and went to some hotel. And on the way back they started bringin' me gifts. I had shirts that was that long, I had shirts that was that short. I had sweaters. Oh, my God! They bought me everything under the sun, and each one of the girls gave me a $100 bill. I'm trying to think. What school is up there? I don't know. Oh, they were wealthy girls all right.

As I told you, a lot of people ignored the Pullman porters. They never paid no attention to him. Lot of times the bell would ring, I'd knock on the door, they said, "Who is it?"

I said, "This is Garrard, the porter. You rang for me?"

"Yes, come in here. Would you get my bag from undernea   he bed?" And she's sittin' on the damn toilet. They don't pay no attention to you 'cause they trusted the porter.

One lady one night couldn't sleep, and she come out into the lounge, and we was on the Lark, and there was no place to sleep because the train was sold out. We had to sleep in chairs. And so the next morning I got up, was fixin' breakfast and everything like that, and the bell rang, and so I went to her room. She was in room A.

So she said, "Porter, I've been woke half the night. Why were you all out there last night?"

I said, "Well, there's no place to sleep. We have to sleep in the chairs."

She said, "Who sleeps there in that berth?"

I said, "Nobody."

"Well, you could have had that berth."

I said, "No!!!"

She said, "Well, that's all right. I paid for this room."

I said, "That's still not the company policy, my dear."

No! No! It might be a spotter or anything like that.

In '39 I came back home. They wanted me to transfer permanently to Chicago, and I was reluctant, but I was thinking about it. My family's all here in Los Angeles. I happened to go downtown to Chicago one day, and that cold air come off of that lake and hit me in them California clothes—I was ready to go home! So I went up and saw Mr. Allen, and he says, "G. W., we were just thinkin' about you. Have you made up your mind what you want to do?"

I said, "Yes, I want to go home."

He said, "Well, we got a telegram here from Mr. Leach that there's an opening for you in Los Angeles."

I spent about two days there, and they told me to go over to the Riverside yards, and there's a car out there that's gonna be deadheaded back to Chicago by way of Buffalo over through Canada and come in through Detroit. So you just get on that and just deadhead back home. They forgot the car's out there! I spent about a week out there. Yeah! In the yard! And I was getting broke and getting hungry. I'd have to tell the fellows, "Look, I'm going up on Riverside Drive to eat. Don't let 'em move this car before I get back."

So finally, after about a week or so, I called up down at the commissary and talked to the fella, I says, "Hey, this is G. W. Smock."

He says, "Where in the hell are you?"

"I'm out here in this car in Riverside yards, where you told me to get on."

He said, "What's the name of that car?"

"I can't think of it. Malcolm so-and-so."

He said, "Jesus Christ, we been looking for that car. Well, you go back and get on it. We'll pick you up this evening."

I said [laughs], "Well, what am I gonna do about my time?"

"Well, you get back to Chicago, and you explain to Chicago, and you tell them what happened."

So they paid me eight out of every sixteen hours that I was out there. Man, I had gotten broke. I'd buy me a sandwich—eat half of it for lunch and half of it for dinner. Yep!

I transferred to Oakland and worked out of Oakland for a while. Yeah, we worked the Cascade, we worked the Shasta. The Shasta was the old hummer, in other words. It stopped at every stop. Jimmy Steele and I were up there together. The atmosphere was different. The clientele was different. I say the clientele was different because you had a different breed of people. Now you're associating yourself with the northerner with, I would say, the San Francisco–type person who was the flamboyant person. And they cater to themselves in that way. They're more of a flamboyant people than there is here in Los Angeles.

In the fifties I started going east. I started working the Golden State roughly around 1954, something like that. I rode the Golden State for almost six years. It was a train going back east where people would take their families and something like that. The Golden State, we had a barber shop, we had dining car service and lounge service.

The summer months, it was nothin'. My car would go out today with not a passenger on it and make a complete round trip to Chicago with nobody. The car had to go because there was one leaving Chicago, there was one en route, and there was one in Los Angeles—one passing each other on the road and two at each point.

But in the wintertime is when our business picked up, because the people from the East would leave and start headin' to Palm Springs, Indio, Coolidge going to Phoenix and Tucson, going off to all the various clubs there. Oh, starting from the latter part of October up until around about March, when we'd catch 'em coming this way when we start taking them back. Then after that it was all over with.

There was an incident that happened in the train. We used to have a gentleman rode the train with us. He couldn't eat nothing but baby food—J. P. Morgan. He had ulcers so bad in his stomach, he couldn't have nothin' but baby food. This passenger I had in my car in the drawing room, him and his wife went up to the dining car, and they ate. And this guy come in and sit down next to 'em, and so they got up and come back to the car. So I said, "What was wrong?"

He said, "They let anybody come into the dining room. That fellow up there looked like a bum."

I didn't say anything. That was leaving Tucomcari.

So when we got to El Paso that night, they went back to the dining car, and he was there but wasn't sitting next to them. So they come on back to the car that evening after they got finished, and the lady says, "Porter? There's something mysterious about that man."

I said, "What do you mean?"

She said, "You all seem to know him, and you talk to him, yet he shuns away from everybody else. While we're on the platform this afternoon at Tucomcari, he was standing way over in the corner over there, and he still looked like a bum."

And I said, "And he'll continue to look like a bum till he gets where he's going."

She says, "Why?"

I said, "Well, because he doesn't want no notoriety. That's J. P. Morgan, Jr."

She says, "Is that right?"

I said, "That's right. He just acts like that, and people stay away from him" [laughs]. Yeah, he didn't wanna be involved with 'em.

I think the best passengers I ever ran across was leaving on the Golden State going to Chicago. I got to Palm Springs, and I saw on my manifest where I was picking up Mr. and Mrs. Warner, Linda and Ross. So when I got to Palm Springs and dropped down, here they come walking along the platform. And I didn't know till later on that he had fell off a horse and fell in the mud, and he didn't have time to change clothes. They were the raggediest-looking people I'd seen in all my life. I thought, "Oh, my God, what now?"

So they came down. I said, "Mr. Warner?"

He said, "Yes. This is Mrs. Warner, this is Linda, and this is Ross. Now, I've got all four rooms. I want the baggage to go in room number A, Ross will have B, Linda will have C, and Mrs. Warner and I will have the drawing room."

I said (to myself), "Gee, this cat must got some dough. He got all four rooms, and one room is for luggage!"

Now Ross, his son, stuttered, and let me tell you, Ross couldn't tell you nothin'. Ross is about 11 or 12 years old. I'd say, "How are you, Ross?"

"Ab-ah-aba-ah-ab-ab-ab. . . ."

I said, "Okay, forget it."

So that morning—they had done away with the barber on the Golden State—and I was sitting in the barbershop, and I said, "Come here. We gonna get together."

He said, "Ah-ah-ah. . . ."

I said, "Don't you say nothin'. You just sit down in that chair, and when I ask you a question, I want you to just stop. Don't say nothin' until you feel that you can tell me. You understand?"

"Ah-ah-ah. . . ."

"What did I say?"

So he said [*pause*], "Yes."

I said, "Now we're getting somewhere. What's your name?"

"My na-na-na . . ."

I said, "What did I tell ya? One at a time."

So he says, "My n-n-name is Ross."

I said, "Now we're getting on the ball."

And I sat up there and talked to Ross for about an hour or so. Then he got up and left. And pretty soon he got back. And all during that day, when I didn't have anything to do—the bell didn't ring—I would sit there and talk to Ross.

We left Los Angeles on a Monday. This was a Tuesday, and Tuesday night the bell rang, and I went to the room. They was all sitting in there. So Mr. Warner said, "Garrard?"

I said, "Yes, sir."

Ross says, "Ah-ah-ah. . . ."

"What did I say? What did I tell you?"

So he didn't say anything. Mr. Warner didn't say anything, neither did Mrs. Warner.

So I said, "What do you want to tell me, Ross?"

He said, "Will—you—" and them last words he just let it out right away—"come visit us?"

I said, "Yes, I will."

So Mr. Warner said, "That's what I want to tell you about, Garrard. We've been listening to you in there. Now, we pay good money to a tutor for Ross, but you taught Ross more today than that tutor has ever done, and I'm gonna get rid of him when we get back to Chicago. Ross asked you would you like to come visit us."

I said, "I would very much so."

So Mrs. Warner says, "We've got a single maid out there" [*laughs*].

Mr. Warner says, "Are you a married man?"

I said, "Yes, sir."

He says, "Well, you just done ruined his marriage right now."

Well anyway, next morning they got off the train. And so I was talking to Mrs. Warner, and she told me, "Garrard, I want your schedule as to when you will be in Chicago. Now, when you come in next week, you call, and you catch the train over at the Northwestern station and get off at Winnetka and call, and somebody will meet you."

So I said, "Okay."

I dressed up in my finest, and next trip I got off and went over to Northwestern station, caught it, got to Winnetka, and she come meet me in the station wagon. They took me to the house, and they introduced me to the maid, as well as I know her name now. She's dead, may her soul rest in peace. Anyway, we was laughing, talking and everything, and she's fixin' dinner. So finally, Mr. Warner come in, and so he said, "Hi, Garrard, how are you? Come on up front."

He took me up in his big library, and he fixed cocktails there for us and everything. Finally,—oh, what is her name, now? Had many a good day with her, too.

She said, "Mr. Warner, dinner's served."

And they had me sit right there at the table. I had dinner with them. I was just a part of the family then.

Then she told me, "I've set up a big dinner party for some of the representatives of the Bell Telephone Company. They will be here for a dinner. I want your size for your tuxedo and everything."

I got out there that day and had a tuxedo. All I had to do is open the door and take the gentlemen's coats and take 'em and put 'em in the other room. That's all I had to do. She had caterers and everything.

Billy Gibbs!! [*remembering the maid's name*].

And it was nothin'—$100 bills—just passed out $100 bill. 'Course, he's very businesslike. He gave me his in an envelope, see. But I fell in love with that family. I was out there all the time. I finally nicknamed her "Princess."

It was an easy job, and it was easy come—it was easy money. And I think the biggest problem was—it happened years and years ago when this Pullman porter wrote an article for the *Saturday Evening Post* of how the money he made from tips sent his children through college. The IRS picked up on that, and from there on all tips come declared. Oh, yes. We had to declare it, and you had to put it down even though they didn't believe you.

I remember one time I was called in for Internal Revenue right uptown, and I could look out the room I was sitting in and look at the Union Station. And this guy didn't believe that I didn't make so much money.

I said, "Well, sometimes the car goes out empty, and I don't have no customers."

He said, "Well, I've never heard of such a thing."

So I said, "I'll tell you what. Since you don't believe me, that Golden State right now, if you turn around and look, is heading out of the station headed to Chicago. Would you call up a number I give you, the Pullman office sign-out, and ask him how many passengers car OB-3 has on it today?"

So he picked up the phone and said, "Who do I ask for?"

"You ask for a Mr. Ross."

So he picked up the phone, he said, "Mr. Ross? I'm calling from the Internal Revenue Department. I just noticed the Golden State leaving out. Could you tell me how many passengers car OB-3 has on it today?"

And Mr. Ross is one of them kind who like to hum first. [*Imitating Mr. Ross*] "Mmm, mmm, OB-3, mmm, OB-3's blank today. No passengers."

So the man told me, "How can they do it?"

I said, "It has to go. There's a car leaving Chicago today, and there's one leaving Los Angeles today and there's two trains en route. So they've got to have the cars at either end regardless if it doesn't have no passengers. They still got to pull that car."

So he said, "Well, you convinced me," and that's all there was to it. But they were sure defiant.

I don't think the public would've accepted white porters. I really don't know. They didn't accept the Filipinos, because they felt that that was a black man's job, and they'd rather see a black man. I remember an incident one morning for breakfast. Ed Garrerra was my waiter, and Steele was the porter, and I was the cook. And Ed's mother was a Filipino, and his father was black, so naturally he came out as a very light-complexioned person. And as Ed went out in the dining car that morning, this lady come in with this little girl, and he set her down and set a menu down in front of the lady, and this little girl looked up at Ed and then looked over to her grandmother and said, "I thought you told me a black man was gonna wait on us?" And the little girl said it so loud, it disrupted the whole lounge. People just busted out laughin' [*laughs uncontrollably*] The lady got up and snatched the little girl out of the lounge. Ed come back in there laughin'.

I said, "What's wrong?"

He said, "You should have waited tables this morning, Smock." Then he told me what happened.

But I don't think that they would have accepted whites. This is a new day. They have some now. Yeah, so it's changed around now. There was no

(Above) Babe, Virgil, and George Smock, about 1946. *(Below)* Babe, Virgil, and George Smock, 1987.

discrimination during that time, where fair employment was a big issue, but it's an issue today. I can look back to during that particular time, and the average elderly porter was not knowledgeable to a great extent as far as education. There were a lot of "yassirs" and "no-sirs" and stuff like that, and that would not have been a type of words that you would have used. The public was accustomed to that of the old porter, you know what I mean. He's half stooped over makin' the beds, and he's grouchy, and they got along with that, they contended with that. Like some of the passengers used to say, "The only time the porter smiles is when the train gets to the station, 'cause he knows he's gonna get him a tip" [laughs].

But I don't think it would have actually worked [with white porters]. Maybe. When they rode the *Queen Mary* and the *Normandy* and all of those ships, there was no blacks in that capacity. If he was, he was down in the hole somewhere. So they accepted [white porters] on that side of the fence, but would they accept 'em on this side of the fence? When you go back 40 or 50 years ago, I don't think it would have been acceptable.

It was handed down from generation to generation: if the father worked for [the railroad], the grandfather was working for it, and the children all worked for it. It was like in the plantations. George tried to trace it at one time. The Smock is of a Dutch name. I remember years and years ago my father received a telephone call from some people who wanted to know something about the family, and I don't know how the conversation came up, but when my father said he was a Negro, they hung the phone up in his face.

My grandmother's Bible when I was living with her had the history of her mother, all of the folks—she was born in Winchester County, Kentucky— and her sister and all the way down the line. I could take you to my family Bible right now, and you open up that page, there ain't nothin' in it, not even my own name on it. But family history used to be tradition back in the olden days. But no! I don't see half the kids today of the younger generation got Bibles, 'less they're interested in church. Yeah!

So I don't know what would have been the outcome of [whites as porters]. But I can sit here and look back to the time of Uncle Billy McCormick and Joe Woods and all of them old porters. They "yassir, yassir," you know what I mean? That younger generation ain't gonna do that now. I don't know, with the way railroading is today, whether I would advise anybody to go into that field.

When Pullman pulled off all of its buffet cars operating out of Los Angeles in May 1960, a lot of attendants were left without jobs, including Babe and his brother Virgil. No severance pay was allotted to these men, owing to a Pullman clause stipulating that as long as one Pullman-operated buffet car operated in the United States on any railroad, no severance pay would be issued to any buffet car attendant. Pullman suggested to attendants that they transfer to other districts where buffet cars were still being operated. This catch-22 suggestion resulted in the retirement of dozens of Pullman employees who neither desired nor could afford to relocate.

Babe and Virgil stated that when the Interstate Commerce Commission held hearings on the abandonment of buffet cars on the West Coast, the Brotherhood of Sleeping Car Porters was not represented at the hearings. It is unclear whether this issue could have been rectified if the Brotherhood had been present to fight on behalf of the buffet attendants. The Brotherhood's exclusion still angers Babe and Virgil, who chose not to relocate and thus ended their long careers with the Pullman Company.

In May 1960 they informed me leaving Chicago that this was the last trip that I would make. They were cutting that buffet car off. So that was it. When I come back to Los Angeles on the first of May, they terminated me and put me on what they call "standby board" in case anything happened. 'Course, they asked me, did I want to transfer to Portland, Oregon. I told 'em, "No!" I wasn't going to Portland. So I just stayed in Los Angeles.

When I first was furloughed in 1960, I applied for the city of Montebello as a garage attendant. I applied for a custodian job for the city of Long Beach for the county. I went down to the post office; they wasn't taking any applications. I went to L.A. transit. During that time they had an age limit of 38, but they'll take anybody now. They told me no. I went out to American Airlines to apply for that. Meanwhile, the next morning, I stopped by an employment agency, and I stopped in there. The lady asked me, and I said I come to apply for the chauffeur's job. She said, "There's no such thing as chauffeur's jobs. We have chauffeur-butlers."

Well, I said, "Okay, fine. That's okay."

So she said, "No, no, no, no! Wait a minute! Wait a minute! Let's take your application."

So I told her who I'd worked for and everything like that. She asked me, have I worked a private family. I said, "Not since 1937, and they've all deceased since then, but I do day work for some ladies here in Los Angeles: a Mrs. Warren and Mrs. Bolin. My brother right now is at Mrs. Bolin's house."

So she said, "Well, let's call Mrs. Bolin."

So she called Mrs. Bolin, and finally she got finished, she told her lady friend there, she says, "We just got to find this boy a job. He comes highly recommended. What about that Gilfillan case? I think that's still open." So she called Mrs. Gilfillan and asked Mrs. Gilfillan, was she still interested. "Yeah," so she said, "well, send him out." So I went out to the Gilfillans. They were an electronic firm. He was a self-made millionaire. Well, anyway, I went to work for them, and I worked for them for 13 years.

You look back at it and just see all the laughter and the gaiety and the things that you done and the things you got by with and how lucky you were to get by with it. Everything! Yeah. It was a fun deal. It was really enjoyable. It's just like going through boot in the marine corps. Once you come out, you look back and see how funny it was.

I've been blessed all my life. I'm not a wealthy man. I get along, so what I have I can share. It's not killing me. I have a lot of people who say, "I don't have no luck." Anytime you wake up and raise that shade and see that light and smell that air and hear them birds, you've got your health and wealth. You've got luck. Yes, sir!

James T. Steele

4

JAMES T. STEELE
Pullman Buffet and Lounge Car Attendant
1936–1960

James T. Steele was born the thirteenth child of his family in Atlanta, Georgia, in 1910. After the death of their mother, his older sister Annie Mae took him to Dallas, Texas, where he was put in a Catholic boarding school for about a year. Annie Mae was doing domestic work for a couple who persuaded her to enroll James in public school. Her employer drove James to school and let him take the streetcar home in the afternoon.

After graduating from high school, "Jimmy"—as his friends affectionately call him—came out to California, where he found work at a bank for about a year before chauffeuring and cooking for a wealthy couple who owned a spice factory. In 1936, at the age of 25, he discovered the Pullman Company and began a 24-year career that lasted until the Pullman Company discontinued the buffet car in which he was working on the Southern Pacific Lark.

On 5 December 1942, the rear observation car Jimmy Steele was working on the Lark was rear-ended by another train, seriously injuring him and killing one passenger. Burned over much of his body by the scalding hot steam and water from the car's kitchen compartment, he was given up to die by doctors at the army medical facility where he was taken after the wreck. But his strong will to live enabled Jimmy Steele to survive to tell his story.

After his retirement from the road in 1960, Jimmy Steele found a domestic job with the family for whom his wife worked. His attention to detail so impressed his employer that in 1962 he hired Steele to work at his airplane manufacturing plant. Beginning as a janitor, Steele worked his way up to department head and was highly commended when a visiting plant inspector from Washington, D.C., said that it was the cleanest plant he had ever seen. Aftereffects from his railroad accident gradually began to restrict his ability to work, however, and he was forced to permanently retire.

I had been out in Beverly Hills looking for a job because I quit the job I was on. When I got off the D car to catch the U car to come home, a friend of mine had a bag, and I asked him where did he go. I said, "Have you been traveling?" because he used to cook out in Beverly Hills not far from me.

He says, "I'm a Pullman porter now," and he pulled out a handful of dollars and change and stuff like that.

And I said, "Well, do you get paid every trip?"

He said, "No, this is the tips that you make. Your salary is $77.50 a month." So I went up there, and I inquired about a job. During those days, if they had openings, they hired you—if they needed you. And in some places where there was a lot of porters, they would transfer 'em out of here. A lot of club-car men that we had came from back east.

So this gentleman by the name of Mr. Schulte, he told me that they had quit giving out applications. I told him, "I'm gonna leave my name and address with you. If the opportunity comes up again, please let me know."

So when I was going outta the door, a gentleman say, "Just a minute, young man." I turned around.

And he says, "Do you go dressed like that all the time?"

I told him yes. I happened to have on a white shirt and blue suit, and my shoes were shined—and my tie. Everything matched.

And he said, "Give this man an application, and let him fill it out right away. And send him to the doctor."

And I think I worked for about a month, and they had this Rexall Special comin' through, and I was supposed to go there and relieve the cooks and things, pantry man and on down, and that's how I got on workin' for the Pullman Company. I was gone six months. When I came back, I had six months' wages waiting for me.

On that special I think they had about 12 cars. It was a big blue and white train. They said it was a streamlined train, but it was old cars that were redone and plastered together, you know. They were set up like a drugstore, and they had different names, like Cara Nome was one of their products. And we had an orchestra with us, and we had two cars that they entertained in, that they danced and have lunch or whatever they wanted. When we stop at these places, maybe three or four days, well, they'd come through the train. Naturally, the Rexall Drugstore owners that was at this place, they would all come, and they had their convention, see. And then after they had the convention, then if they was supposed to stay for lunch, we would serve them lunch. We had a diner.

Let me tell you one thing. The most beautiful thing you could ever see is a dining room on a train. You got the white tablecloths, you got the silver that's shiny as gold, see, and it had a good atmosphere to it. We had a private car where Mr. Liggett, who was president of the Rexall Drugs Company—he was a very nice man. He commended me on the work that I did. I was serving as a waiter, and I did janitor work. Whatever kind of work that was to be done in order to keep those cars clean, we all did it, see. And when we stop at these places where we would be two or three days, that's when you send out all your laundry, and that's when all the commissary things that we had to have, like napkins and tablecloths and things like that, well, they were right there waitin' for us. I would put 'em on that big truck thing and pull it myself and put it all away. And that was the time that Mr. Liggett commended me, when I was doing all that work by myself, and he says, "Every time I see you, you are busy." And I told him that's what I'm supposed to do, is to be busy.

We had a very nice time. It was a lot of experience for me because I have a big family, and by visitin' 48 states and 155 principal cities, I got to see my whole family. It was very interesting because, you know, travel-wise, you saw a lot of places where, an ordinary citizen, you wouldn't have seen, see.

Pullman has always had a reputation as to keep the black man on the train. That was by George M. Pullman. That is what he said. He wanted Negro boys—men—on those Pullman cars. That was his doings, not no whole bunch of people, see. And in them days—he was named George Pullman, and a lot of Pullman porters, they would call 'em George.

There has been, as years went by, before things folded up—I remember them telling me that they had hired some white boys back east, but not out here. Only thing that we had was Filipinos. And they were very nice to get along with. In fact, I worked with one for about six or seven years together.

When I was ridin' the Lark, when I first started there on the Lark—you see, the only thing that rode the Lark when I first started was businessmen and you know who [prostitutes]. I won't call no names. Yeah. Oh, you made the money then! [*laughs*]. Oh! You made money till you got tired of making money, serving champagne and making sandwiches and takin' 'em coffee and stuff. Sure! Yep.

And during those days when I first started, you would have sometimes eight and nine sections of the Lark going to San Francisco or Berkeley for football games to Stanford University. You'd always have sometimes as many as 11 sections, 11 trains, one right after the other. I liked the heavyweight equipment better because you were safer in a heavyweight than you was in the lightweight stuff, see. I wouldn't say they ride better, but your chances are greater.

Now, I also ran from Los Angeles to Chicago [on the streamlined Golden State] while the club car [on the Lark] was being overhauled, you see, painted and everything. Those club cars over there were a lot better than the ones we had on the Lark. I worked over there for quite a while, and you got to meet a lot of rich people from New York and back east coming down to Palm Springs. I liked the Lark better than I did the Golden State. In the first

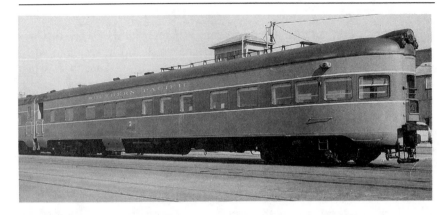

Buffet-observation car #9501 on the Oakland Lark worked by the Smock brothers and James T. Steele, First and Broadway, Oakland, California 1951. Photograph by W. C. Whittaker.

place, you see, you were three days gettin' there and three days comin' back on the Golden State, and over on the Lark it was overnight and back.

But I tell ya, by being a Pullman porter or an attendant or whatever you supposed to be with the Pullman Company—it's a very interesting thing for you to be a porter, because you see a lot of things that you wouldn't think would happen. Like somebody say, "There's President Reagan," or something like that, you see. You get to meet a lotta big people. I had Bing Crosby. He would get on at Glendale, and he had the drawing room in my car. Oh God, $25 every time I caught him! Yeah, but Jack Benny wasn't [a good tipper]. He just like they say he was. Yeah. And oh, what was that child's name? Shirley Temple. I used to have her all the time. Very nice. And I had Humphrey Bogart and his wife.

Well, I tell you what happened one night. Bing Crosby was on, and that's when I was on the front car first, see. Bing Crosby came back, lay down on the floor, and sang the most beautiful songs that you ever heard. And we would sell more whiskey and champagne than we could bring out, see. When Bing Crosby was with his wife, he'd always have the drawing room. I would keep all his bags out but his golf clubs and an overnight bag. I'd bring that in at night, that evening when he got on. And then I'd go get some glasses and a big bowl of ice. He always carried his whiskey in his golf bag. I'd get out a fifth or whatever you call it and serve him until he got ready to go to bed. Then I'd call him [at breakfast], and I would bring a large orange juice and two pots of coffee. I knocked on the door, and when you went in there, he was singing to his wife. He was a very nice man.

One time I caught him at Bakersfield [on the train West Coast which ran from Los Angeles to Portland]. He got on, and nobody knew him. No, because he was all—hair [*motions to beard*], see. So he came back to my car. He was looking for a Pullman buffet car.

So he saw me, he say, "Steele?"

I say, "Yes, sir?"

"This your car?"

I say, "Yes, sir. You have the bedroom in my car?"

He say, "Yeah, it's 2:00 [A.M.], and I'm hungry."

"What do you want?"

He say, "Well, fix me a nice combination sandwich and bring me a high-ball."

I said, "Well, you know it's way after 12:00. But you know I'll bring it to you."

And I did. And I always got that $25 tip. There was several of 'em that I made nice money off of.

Bob Hope was going to Watsonville, and he wanted breakfast an hour before we got there. It was in my car. He says, "I'll take care of you later." And we served all them a big breakfast and got their bags off, about 20 of them, and he didn't even say good-bye! [*laughs*] I knew everybody. I knew people who could do me some good, like lawyers, doctors. And when I [adopted] my son, this gentleman—he's a very wealthy man—he asked me how was my boy, and I told him, he's doing fine. He says, "Your wife?" I says, "Well, she's so heavy, and she has to use the streetcar, and I told her I couldn't get no car right now, and maybe later on I could, see."

And he told me, he says, "You have taken care of my dad so well and all the rest of my family." He says, "I'm buying 24 Chevrolets brand-new, and they allow me $800 as turn-in. I will pick out the best one for you, and all you got to do is take this pink slip when they bring it and take it down and have it put in your name, and you pay $35 a month, no carrying charge, no nothing, and if you don't have it, just call me and tell me."

And when they brought the car out, they told me $75 a month, and I told 'em, "No, that wasn't what Mr. Kuelle said. You just take it back." So they did, and when they got back, they had to bring it right back to me, see, and I paid him $35 every month. And his father was a very nice man, because he asked me, he says, "James, did they give you the car?" I told him they did. He says, "Okay, if there's anything else you need, let me know."

And you take all of your governors and things, Earl Warren and all of them, and Mayor Poulson, Fletcher Bowron. If I needed advice, I could always go to one of the lawyers that I'd know. Anything that I wanted, I'd see them, and you can get it just like that, see.

The evening of 4 December 1942 started out pretty much like the countless other nights Jimmy Steele had worked the Lark out of Los Angeles. Because of

*the war, dozens of military uniforms could be spotted on the station platform
awaiting their departure; the Lark was sold out.*

*Pulling 20 cars that night, the streamlined Lark eased out of Union Station,
creaking through the maze of complex trackage that guarded the approach into
the terminal. Once under way, Steele busied himself with the numerous routine
tasks that were second nature to him. After six years with Pullman, he could
work most any car on the Lark blindfolded. The drinking crowd always kept
him jumping, and when serving passengers aboard number 401, the rear-end
observation lounge, he could expect nonstop business until closing.*

*As the streamliner rolled steadily into the foggy coastal air just north of Santa
Barbara, Steele glanced at his timepiece and noticed it was getting close to time
for announcing "last call" for the bar. He also noticed a distant yellow glow
through the rear-car window that had been following the Lark for some time.*

The night that I got hurt, we left Santa Barbara and we were streamlined. I
was on the rear car. There was a heavyweight behind us—troop train, see.
And before we got outta the block [section of track controlled by automatic
signals], he was right there, and he kept following us and following us, you
know.

I told Roy, he was the rear brakeman, I say, "Watch him. He's following
us too close."

I told everybody back there that the second section was following us too
close and to go up to the big lounge. I had Dr. Strubs and Doheny in my
club car, and they got up and left. And there was two army captains that
was getting off at San Luis Obispo. They had given their room up for a lady
and her children because the rooms was hard to get during the war, you
know.

I told the two captains, "Sir, you're getting off at San Luis Obispo, and I
would move from back here if I were you because it's too dangerous. If you
go up to the big lounge, you'd be right in front of the station."

And when everybody left, one army captain left, and one told me, says,
"No nigger tells me what to do."

I say, "You just stay right where you are."

We drop off the hill, and we turn to go in front of the station. That left
my car sticking out in the back. So I got back to the kitchen to close the
door and the porter [L. "Hi" Hyde] came back and wanted a sandwich. And
I told him I'd been closed long time ago. When I fixed the sandwich and I
told him to get outta here and I got to go, he said, "Well, give me a little
more mayonnaise."

And I did—the train hit us!!! He went through a caution light. He went
through torpedos, and he crashed the red light. When he saw my car sticking
out, he can't stop like you can a car—he have to set his brakes. And he hit
us, and he threw Hi on top of me.

The hot water and steam broke loose in there, and we both laid in that hot water and steam for about a half an hour or so, because he was on top of me, see. And this brakeman was up front, and he came back. He knocked on the window. He say, "Steele?"

I say, "Yeah."

"Are you all right?"

I say, "Yeah."

He say, "Where you situated?"

I say, "Right by the door, only Hi's on top of me, and he's trapped in the closet door."

And Roy broke the window, and when they got us out, they laid us on the ground. Dr. Strubs came back and told the Pullman conductor to get two blankets. So they put the blankets over us, and Doheny gave us a drink of brandy. And this army captain came back and said, "Steele, I hope you'll be all right. My buddy, they just washed him off the head of the train. He rode it all the way through."

I got hurt at Casmalia, and they took me to the army camp up there at Camp Cooke. And there was two white nurses—army nurses. They rushed me in the room, and this major, whoever he was, captain, he say, "Steele, you're in pretty bad shape. I'm gonna do all I can to save you."

This other doctor that was working for him, he says, "Them two niggers' lives ain't worth that captain that lost his life."

So this man told him, "The best thing for you to do is get outta here and get outta here fast. I will report you tomorrow."

So he asked me, "What religion are you?"

I told him, and I say, "If there's any more, call Him, too."

My eyes looked like red paint, boiled in oil like a fish is. The doctor told me, "Steele, you pray. I'm gonna pull you through, at least for a day or two."

They put me in the ward, and I was laying in bed—this arm swollen and that leg—they had cut my clothes off. So it was time for the big boss to come through. And those soldiers that were in bed, they had to stand up and hold their hands out like this, see (extends palms face down). When he got to one soldier, he says, "Mae West, didn't I tell you to cut them fingernails off and all that shiny stuff you got on there? What are you, a master sergeant? You are now a private first-class."

He came over to my bed. He said [laughs], "What the hell you doing here?"

I said, "Man, I was in a train wreck, and they brought me over here, sir."

He said, "Go get the barber to kinda clean this man's beard up and get all that blood and stuff off his face. I will be back." So he went over there, and the barber told him he didn't know nothin' about working on niggers [laughs harder]. Told him, say, "If you don't know, you got a damn good chance to learn. I want him cleaned up, and I'll be back here."

So he came back, though he's a little bitty old guy, and he told me, "There's gonna be lawyers coming out here. Sergeant so-and-so, he'll be right over there. You call him."

About a day or two later here come this little Jew. He had one of them short coats on and everything. He started askin' me questions. "Vell, can't you hear me?" [*imitating accent*]. So this great big white sergeant man [*barely controlling laughter*], he looked like he had football pads on, you know, and he looked like he didn't wanna be in the army, no way. So he went over there, and he grabbed him and shook his ass right onto the door and dropped him. He say, "You won't be worrying with him no more."

But they kept me there. I woke up, and they screened me off, and the lady told me that I was gonna die. And they sent for my people. I told her, "You go to the PX and get me a box of cigars."

She said, "You're not supposed to have 'em."

I said, "That's my dying wish, and move all this stuff away from me."

They give me up to die, but I was still living!

The doctors rushed in there. "Are you all right?"

I say, "Yeah."

He say, "Squeeze my hand."

I had big hands, you know. I waited till I could get set, 'cause I didn't use this one, and I come down on him, and he hollered, see. I said, "I'm leaving here Christmas Eve, and I wanna say goodbye to you."

And sure enough, [on Christmas Eve] he said, "You sure kept your word, didn't you?"

I said, "Bye."

Christmas Eve they brought me down to Los Angeles. I got to Los Angeles on Christmas. I got about $13,000. Hell, if that would've happened now, why, good God, I'd own the railroad. You see, this arm is skin graft. This leg is skin graft. See? And all my buttocks are skin graft. And the donor area was from my stomach and my thighs. But as a whole, it was a good experience.

Listen. During those days—let me tell you something, not only on the trains, the whole state of California and the United States was a tremendous amount of prejudice, see, especially in '42, when everybody was coming out here working in them shipyards and things like that, see. You take in the early history of railroads, they'd have coaches for Negroes only. Now down there in the South, before I was railroadin', you had a car right next to the baggage car. And during them days, they burned coal. A lot of times you had to screen your windows to keep the coal and dust out of 'em. During them days the porter slept in the men's bathroom. They had a bed in there and curtains that you put up. In the station you had a certain place you had to sit. Hell, yeah, I remember when Annie Mae [his sister] went to Atlanta, Georgia, when I was seven years old, and she brought me back. During those days, when you stop in the towns, people would make all kinda sandwiches and things and sell it to ya through the windows. But you couldn't go in no dining room. Didn't allow you in there. They had them guys that went through the train sellin' magazines and candy and stuff like that. That's what you got. If he had sandwiches, you got 'em.

As years go by and things began to change and this and that and the other, then they cut out the Jim Crow [segregated coaches]. But when I first started, you had to be careful. It was no joke. Oh, listen, during them days, if the white man could kick your butt, he did. But if you showed him that you'll kick his butt back, he wouldn't bother you. I tell you how I dealt with it— by ignoring it. As long as you don't put your hands on me, I won't bother you. Now, during the war, we were coming down from San Francisco. At twelve o'clock—ten minutes to twelve—I said, "The bar will be closed in ten minutes. If you wish any more whiskey, you'll have to order it now, because after twelve o'clock I'm not permitted to sell whiskey." So everybody got up and left. This left an army captain and his wife back there. He had been drinkin' and tellin' everybody how he killed Japs with his bare hands. So he rang the bell. I went back there.

"We'll have two scotch and sodas."

I say, "I'm sorry, I announced ten minutes ahead of time that we closed at twelve o'clock. I can't serve you."

So I walked away from him, and he gets up and comes to the kitchen door, and he starts raisin' hell. He told me what all he'll do to me and this and that and the other. So I reached and got the steel that I sharpened knives. And I got a French bread knife, and I hit it four or five times. I told his wife, "If you don't want his guts emptied on this floor, you better come and get him."

And she did. Then the conductor heard about it. He came back there.

"Steele, what happened?"

And I told him.

He says, "Okay, it won't happen no more." And when we got to Salinas, the MPs was waitin' for him.

Them people knew what they were doing on the Lark. Now there's a man named Slauss. He never did see me before. That's when I came back to work from the wreck. Virgil [Smock] and I were running together. And Slauss came up to the kitchen. He says, "Hey, nigger, give me a scotch and soda."

I say, "Well, my name is on the door out there: 'Steele,' see? And I don't appreciate you callin' me that. And if you don't want to get knocked on your you-know-what, don't call me that again."

He says, "Well, I'm sorry," and he gave me $10.

That old saying, the passenger is always right—whether it's black, red, or blue, your passenger is always right.

I'll tell ya, we had conductors that did everything in the world to make it hard for ya, see. And we had a man on there, a gentleman by the name of Gale, he was the inspector, you know. And he would tell different porters about him being a ex-policeman in San Francisco—he had kicked a million niggers' ass. So he said that to the wrong porter one time, and this porter laid him out. And they squashed it. Nothin' was said about it.

You had all kinda conductors from all parts of the country, mostly the South. But you had to swallow so much. The conductors are right, you're always wrong.

When I was on the train that went to Portland, Oregon, the West Coast, I ran outta milk when we got to this place, and I went over to get some milk. No, it was before I went—I was locking the door. And this lady said, "Look out, porter." And I ducked. This man was swingin' at my head with a fifth bottle of whiskey, see. I looked at him. So I went on and got my milk and put it in the kitchen. Then I went back outside, 'cause we stayed there 15 minutes. They changed train conductors there, too. So he told the Pullman conductor what all that I did to him and this and that and the other. The train conductor was right there. And the Pullman conductor said, "Well, I'll have to pull you off, and you deadhead back to Los Angeles."

I said, "It's quite all right with me."

By my club car being way up there, the train conductor would be there, too, and the head-end brakeman was to ride up there. So when this guy was raising all that hell and the Pullman conductor told me, "You'll have to get your bag and get outta here, we don't go for that," the train conductor said, "What the hell'd you say?"

He said, "Well, Steele insulted this man . . . and I'm gonna pull him off."

He says, "I run the train, not you. Steele, you get back on that train when we get ready to pull out."

And he stated right before the man, "If this son of a bitch tries to hurt you, you kill him."

And I got on. [The man] got back on the train, and I was mixing drinks and everything, and he stopped there and looked at me, and I said, "Look, man, you heard what the conductor told you, didn't you? Don't you mess with me, 'cause I'm gonna tear you in two."

So he left. And about four women handed me four letters to turn in to the Pullman Company concerning him.

When I got back in town, they pulled me off, told me to come over right away. Mr. Armstrong was his own superintendent, and he was a toughy. He says, "I wanna know about this."

I say, "Did you get the letters?"

He says, "Yeah."

I say, "Well then, you don't wanna see me about nothin'." I told him, "I was told that he was one of the vice presidents of the Pullman Company out of Chicago. Is that true?"

He says, "Well, Steele, you can go, 'cause we know you're all right."

You had to swallow. I could tell you a million things. I tell ya. I was a young man. I was 25 years old when I started on the road, and I weighed about 200 and something pounds. When they looked at me, they would think twice, see, 'cause I was always smiling. I'm waitin' for you to raise your hand to hit me. If you do, I'm gonna knock the hell outta ya, I don't care who you are. All I can say is this. You're on there to do a job, and you are a Pullman porter. You are supposed to take everything the passenger puts on you—you're supposed to take it. I swallowed a lot of times to keep from losing my job, 'cause I had Sears to pay, and all them stores, see? So I'd walk away. A lot of times, because you don't say anything, that doesn't mean you're a coward, if a man is cursing you and things like that. Oh, I've been cursed out a lot. I just look at you and laugh. Now, just like I say, during those days you had a tremendous amount of prejudice, and you still have it, but not as bad as then because more opportunities have been opened up to the black man. Now, in some of these big white stores you see a lot of big dark men—or black men, as you call 'em—is vice president or just like the RTD [Los Angeles bus system]. There used to be a Negro man in there that had a high position. I can't think of his name now.

Right now you've got prejudice. You know what? I'm gonna tell you somethin'. I bought a new Buick out there, see, and when you close the door, the bell that rang—the buzzer—would still buzz, see. So we put a piece of leather and taped it, and that made that thing stick out more and connect, and the buzzer would come off. And right on the round part of the seat there was a kinda tearin' a little bit, see, so I went over there [the dealership], and this man came over to me, he says, "What's wrong?" And I say, "Well, I had trouble with the door there, and we finally stopped it by puttin' a piece of tape on it."

He said, "You didn't have to do that."

I said, "Well, we didn't know." So I say, "Now the seat over there has to be repaired."

[*In gruff voice*] "Oh, I know all about that."

Now that was a man that he could see a Negro pull up in a nice fine car like I got out there, see. Now when the white people come up . . . [*imitates salesman smiling and greeting customer*]. When he looked at me, it looked like he puked, and I told Bobby, "Bobby, I oughta let him have it," and Bobby say, "No, we don't need that trouble."

I'm gonna tell you something about people during the time that I started working for the railroad. Those men, they knew who not to mess with, and they knew who they could cower down, see, because some of them porters would grab them men and fight 'em just like he was a colored man and thought nothing of it and tell the conductor, "Damn, you wanna pull me off the train, I'll get off the goddamn thing. He had no business doing so-

and-so to me." All that was squashed, see. Now just like this guy out there at the Buick place. I'm waiting till I have to take that car out there, and I do hope I get him so I can tell him in a nice way—I don't mean curse or anything like that, see, because man, he really hurt me.

The Pullman Company was often sued by unscrupulous passengers who saw the company as an easy target for making money by pretending to have been injured while the train was in motion or to have been sexually harassed by a porter. The possibility of sexual harassment by Pullman porters was of major concern to the company—so much so that it hired female spotters whose job was to try to seduce porters. Naturally, with thousands of men on the payroll, it was not unreasonable to expect that some of them actually were guilty of making sexual advances to their passengers. But for the thousands who did not succumb to the spotters, their presence was a constant lesson in restraint.

You had to be so careful when you catch a lot of single white women, because a lot of 'em are put on there to try to trap you, see? And you got to have damn good willpower not to get yourself messed up, 'cause [Pullman] would pay you $77.50 a month, and they pay $2,000 to get something on you. See? A lot of porters was caught, and you had to be careful.

One guy, this lady had left her curtains open where he could see her, and he'd come right in and peek. Then she would ring the bell like she wanted something, see. And he'd go there, you know, and she'd just show him everything. He'd get ready to crawl in there, then the inspector is over here. Just as [the porter] got in there, the man tapped him on the back. We got ya! You get *fired*!! The minute you get in, your check is waitin' for ya. That news gets down to Los Angeles before you do. And when you get off the train, they right there waitin' for ya. And you had to be very careful.

If it's with a woman, they got to prove that you did that. Now we had a porter, Forsythe was his name, he was way up in age. This white woman say that he screwed her twice. They had that big hearing. And the guy that was representing the Pullman Company says, "This man is 67 years old, and he has worked past the time for him to retire." This lawyer told the judge, he say, "Judge, I want you to read this letter."

And he read it out loud. It was signed by one of the biggest doctors here in California. And he was a white doctor, too. You know what it was? He couldn't raise a hard-on. That's what it was. And he told the lady, "We should be suing you. Now there's a man ain't raised a hard-on in years, and you gonna say he screwed you?" And after that hearing they told him, "We don't have anything against you."

Look, if they wanted it to be aired out, they'd have it in court and have the lawyers and all that. Let me tell you one thing. If the woman says that you tried to screw her or you did screw her, and then she makes a fuss about it, well, naturally the Pullman Company will pay, regardless of how much it is, in order to squash it. But they gonna let you go.

If at night, say around nine or ten o'clock, the bell ring, and you look at it and it says room D, a lot of times it's just one woman in there. She'll say, "Come in. I wanna give an order."

I say, "You can tell me right here at the door what you want."

"I would like a scotch and soda." Well, you're supposed to open the whiskey before the passenger and pour it, see? And I mix a drink for her, and she says, "You can come in. I'm not going to bite you."

I said, "Why you think I left that door open for? So everybody could see in here what I was doin'. I don't know anything about you, and I'm not supposed to stay in a room with you. I'm here to serve. Your bed is made, and if you want this drink, we'll leave the door open," 'cause she'll say anything.

Whether it's a setup or not, you know you ain't got no business there. If you open the door and you see that, then you turn around and close the door. I don't give a damn how many times you ring the bell. And if she keeps on ringing the bell, then you go get the train conductor. Say, "I want you to go in there with me to serve this drink. This woman ain't got no clothes on."

He'll knock on the door. She says, "Come in." He walks in first. She grabs her robe and puts it on right quick. "Oh, I'm sorry." Then she mixes her drink, and the conductor tells her, "Look, I don't want this happening no more, or we'll put you off the train."

Now, on a trip to Chicago we stopped at Palm Springs to take on a millionaire, and this one particular lady got on and had the drawin' room, and I put her baggage in there. She looked like she was a brown-skinned Negro woman, and I told her, "I'm sorry. We're not allowed to sell whiskey to Indians."

She says, "I'm not an Indian," and she pulled [her dress top] way back where I could see all her white meat. And I said, "I'm sorry" [laughs]. So I served her.

If you are a man—'course, you're young when they hire ya—if you are a young man, and this job is business to me, I gotta wife at home and two children and I know if I steal, if I fuck around with the women, I'm gonna get fired. What I'm gonna tell my wife? All right. Now, there was no way in the world that a woman could get me on the train to go to bed with her. I don't care if she showed me her natural butt. That meant nothin' to me but a dollar three cents for that scotch and soda, and give me that and I'm gone. You can show your ass to whoever you wanna. But you got to be strong. You got to be strong, see, because I'm gonna tell ya: temptation is great.

Now we were coming into Santa Barbara at breakfast time, and the train made a bad stop, and it kinda threw this lady back against the wall, see. So I went over to her, and I says, "Are you all right?"

She says, "Yes."

I say, "Did you get hurt?"

"No."

I say, "Well, you put this down on this paper." And she did.

Two days later they call me in, and they say that you had a Ms. So-and-so on the train, and the train made a bad stop and knocked her back against a wall. The big boss told me, he say, "She's gonna file suit."

I say, "Well, wait just a minute. I'll go get my bag." And I went and got my bag, and I opened it up, and I handed him the paper dated, and she signed it with her name. I say, "This what you're talkin' about?"

He says, "You mean to tell me you did that?"

I say, "That's the sensible thing to do. I'm in charge of the car, and I just figured she was gonna do that, so I had her write her name and address down there that she was not hurt or nothin' was spilled on her."

He says, "You sure savin' the company a lot of money."

And I say, "Well, here it is."

So being on a car is just like being in the South. When you're walking down the street and a white lady's coming this way, you're supposed to get your black self outta the streets and let her go by. Then you get back on the sidewalk [laughs]. That's true!

As the years went by—which was a struggle for A. Philip Randolph, when he got us together and we formed the Brotherhood of Sleeping Car Porters—you had a chance, you had a union. But when you didn't have no union, your ass was just out to the wall. If you want something, you got to fight for it, see. And do you know how much money it cost us for A. Philip Randolph to get a seat with the AFL and CIO? Fifty thousand dollars they taxed us, and we got that money up before you could turn around. We had a damn good union. We had a guy that was head of the Pullman Company union, and the minute you got to be a porter, he would grab ya and tell ya, "You don't wanna belong to the Brotherhood of Sleeping Car Porters. This is the union you should belong to. We can do this, and we can do the other." Then he turn right around and walked to the white man, tell him every damn thing you told him [laughs].

When A. Philip Randolph got in there, then the salaries began to go up. He was in there way before I started working for the Pullman Company, but they hadn't got strong, see. When they got strong, then you had a chance. But before then, if this white woman say you felt her legs or you tried to do so-and-so to her, they would take her word and pay her so much money and kick your ass out in the streets. I will say this. I know I belong to the union, and I know out of all them rich white men and businessmen that's on the train, here I am just a little $77-a-month porter on the train. Why would you try to get me? Now I ain't got a damn thing, and here's all these rich men down around here just layin' for ya, see. So you've got to have willpower. When they first approach you, walk away. And if she keep nagging ya, go get the train conductor. Not the Pullman conductor, the train conductor. He's the boss, see, and you tell him what's happening, and he'll tell her, he say, "Now, if he reports you one more time, we're gonna have to put you off the train at the next stop." That's what unions'll do for ya. But if you didn't have a union then, you ain't got no voice.

I'm gonna ask you something. You going down the street there, and it's a rattlesnake about four feet long, and you hear him rattle. You gonna turn around; you're not gonna continue goin'. You're not gonna move right away; you're gonna stop to get the range of his rattle where he is, see, and if there's any way you can get back to where you were goin', you gonna do it, aren't ya? So when you go to the door to carry a drink, and she's got on one of them short nightgowns and showin' all her titties and things, you just say, "Well, lady, I'll mix it outside." Then I'll have the conductor collect the money, see. But if you're one of them kind that's wantin' to see this stuff and wantin' to do that shit, you're gonna get caught. You're gonna get caught. So you're on there to work and to tend to your business, and if the passenger bother you, you go to the Pullman conductor. And if the Pullman conductor don't do you no good, then you go to the train conductor. And maybe he had to walk through about ten cars, and when he get back there he mad, see. Then the passenger say, "Well, he did so-and-so." The conductor'd say, "Well, I've been riding with this man for years, and I want you to let him alone or we'll put you off the train."

Now the Pullman conductor's gonna say [imitates milquetoast voice], "Well, I don't know. . . ." But the train conductor, he is the boss; what he say goes. Now, we had a big rich man had a big meetin' down here in Los Angeles at ten o'clock. He raised so much hell on the train, till they put his ass off at Salinas, and he had to charter a plane to come to Los Angeles for that meetin', see. Do you think they say anything to the train conductor about that? No. He's the boss. You don't say nothin' to him about that. But the Pullman conductor, shit, he'll go in his shell in a minute [laughs]. He's scared of his job.

Sam Turner

5

SAM TURNER
Santa Fe Utility Man and Cook,
Amtrak Sleeping Car Attendant
1946 – 1988

Sam Turner railroaded for over 40 years, starting in the kitchen for the Santa Fe Railroad and ending his career in an Amtrak chair car. Born on 26 November 1926, Sam was raised along with three sisters and a brother in Eudora, Arkansas. By 1946 he was out on the road for the Santa Fe. From the confines of a café car on the Oil Flyer to a kitchen on the internationally famous Super Chief, Sam worked his way up the seniority ladder to the enviable position of being able to pick and choose the trains he worked.

With the formation of Amtrak in 1972, the railroads handed over their passenger operations to the government, abolishing many fine name trains throughout the country. Sam decided to go with Amtrak and began in the kitchen because of his extensive experience with the Santa Fe. He had always wanted to work a sleeping car, however, and bid on a sleeping car run as soon as he saw one posted on the board at the Los Angeles crew base.

By the early part of 1988, the demands of the sleeping car proved a little too difficult, and Turner spent his last few months with Amtrak working the chair cars. He retired on 2 November 1988.

When I was a kid, I used to be in a place in Arkansas about 60 miles from Little Rock, and the Missouri Pacific track used to come through this little town of Dermott. I used to stand up on the side of the railroad watchin' 'em, said, "One day I sure want a job on the train like those guys." They had their white coats on, the porters be lookin' out the train, and the brakemen had their black suits on. I say, "I'm gonna get a job like that."

My granddaddy, he was a brakeman on the train, and he worked for the Missouri Pacific. Yeah, he worked there 30 years. I had an uncle worked on there also for 20 years, and he was a trainman. Then I had another uncle down there in Texas, used to work on the log train. He was an engineer. Didn't have no education, but he was good, and he worked on that train for a long time. He'd blow that whistle—you could hear him a mile away—they knew that was Bradley comin' into town. And that's what made me want to railroad.

I was born in Eudora, Arkansas, but I left there when I was about 17 and come to Los Angeles in 1944 and graduated high school in '46. I heard so much talk about California, and I read so much about it in the geography and all that, about the kinda weather they had out here, about the movie stars and all that. I just wanna come out and see this place. I don't know, I always had a premonition that I would be comin'. I always saw myself comin' to California, and I did.

I'm tellin' you, I come on out here—it was durin' the wartime then—they had the shipyards. A lot of money was bein' made out here, and I'll tell ya, I never had such a good time in all my life. We had a main street out here in Los Angeles, Central Avenue. Back in that time, they had all kinda nightclubs, and all your movie stars like'll be down, they come out here and walk around here on that street. It really was a jumpin' street, but now the street has gone to pot. But years ago we sure used to have a good time. I never thought that street would die out like that. It's still there, but you know, it's nothin' but the slums and things like that.

I was goin' to school, too, Jefferson High School, and what I did, I worked the graveyard shift at nighttime and go to school in the daytime. They let you work six hours, you know. That was good money then. Not much time, but you made some good money when you was doin' it, though. They had ships comin' in from all over the world, from Russia, from everywhere. It was somethin' to see. It was exciting.

I was a scaler, a chipper. I would chip off the rough edges. I had a machine that chipped off the rough edges on the ship, then the other guys would come back and smooth some over. Lot of times, a guy'll weld and leave those rough places; well, I chip 'em off and make 'em smooth. I did that for about a year and a half. I made some of that money, but it wasn't long, though. The war was soon over. Then I worked at a cafeteria down there on Broadway for about six months. That was all right, but I soon put that down and went to the hospital. I worked at the Los Angeles County Hospital for a year, then I heard about the railroad. Sometimes I wish I hadda stayed, 'cause you can go and take up trades out there. You can be an X-ray technician or you could be an intern; you could go to school, become a registered nurse. They had some good breaks. But I wanted to railroad; I wanted to travel. Travelin's just in my blood.

I used to see a fella workin' on the Southern Pacific—he was a chef cook— and he always had all that time off. I asked him, "How 'bout one of them good jobs?" Well, he was workin' on the extra board, you know, sometime he'd be in town a couple weeks, and then he'd be gone a week or so. I thought that was the easiest job in the world.

So finally, I was supposed to work at the Southern Pacific, but I went to Santa Fe. I was about 18 years old when I started for Santa Fe. I've been railroadin' ever since. It was 1946 on my birthday. They were to hire me out as a waiter, but they hired me out as a cook and said, "We gonna give it to you later on." They tricked me. They never did get me out the kitchen, and I always did want to be a waiter.

My first assignment was fourth cook. That was a dishwasher then. Then I worked all the way, fourth cook up to third cook, which was vegetable cook and the pot washer. Then the second cook is the one who cook all the meats, and he's assistant to the chef. But it did take you a long time in those days to work yourself up. Sometime it took you at least ten years to work up to become a chef cook.

Santa Fe had some crack trains. They had the Super Chief. The El Capitan. Then they had the Chief. Old California Limited. I tell ya, the first train I worked was the Grand Canyon. That was the train that was mostly the pass riders and the little local towns. We called it "that old covered wagon" 'cause it went so slow. It stopped at every little pig trail, every little stop between here and Chicago. And finally, I went to one a little better than the Grand Canyon called the Old California Limited. It was the old equipment, but it was that pretty heavyweight equipment. The Old California Limited. I will never forget.

The California Limited had a crew of five cooks: two second cooks, one third cook, a fourth cook, and a chef cook. And we had six to seven waiters on the train. The seventh waiter was the one we call the upstairs waiter. He would take the people's orders back to 'em—like if people didn't feel like comin' in the dining car, he always took their order up front [to the Pullmans]. Every waiter had a different job. We had one silver man. He take care of the silver after the meal is over. Some take care of the salt and pepper shakers. Then we had one man made all the salads, all the dressin's, clean the chicory and the lettuce. He was the pantryman, and he kept the pantry and all. He had a little small space. Sometimes I don't know how all those fellas could turn around in that space, but they could manage some kinda way and get their orders.

I worked the Oil Flyer, and I worked the Texas Ranger. The first time I got a job when I went to Chicago, I went from Chicago to Fort Worth on the Texas Ranger. I got out with the boys and went out there on the street that night and got clipped. Pigeon droppers got me. They told me, say, "Take your money, and put it with my money." I act the fool, they got my watch and everything. I opened the envelope—lots of cut-up newspaper. But I learned that lesson. I can spot them people a mile away, and that happened to me over 38 years ago. I never will forget. Right on Ninth Street in Fort Worth.

Then they had the Scout. The Scout wasn't nothin'. Now, the Scout carried a lot of soldiers and a lot of poor people on there. See, on the Scout, when they cook your breakfast, they have scrambled eggs. They never would fix their eggs no way but scrambled. They put everything on one plate. But it was cheaper. It was about $20 less in fare. The waiters and cooks would call it the "greasy spoon." That stopped round about 1949. Then I had a little small run from Los Angeles. That was over 38 years ago—just a little small train. I can't think of the name. Used to run from Los Angeles to the Grand Canyon. You'd go overnight and be back the next day. It was beautiful, too. We go to the El Tovar. That was that nice hotel there in the Grand Canyon. And we run there all the time.

We had a lot of little short runs. On a little short run from Chicago to La Junta, Colorado, we used to stay overnight there. A lady, she had a little roomin' house. Put two of us to a bed. I never forget them old iron beds. Then they had a place for the white crew to go to. Yeah, we didn't like that, but it's one of those things you couldn't help.

When we was workin' outta Kansas City, they only had one cook, he was the chef, and they had two waiters. It was a café car. You had a little kitchen right in the center of it, and then they had the stools right around the counter there. You had one man that was in charge. They called him the waiter-in-charge. He had a helper with him. Sometime I've been on there with nothin' but a waiter-in-charge and myself. We serve 22 people at a setting. We serve 'em, then we clean the place up, and we clear all the plates off, then we start again with another setting. That was fun. I liked that. I did that for quite a number of years, too, run outta Kansas City.

We used to have these old diners, and in the floor they had what you call the possum bellies. They had these bunk beds, these beds you could fold. You pull back the carpeting back over it in the daytime, but at night, when we get through serving the people, we take 'em out, and the crew would sleep in the diner at night.

Then we got so they had an old Pullman they would give us that you had the curtains you had to hang up—section cars. We had that for a while. Then they got better, where they made us a dormitory. We went through all them phases.

On 18 May 1937 the Santa Fe inaugurated the new all-streamlined Super Chief on a 39½-hour schedule from Chicago to Los Angeles. Internationally famed for its first-class service and clientele, the Super Chief was the pride of Santa Fe's passenger train fleet. To work the Super Chief, whether in the diner or the Pullmans, an employee had to have quite a number of years under his belt. *By the time Sam Turner worked the Super on a regular basis he had the necessary seniority.*

In 1956 the El Capitan chair car train from Chicago to Los Angeles was reequipped with Hi-Level cars delivered by the Budd Company. These stainless-steel beauties offered "penthouse"-style seating and eating facilities on the upper level of each car. The lower level of the chair cars contained the vestibule and the restroom area, as well as ample baggage storage. Sam also worked the El Capitan during his years with Santa Fe, and it remains one of his favorite trains.

By 1957 the Super Chief could not support itself during the off season; it was combined with the El Capitan into one long train, although onboard the two trains were still separate entities.

I worked the Super Chief—I was second cook. I stayed on the Super Chief for ten years one time. I liked the Super Chief. You worked hard on there, but you learn how to cook many different things 'cause they had the most fanciest things in the world. All those filet of mignons, those sirloin steaks. You had a lot of turkeys to cook, and dressing. Prime ribs. Cornish hens. You had those trouts, and you had to bone those fishes out. You learned a lot on there. You didn't have no canned goods or nothin'. No, you had to bring it up from the nub. If you had string beans, you had to take a knife and French-cut 'em and then put your almonds in there and cook it up. You just had so much to do, but you had to do it from the nub. Make all your soups. Big old stockpot. Have your bones in there and make your stock, then you make your soup from that. You had your Philadelphia pepper pot and cream of mushroom, your cream of asparagus, vegetable soup. You had all those different kinds of soup mix.

But now they got stuff in the canned goods. It's easy now. The cooks got it made. They ain't got nothin' to worry. But everything was brought up the hard way. Make all of your puddin's, all your sweets, and all the stuff en route—right on the train.

You had to specialize fixin' that French toast. See, the Santa Fe had the prettiest French toast in the world. You really had to know. Couldn't every-body cook that French toast 'cause a lot of 'em cook it would fall down. There's a certain way you had to cook it for it to stay up like it was. It was a specialty. I learned from a chef—old German chef taught me. You had a knife, you would trim that toast, and then you soak it in the cream and egg batter and salt and pepper. Then put it in some hot grease right there and then. And when you cook it in that grease, it makes it real fluffy and round. Pretty! Then you run it in the stove. It will stay up, but you got to have the stove a certain temperature, too. You could just about gauge it because you been doin' it so long, and you know whether the stove was cold, wasn't too warm or it would fall down. You let it finish cookin', and you put all that powdered sugar on it real neat. Then you put it on that silver platter. Put a doily on it, and take it on out there to 'em. And that was Santa Fe's pet pea—French toast.

At that time you had a 46-seat diner, when I was there. But the kitchen was small, and then it was hot. It was extremely hot down there, all that metal. You talk about hot! We used to pass through Needles, California. That's the hottest place in the world!! That's the first place I ever come through that when you pass through Needles, it'd be so hot in June, July, and August, you stick your head outta the kitchen door your head was more hot out there, the atmosphere, than it was inside the kitchen. Now, they say it'd get 120-something in Needles. You take an egg and just put it on the ground, and it'll cook. Sometime there'd be so much sweat, it'd run down in your shoes. That little fan didn't put out that much.

On the Super Chief, shoot, for our diner we had to get up around five o'clock in the morning. We open our diner at six-thirty in the morning. But we had to get up early and get a good start 'cause we had everything just like on a hotel to cook for those people. Breakfast would cut out sometime around nine-thirty or ten o'clock, accordin' to how the load was. Sometime we went straight on in from breakfast into lunch. Sometime we stay on our feet all day long; your legs swell up like that. Oh, we have seen it many a times! You just went straight on through. Sometimes we get up in the mornin' at five o'clock and didn't get outta there before twelve o'clock at night, especially in the summertime. Then, you know, your peak season start around the middle of May, a little before Memorial Day, and you know the next month the kids are gettin' out of school in June, lot of people gettin' their vacation. You go up until Labor Day, around the tenth of September. Then it falls down a little while. And a little before Christmastime round about, I'll say about the middle of November, they start back again for the Christmas thing. It'll go up until about the fifteenth of January. That's the way it always has been on the Santa Fe.

Boy, we saw a lot of the top celebrities on that train. One time we had Harry Truman on there. We used to see Alfred Hitchcock, Bette Davis, Rita Hayworth, Irene Dunn, Van Heflin. We used to see 'em all on the Super Chief. Some of 'em ate in their rooms; some of 'em didn't come out. But the biggest of 'em like to come in the dinin' room real sharp, you know, sit around and shoot the breeze—have the waiter bring their cocktail to 'em before they eat.

That was Santa Fe's crack train, and you was proud to work on that train, 'cause when I get in town I'd say, "Boys, I work on the Super Chief." And people really thought you were somebody if you work on the Super Chief 'cause all the big shots rode it. That was a really beautiful train!

And then one time, I tell you what, one time I was on the El Captain, you know, that was the Hi-Level train, all-streamlined chair cars. And I was steppin' over one coach—that was really fate, God was with me that time— I stepped over, and just as I stepped over to go into the next car, it came loose. And they had to back two miles to hook back together, and I just stepped over in a split second, otherwise I would've gotten it myself. But it just wasn't my time. I never will forget. That scared me. My heart was in my mouth for a long time.

The kitchen was always downstairs, and the top was all dinin' room, but they had a lot of waiters. You could feed about 96 people, 'cause that whole level was where the people could sit up there. That's where I was a pantryman on there, a stationary pantryman. I had a little space to myself down there where I sent up all the orders. I had a dumbwaiter, and I would make all the salad and dressin's, take care of all the cakes and pies, and do all the orderin' for the chef. I would order the food supply, and all the chef had to do was cook 'em. I liked it 'cause I had a fan on my side. So I put that kitchen down, 'cause I loved that pantry job.

Yeah, the El Capitan! And it was fast! You know how fast? We've got so fast we could make it from Chicago to Los Angeles in 39¾ hours. That was a fast train. And the Super Chief'd be right on his tail. We always get in maybe 15 minutes ahead. Sometimes the El Cap be racin' with the Super Chief. The Super Chief would sometimes get there 15 minutes ahead of us; we get there 15 minutes ahead of them.

They finally quit runnin' them separate and put the Super Chief behind and put the El Cap up front. They consolidated together, two trains. They had the gates up where the people couldn't go back in there. That was called the first-class section, and the other part was the chair car section. And then they feed a lot of people on there, too. You have about three or four settings. We call it Chico—"We gonna serve Chico"—a cheap meal where you get everything on one plate. Maybe they have about 600 orders of turkey and dressin', corn on there, vegetables, and mashed potatoes and gravy. We'd serve the people real quick with that. They just give 'em dessert right along with it and everything—everything at one time and let 'em get up. They had so many people, they had to do it. It wasn't nothin' for 'em to have seven or eight hundred people on that train.

And then after they feed the first bunch off—they had two classes of people—then the first-class people could come in last. The Pullman people, you know, they didn't throw it at them. They just take their time and wait on them. They could give 'em better service. You get your "sides" and all that. Side dish of this and a side dish of that. If you brought a person a steak, you brought 'em five different side dishes, and it was on a silver platter. They had a plate, and the waiter would take it out and slide it on the plate for ya. He wait on you hands and feet. You got good service on there.

A lot of trains used to have two diners on there. We used to have so many people travelin'. Well, you have one to help the big diner out. And when they get further down the road, they didn't have as many people, so they didn't need it all the way through. But the main diner went all the way through. Now we used to have some diners would go no further than Clovis, New Mexico. One of the diners would go through and the other would turn around, go back to Los Angeles. That was beautiful, too. That was nice. The diners was air conditioned, and as a whole, the Santa Fe kept their diners up. Very seldom one of 'em would go hot on you. It was always so you could get that good air conditioning. They didn't care too much about the cooks. The cooks caught hell and everything.

We used to give the people service 'cause they had a crew to give 'em service. Nice tablecloths on the table, silverware, finger bowls. A waiter usually had two tables to wait on, and there were four people at each one of the tables. Every waiter had a station. Maybe they had about eight stations in there. And by the time you took care of them, you've done a good job, go get this and go get that, you know.

They had some young waiters, and some of 'em was old. The younger waiters was faster. But you had some of them good old men who were just as good as those young waiters. I've seen some of 'em, 65, 70 years old, run a ring around some of them young boys. But you take back in that time, the waiters didn't leave them jobs at no 60 years old. A lot of them waiters died on them jobs. Some of 'em just liked them jobs so well they just didn't retire. The company had to make 'em step down. Yes, indeed! I know a lot of 'em had to be made. I seen some of 'em cry like a baby, they didn't wanna leave.

Some waiters would make as much as a hundred dollars each way, sometime more than that 'cause at that time they wasn't given 'em no big salary. You give the people that good service, and it wasn't nothin' for them to drop five dollars on ya, two dollars on ya. All that adds up, you know. I've seen some waiters make as much as a hundred fifty, two hundred dollars. But you don't make that kinda money nowadays. Naw, that's gone! People don't tip like they used to. They tip, but they don't tip heavy like. But at that time, in your salary, you wasn't makin' but three hundred to five hundred dollars a month (over-time included). And so the people know you wasn't makin' a whole lot, so they tip you good. You could take your time and wait on 'em. I had a friend of mine—now some guys would wait on about ten people? He'd wait on about four people, and he'd get more than the guy with the ten people. And he taught me somethin'. He said, "You know, if you take your time waitin' on people and give them good service, you'll get a bigger tip than you will butcherin' people up just tryin' to get all the money you can, 'cause you can't half-serve 'em decently like you should. But if you take just as many people that you can give good service—take your time—you come out even." And he did, 'cause people like good service, and people like attention.

They had these Harvey Houses along the road, and a lot of times the train would stop, and you go in there and eat, you know, in the Harvey House. That's what they used to do years ago. Take right there in Barstow. That beautiful Spanish station. Now it's all closed up. You see all the windows torn out of it. But they used to have a fabulous eatin' place in there years ago. We get off the Grand Canyon, we go in there for one hour and eat our breakfast in the Harvey House. Then comin' back from Chicago, we went in there and had dinner for one hour. A lot of people stopped in there.

We had a place in Albuquerque at the old Harvey House there. They tore that down. They still got the station there, but they tore the dinin' room facilities. They used to have Harvey Houses like Las Vegas, New Mexico. They had one there. It was a fabulous place years ago. Some trains had a diner, but they still would stop there sometimes. I guess they had so many people they had no option but to stop and try to feed some of them there, too, you know.

When I was a cook, I was liked by everybody 'cause I found out when you get mad it slows your work up, and it just really makes it bad. And you can't get nothin' right the rest of the day. I always try to control my temper—some kind of way I would control my temper. I don't know why I didn't drink or nothing like that. A lot of the cooks drank—drank a whole lot. And the waiters did, too. They just figure, they drink, it'd make the job go easier. Well, a lot of them sneak it and do it. They didn't let anybody see 'em do it, you know. They caught a lot of 'em. Some of 'em was alcoholic. Some of 'em had to go to Alcoholic Anonymous or whatever it was. They had a class for ya to go in, supposed to get the cure, and then you come back. But they can't break that habit. Some of 'em gonna slip and drink, I don't care what's done with 'em.

But the Santa Fe was just like a family. They would feel sorry. I seen a lot of those German chefs, they had alcohol problems, but they go around there and wasn't nobody lookin' and get on their knees to the boss and plead with him. The boss would bawl 'em out, "Get back on that train." And that's all there was to it. They didn't have no hearin', unless you did something awful bad, you know. And see, back in those days, railroads, they had you set in their ways. But one thing I can say about Santa Fe, if you did anything wrong, they'd put you on the ground for a few days, but they'd always let ya come back. They would always give you another chance.

I know we had one fella who I call Cryin' Black. He had about seven or eight kids, and he was an alcoholic. When he was drunk, he'd get left a lot of times, and they'd put him on the ground. So what he would do, he would always bring his family down there and them kids and just put 'em on the boss's desk and says, "Now you all take care of 'em, you done put me on the ground." And the boss would feel sorry, "Get those kids outta here," and let him go back to work. He did that for a number of times.

I missed a train one day in Chicago, I never will forget. I was changing clothes in one of the cars they gonna hook on the train. It was supposed to have been a dormitory car, and when I come out, the car, the dormitory car, was still there and the train was gone! It was supposed to have left out that mornin'. I run up there, Mr. Dykes [superintendent] was up there, and I said, "Mr. Dykes, my train?"

He said, "Turner, that train's been gone an hour and a half ago." It was the Chief.

When you miss a train, they were strict on ya. They put you on the ground for about a month or so, or two trips. "Mr. Dykes," I said, "I didn't know that train was gone. But if I catch that train, you won't do nothin' to me?"

He said, "Turner, if you catch that train, we ain't gonna bother you. But you can't catch it." I said, "Well, you let me try." So what I did, I ran and got me a car. A buddy of mine took me out to the airport. I went to O'Hare, and they said, "The airplane is all filled up. But you're still standby." And I stood on standby. And all of a sudden, I don't know—a miracle—that plane was just closin' its door for 'em to pull off, and it stopped. They opened that door, and the guy run out there and put me on that airplane. And I went all the way to St. Louis.

Then I got on and caught a little ten-seat passenger train from St. Louis, Missouri, to Kansas City. So when my crew got into Kansas City, they looked, and there I was with my grip. They called me the flyin' cook. I never will forget [laughs]. Everybody was just laughin'. They say, "He made it! He made it!"

I had such a good crew. Had a little old Italian chef named Nick Cecconi. He said, "Turner, we got your work done for ya." And so they had my work done for me, and boy, I put on my clothes. They kid me for two years about that. Do you know Santa Fe never did reprimand me about that? I never did get no punishment for that. But you know what? I'd have lost around a hundred and fifty to two hundred dollars in pay. And I didn't want that. And a wife and kids? I couldn't afford "no pay."

Then another time I was in Bakersfield, California, on this Golden Gate [Santa Fe train from Bakersfield to Oakland]. I'm up there runnin' my mouth in Bakersfield right at the station there. They used to let the crews sleep upstairs. Had beds and bunks up right over the station. But I come out there and talk and looked, and that train was easin' away from me like that. I wanted to try to catch it, but the porter wouldn't open the door. He say, "No, you might hurt yourself." So I was worried. I said, "What am I gonna do?" It's a bad feelin' to get left. Oooh, that's the most miserable thing.

Do you know what I did? I had to catch the milk train. They had a little old train they call the milk train. It had a lot of freight and a lot of things they have for the commissary loaded in there. And they had a little caboose on the back end of it. I got in that caboose, and I caught that about an hour later. And do you know, that train got to Oakland the next mornin'? It got there one hour before time for my train to pull out. And so it happened my boss is out there. Well, he saw me get off, he said, "Turner, what you doin' gettin' off that train? I put another man in your place."

So he seen I was sincere, I was tryin' to make it, so what he did, he pulled the other guy off and put me on the train. He say, "I ain't gonna cut your time this time, but next time you mustn't run at your mouth before you have to leave." But anyway, he let me go. I got a chance to make that trip, too. I didn't lose no time.

The major drawback to railroad life is the great amount of time spent on the road away from family. In Sam's career with the Santa Fe, however, the chance to make all that money by doubling out, taking one trip right after another, was too good to pass up.

See, I was a globe-trotter. The way I do, I get tired of it, and then I go and get somethin' else. In the summertime they put on a lot of special trains, and you have your choice, and I had a lot of seniority. The longest time I was out was 24 days one time. I never will forget. And when I got home, I said, "I'll never do that no more." They had been callin' my house in Chicago where I stayed, and they had tried their best to get in touch with me out on the road. They said, "Somebody been callin' you down in Arkansas."

So I called down there and asked 'em what it was. They said, "Your grandmother's dead. We been tryin' to get you for the past eight days. We give up. They holdin' the body out for you to see your grandmother." And I told 'em, I said, "If you all can hold 'em two more days, I'll be down there. I just got the news."

I was gone 24 days, came in, got a check around about [$350]. That was big money in that time, see. Big money. That was long about 1951. Instead of gettin' to Chicago, I'd call the man up over the phone. You know, the Santa Fe, they got a commissary in Kansas City, too. I just call my boss and tell him, I said, "Well, I don't wanna come to Chicago. You send me back out again." I got back out again with another special that was goin' out.

Sometime I go down to Albuquerque, New Mexico. You stay down there five or six days with the Elks until they get through with their convention. Then you bring 'em back to their places. And the Elks, they had all the whiskey in the world you wanted on there, all that good food. They give you a lot of stuff. Those groups would be so good, a lot of times they didn't care about no color or nothin' 'cause they be drinkin', having a good time.

Them Elks, yes indeed! And you'd get all you wanted to drink, and all you could hide and everything else [*laughs*]. It was a good time during that time. I tell you, you caught some good specials on the Santa Fe. And it really made you get railroading in your blood.

I tell ya, that was pretty hard. I did it, but I don't know how I did it. That's one reason me and my first wife separated. I stayed with her 18 years, and I had five kids by her, but bein' gone all the time—lot of times on Christmas I have to be out, or on Easter. She just couldn't seem to take it. She said she took it long enough. Said I'd be gone all the time. But we had some good times on the train. I kept her on the train ridin' with me a lot of times. I'd take her, you know, get a pass for her and take her along with me. But she said it still ain't nothin' like you bein' home. Nowadays, she regrets it, though, she wish she stayed with me.

I had a second wife, put her through college. She's up in age, in her fifties, I believe. She got her B.S. degree with me. Then after she got her degree, she got disgusted, then say I be gone all the time. But you know, on a job you got to have a wife that understands, that's all I can say. She tried her best to get me to quit, but I wouldn't quit.

I'll never quit the railroad for nobody because I've been with it all my life, and that's all I know. I love it, and there ain't nobody gonna make me quit it. That's right. 'Course, I imagine if I had it to do all over again, I would have never started with the railroad, if I'd know'd like I know now. But I can't cry about it, 'cause I have just enjoyed as much of this sweet life as anybody else bein' on the road. And a lot of things that I've done I don't think I could have done if I hadn't of been on the road.

At that time when I started railroadin', you didn't have no black chefs. See, when we first started, we had all German chefs and French chefs—foreigners. Old man Harvey and them dudes, they didn't want no black cooks at the time. They said a black man couldn't cook, but later they found that out better. A lot of those chefs retired, and Santa Fe had no other opportunity but to take black chefs and let 'em go on up. But we used to couldn't go no further than the second cook, that's all you could go. They did that for years. I remember that real good.

Finally, having the war started, they had to go to hiring them all 'cause a lot of those white chefs went to better jobs. Some of 'em died out, and some of 'em just didn't do it anymore. Some of 'em went to hotels. They got better positions. Fred Harvey used to go over there in Europe and get his chefs and bring 'em here. And his stewards was also Germans, too. Finally, during the wartime and after, then they started hiring colored.

See, we played that role so long till it just made us look natural, being porters. The white folks was always used to that because in slavery times, the white man and his family, he always had the maid, she was there at that

Sam Turner working as a sleeping car attendant during his
Amtrak days, San Bernardino, California, 1979.

time. They called 'em the mammies then. She would wait on the children, cook for 'em, and prepare the food. And I guess they just had that in their minds that that is just our regular job, that's what we supposed to be. They just look for us to do it, and they comfortable with us doin' it. They had made up their mind. They feel like it look more natural for a black person to be waitin' on 'em or being their porter or being their waiter than for a white to be doin' it. That's just the way I feel.

I've noticed a lot of white passengers they still can't get it together seeing a white man being a porter and things. But they getting adjusted to it now. After awhile later on as we get further on up the road it's gonna be common. They ain't gonna even think about it no more. It's just something that is gonna take time to wear off.

You can't carry no bitterness and things like that, but you do think about it sometimes. Course you can't carry no hatred in your heart; you got to forgive. If you carry hatred in your heart it's just like an eatin' cancer, it will destroy you and you'll block your own good thoughts carryin' negative thoughts about what happened in the past. That was things that was done

95

under the bridge and so it's been done and there ain't nothin' you can do about it. I don't like it, but it was that way. But it's better now. They're tryin'.

It was fun workin' for the railroad. Santa Fe was really nice to me. And I have had some good times. Since I had the job, I've been overseas five or six different times. I own two homes. I raised five kids, and they all grown now. So I can't say nothin'. The railroad has been good to me. I just come from a railroad family. It's been in my blood all the time.

Sure, I'd miss it. You miss a job like that when you been doin' it all your life. I've seen some guys like those jobs so bad—we had an old steward years ago he lived in Pasadena. He got him a house right by the railroad track— used to pass by there. He had it so bad, he'd wave at everybody passin' by there everyday. Finally, he must have died, 'cause we don't see him no more. But for over ten years he'll be right out there wavin', don't care what hour of night you pass by. He was right there. He's an old railroad man. It just was in his blood.

Now, if I had it to do all over again, I'd go to college. I did finish high school. Thank God, I got my diploma from high school. I wouldn't let none of my kids start on the railroad. They all want to follow in my footsteps, yeah, but I wouldn't let 'em do it. I told 'em, "Now you got wives. You'd be away from 'em all the time. I don't want you all to come up separated like I did." So finally, they gave it up.

They told me 38 years ago they gonna pull the trains off, and ya still got 'em on. But I used to think every year they gonna pull the trains. I be nervous and scared, thinkin' they gonna pull it off. So I don't even pay no attention. There's always gonna be some trains. You'll always have trains.

Jimmy Clark

6

JIMMY CLARK
Southern Pacific Chef Cook
1918–1950

Born in Mobile, Alabama, at the turn of the century on 3 October 1900, Jimmy Clark came out to California by train in 1917. Within a year he was working in a Southern Pacific dining car kitchen washing dishes. His extraordinary memory offers an in-depth look into the prerailroad genealogy of an African American family as he retraces his life from his earliest recollections of rural life in the South through his years as a chef cook on the railroad.

Jimmy Clark is a gentleman's gentleman, with an accent on "gentle." A more peaceful and loving individual would be hard to find. Of all the men interviewed for this book, Jimmy Clark possessed an unusually fond affection for his company. He retired from the road in 1950 because of an arthritic condition that prevented him from working long hours standing in the kitchen. He had served 32 years for the railroad.

My grandfather was Scotch-Irish. He had a brother, and his brother came from Ireland. They settled in either North or South Carolina, I don't remember. One of the Carolinas. They came aboard this ship where you ride down where the freight is kept; they couldn't buy no first-class ticket. If I remember right, it was 1842. I could be a little off on the year, but it had to be somewhere back in that period because he would relate a lot of things to me about their life.

They migrated from the Carolinas to Alabama. That's where my grandfather met this black woman, which was my mother's mother, and they had four children—two boys and two girls—all right there in Mobile. And the two white brothers kept up with their children and visited with them just like as if we were all the same race. There was never any friction. I didn't remember my great-great-grandmother. My mother said when I was a baby she used to come and hold me in her arms and nurse me—talk to me. But my grandfather, I remember him very well. Of course, I was about nine years old when he passed away.

Now, on my father's side, I remember my grandfather. He fought in the Civil War. I had a picture of him in uniform. He didn't have a full uniform. He had a coat and a hat. And you see, that's how they'd come about, how the blacks who fought in the Civil War would come about with a partial uniform. They'd come across a dead Union soldier, and they'd take his coat or his pants or whatever they could take off 'em. If it fit him, they would wear it because all they had in the Union army was rifles and civilian clothes. He used to tell me many times about his experiences during the Civil War. He said he was 19 years old when he went to fight in the Civil War. He said that when they were fighting, bullets would be passing by and soldiers would be falling here and there. He was just fortunate that he wasn't killed. I happened to be running to New Orleans on the Sunset in 1921. I went to Mobile, and my cousin told me where our grandfather was living and took me out to see him. He passed a few months after that time.

He was part African and part Indian. So you see, I have four different bloods running through me—Scotch, Irish, African, and Indian. My mother was fair. You could tell she was a black woman, of course, she wasn't perfectly white. She had a white father and a black mother, and usually a child born by a woman with a white father takes after the father.

My father, he worked for the Mobile and Ohio Railroad for the president of the Mobile and Ohio Railroad on his private car. Then in 1904, during the World's Fair in St. Louis, Missouri, Mr. Taylor, the president of Mobile and Ohio Railroad, told my father that he was going to St. Louis to the World's Fair. And naturally, [my father] was going to be going because he's got to be in that private car. So he told [my father], you have an opportunity to take your family to the World's Fair.

Now, this is the first time my memory started. The first thing I can remember, I was three. I don't remember getting aboard the train that night. Evidently I was asleep. When I woke up the next morning, we were on the train. My father came up from the private car with a tray of food. We was up in the coach, me and my three sisters, and we ate our breakfast from this tray that my father had brought on.

We arrived into St. Louis at the Union Station. While we were at the station, he went back in the baggage car to get a little dog that we had, Daisy. A little shaggy dog named Daisy. He brought Daisy into the station, and evidently he didn't have a leash on Daisy because Daisy got loose, seeing all the people, I guess. He went to try to find her, and he couldn't find her. Well, I remember all that just as clear as if it was yesterday.

He took us out to where we were gonna stay. My mother and father got a job through Mr. Taylor on the pike out at the fairground working in a restaurant. My father was cooking; my mother would assist him. And, of course, my three sisters, they were put in school. I was three years old, so they would take me with them on the job.

This is what happened to my father in 1909. He had this little job, you know, on this private car. And whenever he came in town, he'd always make a preparation for him to get a job so he could exist until [Mr. Taylor] needed him on the private car going out on a trip. No tellin' how long it would be before Mr. Taylor would go out again. So my father was workin' in a little restaurant. I think he had this restaurant across from a bar, because it was in a black neighborhood. He and a white man got in an argument one day concerning rent, and I was listening and looking. This white man grabbed my father round the neck and was choking him, and his fingernails went into his flesh. My father got loose somehow, and he ran into the restaurant. Well, this white man probably thought he was going in and get something to hurt him, kill him or something, and he took off. And he came back with a mob.

My grandfather knew what conditions would be in a case with an altercation between a white and black man. He wouldn't have no chance 'cause they'd settle it right now with a rope. So my father went to my uncle and told him what had happened, and he showed me his neck bleedin' and told me to go home. Well, I went home, and he went and got five dollars and went to St. Louis, Missouri. And, of course, in about a week my mother heard from him. She got a letter from him. He explained to her that he wouldn't be coming back to Mobile because he knew he wouldn't have a chance 'cause he was known, see, and that mob would get him. So he stayed in St. Louis, and he kept my mother and sent her money. I never did see my father again.

My mother, naturally, she was working. My sisters were young; they became teenagers, and as soon as they become teenagers, with no father and mother workin', they became pregnant. The men wanted to marry 'em, but the parents didn't want 'em, so they sent the boys away. They wasn't boys, they were young men. One went to Galveston, Texas, and the other went some place in Ohio to keep from marrying my sister. My youngest sister, that man that got her pregnant, his folks insisted that he marry her. But these sisters that had these babies when they were teenagers had to go to work because they didn't have no husband, and I had to come out of school and take care of the babies. That's one reason why I didn't get any education in Alabama. I had to nurse these babies, wash their diapers, change their diapers, prepare their milk, because there wasn't nobody home but me and these three babies. My mother's at work, my sisters are at work. But we got along pretty good. Got the children . . . raised them up.

I never knew anything about segregation. The elders would always say where you could go and where you couldn't go, and that was it. That was all there was to it. The white people that I knew, that I worked around when I got to be 12 years old, that's when I got me a job as office boy, I would clean their office and go on errands for them. I was workin' for two companies. They had their office in the same building on the ground floor, and I was an errand boy. Each one paid me a dollar a week apiece, and they were very nice to me. I never knew any bad treatment from 'em. They treated me very nice, although I ain't gonna say that about everybody, 'cause I don't know how everybody else lives. I'm only speaking about me. And my mother, she would work for the white people, and she always bring home food. They'd always tell her, say now, "Jenny, when you cook, cook enough so that what's left over you take home to the children." And it was always very nice in that manner.

The toughest thing that I can remember in the South is when we used to sell newspapers on the waterfront. The white and black kids sold papers together on the waterfront. There used to be a policeman, his name was Milton. This policeman would go to a black driver driving a wagon and get his whip. Most of them had long bullwhips, you know, that they could do like that and pop it around the team. He'd go up and just take this whip out. Well, this black man couldn't tell him—he knows what he's gonna do with it—but he couldn't tell him, no, you can't take him out and whip him, 'cause hell, he'd turn around and give it to him. So if the black kids didn't see him, then he could stand from here to that door and catch one of 'em with that whip. One of them black boys got hit one time with that bullwhip right here, and it just split his jaw up to his ear, just like it was taken a knife. And, of course, there was nothing done about it. There wasn't nothing said about it at all. That's one particular thing that I witnessed in the South. We knew that we were segregated, and we knew better than to attempt to go into a place where we weren't wanted.

Now, I've gone into places to deliver things, you know, when I was errand boy, deliver messages or something like that. But that was all. I was always treated very nice by the white people that I knew. I never was brutally treated, only by this cop. Of course, I saw him. I always had a lookout, and I'd get outta the way.

My oldest sister and her husband had come to California—he did in 1915. Had been some other people from Alabama come out here, and I guess that's what encouraged him to come to California, because they had said what they were doing and how well they were doing and the difference between California and Alabama. So he came on out here, and naturally, he sent back for his wife and son. They came out here in 1916.

Me and my mother was the next to come out. When I was working on this job where I was makin' the dollar from each one of these people, they encouraged me to join what they had a Christmas Club at the bank. You start out with a nickel, and each week you increase a nickel. Well, when it got up to over two dollars, my mother would add the rest to it. And when I got my Christmas check for $63, including the interest, and I told these people about my check and plans, my sisters sent part of the railroad fare for my mother. And I got this $63 to help make up the rest. We're going to California! And I'll always remember Miss Ruth. She says, "Jimmy, you're going to California. That's a wonderful place. I wish I was going to California. I know you're going to like it." She gave me a lot of encouragement. These are white people.

I gave up my job, and we got the party together, and we left Mobile and came to California. We arrived in Los Angeles on March the fifth, 1917. It doesn't seem like that long ago to me because everything that I'm relating to you now seems like last week, last month, last year. That's the way it seems in my mind, just like it just happened. And the fact about it, those memories still live with me. When I'm lying in my bed alone at night, my memory goes back to my childhood days.

Only thing I knew about a railroad was the railroad we came from Alabama on. We came from Mobile to New Orleans on the L&N, Louisville and Nashville, and we left New Orleans, and we went to St. Louis. We went on the IC, Illinois Central, and we transferred after we crossed the Ohio River at Cairo, Illinois, from the IC to this other railroad that brought us into St. Louis. We left St. Louis and went to Kansas City. I forget the railroad. But anyway, we left Kansas City and come to Denver on the Santa Fe, I believe it was.

We left Denver on the Denver & Rio Grande to Salt Lake City. From Salt Lake City we came into Oakland on the Western Pacific. We took the ferryboat and came over to San Francisco, and we went into a restaurant on Market Street and had lunch. Then we went back across on the ferry to Richmond, and we got the Santa Fe again and came into Los Angeles.

I think it took us about six or seven days to make that trip. 1917. Sixteen years old. They made us lunch. Every city they'd go in, they'd buy lunch and fix it up until we get to the next city. They had a big old basket of lunch. You think we was going on a picnic. The only time I saw a diner, I think, was when I worked for Southern Pacific.

They had a law called Jim Crow law—segregation on the train. Say, for instance, you're coming west: Jim Crow segregated until you got to Texas and New Mexico, which is El Paso, Texas, just across the Rio Grande River. Till you crossed the Rio Grande River coming west, you segregated. Once you crossed the river, you can go up in the coach—sit in the coach you want to. But you couldn't buy a Pullman ticket for a reservation in a Pullman car out of the South to come through in that Pullman car all the way. They'd sell you a ticket in the chair car. After we got outta the South and crossed that line, then the train conductor came through the car and announced that blacks could move up front if they wanted to or move back or anywhere.

From then on out you sit anywhere you wanna sit. But that was what they called the Jim Crow law. And that was back in the late teens and up until the twenties.

The Jim Crow law had the chair car ahead of the train, see, right behind the baggage car. The first chair car behind the baggage car was for the blacks. And then from that, one or two other chair cars were for the third-class white passengers. Then behind that was the second class, which was the tourist Pullman car for the second-class white passengers. The first-class white passengers was standard Pullman cars behind the diner and the lounge car, see. They had the lounge car privilege where they could go in and have their drinks, you know. Then from there they'd be right next to the diner. They didn't come in contact with the second class nor the third class.

And the porters, when they'd come into the diner to eat, they had curtains that they'd pull to separate the part of the diner where the black passengers or the Pullman porters used. They'd have to eat behind the curtains. I think it could seat about six people, and if there was more than that come in to eat and there wasn't a seat, they'd have to just stand and wait or come back when there was a seat. I know this was on the Southern Pacific, and I'm quite sure it applied to all public accommodations.

When I got to Los Angeles and I got a job, they told me I had to go to school. I was shining shoes in this barbershop, and this truant officer came looking for some kids that had been outta school one day and was checking on 'em. He saw me, and he asked me why I was not in school. So I explained to him that I had just got here from Alabama, me and my mother, and we spent our money for railroad fare. And, of course, we both need a job, and I got a job, but I do intend to go to school as soon as I can get back on my feet again.

He grabbed me by the wrist. He say, "Boy, you're going to school now."

I went to school, and that's when I went in this cooking class. I went to 14th Street School, and they had a cooking class. I went a half a semester to school because I was 16 years old when I came here. I was in there from February to June, and instead of going back when school opened in September, I got this job on the railroad. This friend of mine that took me there, he was working on the road. He was a year or two older than me, but we were friends—one of the first friends that I met when I came to Los Angeles. He knew I was going to this cooking class in school, so he said, "I'm gonna take you down to the commissary and get you a job on the road."

I said, "Man, I'm too small. They ain't gonna give me no job on the road."

He say, "You're 17 now. You can get a job."

I say, "Well, I'm in knee pants. They ain't gonna get me no job in knee pants."

He say, "I'm gonna take you down to Goodwill and get you some long pants."

So that's what he did.

So I went in there. I was scared to ask the man for a job, you see, because I was small for my age. So pretty soon Mr. Kendall got up from his desk and came out on the platform. I went up and asked Mr. Kendall for a job, and he looked down on me, and the first thing he asked me, "How old are ya?"

I said, "I'm 17. I'll be 18 next month."

He said, "Well, I can give you a job. But if you had been under 17, I wouldn't think about giving you a job. The school authorities would be right on my neck."

It was 1918 when I started as a dishwasher. I'd never had a job as a dishwasher, porter, or anything of that type, so naturally I was all green to the job. The first trip was on a train we called the Coaster. We used to leave Los Angeles serving dinner, and we'd go into San Francisco the next morning, serve breakfast. I remember because Mr. Kendall, the sign-out man, he gave me my instructions. I had my cook uniform and all, and he brought me into the diner. None of the cooks had reported yet. I was the first there. But some of the waiters were there changing their clothes and getting ready. So he explained to the waiter that I was the fourth cook. That's what they call them, "forty."

So the waiters, they started to kidding me about "forty," you know, the cook. They say, "Now, forty, when you get back there in that kitchen, you make a good pot of cold good soapy water and cook them dishes nice and clean." And it was really nice but one thing—I found out that there was a whole lot of dishes on a dining car, more than what Mama had at home in her kitchen. Oh, man!!

Going by the ocean, you know, before you get to Santa Barbara? The waiter say, "Say, forty, you see the Mississippi River out there?"

I say, "Man, there ain't no Mississippi River out here. I might be dumb, but I ain't that dumb. I know the Mississippi River don't come out this far."

They say, "That's right, boy. That's the Pacific Ocean. You see the Pacific Ocean?"

I say, "No, I haven't seen no ocean. Only ocean I've seen is this big tub of water here washing these dishes."

Prior to the adoption of all-steel passenger cars, the equipment was constructed of steel underframes with wooden bodies, commonly referred to as composite cars. The hazards of such cars are obvious. In a derailment, the car bodies were prone to break apart, with no protection for passengers or crew. And because car heating during this era relied on coal-burning stoves, the danger of fire in such a wreck was great.

The wooden diners, they would make a whole lot of noise. They'd creak and make noise just like you don't know whether they're coming apart or not. And then they were dangerous in case of a wreck, whereas if the steel diner'd go off the rail, they gonna stay in contact. But those wooden diners, they just be like a cracker box. They go to pieces, and you could get a sliver in you or get a door broke off and hit you or anything.

They was all wood. Just a small place to work in, and hot! They had water tanks, two cold-water tanks above overhead. Then they had a short one over the steam table which was the hot-water tank. And that's another thing that we had to be very conservative about, using water. You run out of water, and you wouldn't get any water till you got to the next division, which might be Tucson or Phoenix, Arizona or Yuma. See, they had these different divisions where they changed train crew, conductors, and the brakeman, and so forth—the engineer and the fireman. They changed from five or six times before they got from Los Angeles to Chicago. But the dining car crew and the Pullman porters was the only ones that went all the way through on the train.

We had two trains that had steel diners. The Golden State had a steel diner, and the Sunset Limited had a steel diner. And they was 36-seaters. The other diners were 30-seaters and all wooden.

I was in a wreck, but I was in a steel diner in Mexico, so there wasn't any damage done to the diner. Only turned over and broke up a lot of dishes and upset the food and all. My diner went over on its side, and the diner that was connected to me was on an angle like that. That's the way we were when we was in this wreck. Kitchen to kitchen. It was fortunate that nobody got killed, but one porter was hurt pretty bad. Me and the second cook went up in the Pullman car—Pullman car was over on its side—and we helped some of the passengers to get out. They weren't hurt, but they were frightened, naturally. We helped 'em out because they didn't know which way the door was. The train turned over on its side. You wouldn't know which way the door was, and we had to reach down and pull 'em up and help 'em up like that.

We had a wreck in Liberal, Kansas, and we lost a chef and a waiter in that. They were sleeping up in the dormitory car. That's another thing that changed. We used to sleep in the diner, and, of course, the steward slept in the Pullman car, because of segregation. In later years that was broken up. They furnished a dormitory car ahead of the last chair car up front for the crew to sleep in. That would break up this sleeping in the diners. Well, the chef was sleeping in the dormitory car, which had Pullman sleepers, and he was in a lower berth. The waiter, I think, was in the upper berth. But anyway, they hit this soft spot, a washout, and the engine got over, but the other part collapsed when the dormitory got there, and it went down into this puddle. The chef was killed by the upper berth falling down on him. And the waiter, I think a similar thing happened to him. The other members of the crew was injured, but not too serious that they didn't get over it.

After I got in the diner and heard 'em talkin' and seen how things were going, then I thought that I would have an opportunity to work up, which I did, see, work from dishwasher to chef. The men, they put their arms around me and trained me from a dishing job clear through to third cook, which is a vegetable cook. A second cook cooks entrées and fry, combination. He had to work the range for breakfast, you know, and turn out the ham and eggs and the hotcakes and omelettes and all that. That's the second cook. Well, I moved into that place. From the second cook's place, I moved up to chef. All this with the training of those good men, those wonderful men that I'd worked with, took me by the hand and trained me just like a father would in the home. And being of the disposition and desire and willingness, all those things tended to help me, because the fellas would hear about me even before they got to work with me, they would hear about me, and naturally that made a big hit.

I remember one time the sign-out man, Mr. Kendall, said to me, "Jimmy, what kind of a man are you? Everybody wants to run with Jimmy Clark, Jimmy Clark. Everybody can't run with Jimmy Clark. Only so many men in a crew."

Well, it's the way that I guess I attracted myself to the men, the way I worked. Cooperative. Peace. Get along, you know. Get the job done. Do the best you can. Put your very best into it because these people that's riding these trains and eating in the dining car, they're the ones who are supplying our jobs. They're the ones who's making it work for us, see. And it made so much common sense to the majority of the men that they just grasped it, it worked out fine. Worked out wonderful!

I used to put 'em in my place. I'd take the dishwasher, put him in the third cook's place. Third cook, I'd put him in the second cook's place. The second cook, I'd put him in my place. Then I'd get down there in the tub where I started, and I'd say, "Now, I'm gonna give all of you instructions, and all your orders that come by, they got to come by me because I'm gonna see what comes by before it goes into the pantry to the waiter. Be sure to get everything just right and looking good as well as to taste good to our passengers."

That's the way I used to instruct them, and I said, "Now, when the time comes for your promotion, you won't be puzzled or wondering how to do this or how to do the other. You'll be well trained, and you'll fit right into your job just like as if you'd been doing it all along." That's the way I used

Jimmy Clark (left) and fellow cook in Portland, Oregon, 1925.

to talk to them, and a lot of fellas called me "Daddy," you know. There's two or three of 'em still living that still call me Daddy, because I did the same by them that had been done by me.

After I got promoted to chef, I was a relief chef for quite a while. We had white chefs. Let me see now—Milton, Hawkins, Lankershim. They were on the Lark and the Padre. Those chefs would work so many days and then get many days off, and I would be the relief chef. I'd go on for four or five days, whatever number of days they were off on their layover. Then I'd go over to the next crew and relieve that chef. That's when I was first promoted, because I didn't have enough seniority to hold a regular line. So I was, you might say, a utility chef.

Finally, I worked up to enough seniority through some of the old chefs passing away, and one or two of 'em quit. That would put me closer up in the seniority list. And finally I got enough seniority to hold a regular line. But I used to catch these specials, too, before I had a regular line, because these stewards liked me, and the waiters liked me from second cook, third cook, when I started to cooking.

I was always anxious to satisfy and please, and I know that if I satisfied and pleased, I'm bound to get along, sure to get along. No problem. No troubles. And that's what I did, see, and that helped me in my promotion because there are some waiters and cooks would get in an argument over an order, you know, and tie up the whole works. Well, now, I didn't permit that in my kitchen. I said, "Now, there's only one person who is supervisor in this kitchen, and that's me. If anything goes wrong, any mistake or what happens, I'll come down and straighten it out. You keep on cookin'. No third cook or second cook is gonna argue with the waiter or discuss anything with the waiter. He's gonna catch the waiter's order and get that order out as fast as you can. That's the way it's gonna be, and if anything goes wrong, I'll go down and straighten it out." And that's the way I managed. They used to say, "He's not the nastiest, but he's the fastest." That's what these waiters used to tell the other waiters that was coming on, "If you ain't ready for your order, don't put it in till you're ready, 'cause if you put it in, Jimmy's gonna say 'pick it up.'" Just like that, see. Well, they naturally liked fast cooks, because people come in to eat—other people waitin' to get a seat. Just get 'em out and accommodate the passengers, see.

I was concerned about those passengers just like I was concerned about myself. And I know that, we please those passengers, they gonna recommend Southern Pacific. They gonna praise Southern Pacific and their service. And that's what I was concerned about. You give 'em the best service, the finest service—and that's one thing I always insisted on the food leaving the kitchen. Be sure that food looks good as well as tastes good, see, and garnish it nice so when the waiter sets it down before that passenger, that passenger say, "Oh, that sure looks good. I hope it tastes that good." And when they ate it—tastes as good as it looks. And I was just as concerned about that passenger out there being satisfied as that waiter was serving expecting that tip, because I knew well enough that if we give our passengers the best that we have, we're doing something for our company as well. And our company is looking out for us.

I was the youngest chef at that time working for the Southern Pacific. They called me "the baby chef." But the thing that I did that meant more to me was to carry out my instructions. Whatever the rules of the company was, I lived up to that rule. There was no smoking in the kitchen. I didn't smoke in the kitchen, and I didn't allow none of my members of my crew to smoke in the kitchen. Anything that was ordered by the company, that's what was carried out by me, and I put the very best into my work. Whatever they taught me, if there's anything that I could add to it to improve it, I would do it. The experiences that I've had with passengers was sometimes they'd stop by the kitchen door, you know, to look in and see the kitchen and speak to the cooks. That's about as much experience as a cook would have with the passengers, because we wouldn't have an opportunity to go around while they're eating, you know. You had to be in the kitchen gettin' out those orders. Sometimes the passenger would ask the waiter if he could get a recipe for this particular entrée on the menu from the chef, which I would gladly do.

We had about five or six different entrées. We had steaks, chicken, fish, soup. Two or three different kinds of desserts—pie, ice cream, cake, and puddings—rice and raisin pudding, bread pudding—apple pie, berry pie, pumpkin pie when pumpkin's in season. And we used to make all of it right on the dining car. The only time we'd get any assistance in cooking from the commissary would be when we'd stock up in the afternoon when we reported, say, for three o'clock, and we gonna be leaving about five-thirty or six o'clock, and we're serving dinner leaving town—the commissary would give us a supply of pies. We wouldn't have time to make pies and then bring up all of the rest of the entrées and use the oven at the same time roasting meat. See, you couldn't bake your pies 'cause your oven is full of roast meat.

For some reason or another, you know, when it'd come time to go out, I'd just be so glad and happy I'm going to work. I'd get my bag all packed with my clothes and necessary things in it, and catch that streetcar. This was dirt roads, bus wouldn't come down here. I'd walk up to 103d Street. I used to get up there to catch that first five o'clock car leaving 103d—which was called Main Street then, the only street with the gravel road—and that local car would leave at five o'clock. That would be the first car going to Los Angeles. I'd be up there waiting for that car to pull outta the shed to come on down to pick up the passengers. I used to get off at Ninth Street, and I'd walk through the PE [Pacific Electric] yard about three blocks down to the old Southern Pacific station, Fifth and Central. I could walk down there in about 25 minutes after I got off the streetcar.

You had to stock up. Naturally, that was the first thing. And another thing that I practiced—and I lived up to it because I learned this at home, my mother taught me this—that if you're supposed to be at work at eight o'clock, you'd be to work at a quarter of eight. See, never late or never be on time. Be ahead of time at all times. And I lived up to that, because when I got to work, I'd have to change clothes, put on our uniform, and then go into the commissary and check out with the steward and the pantryman all our supplies. And I'd get aboard and start my fire—charcoal on the broiler and hard coal in the range. See, we'd stock up today going out on the Daylight [Limited, a prestreamlined train] in the morning.

So what I'd do, I'd set my fire, see, put my paper in and some wood on it and a little charcoal and some hard coal. Then the next morning, when I get on the train early in the morning, all I do is strike a match and pretty soon I got a fire going. I get everything done that I could do while we're stocking up, so when I get in there the next morning I would have that much ahead—on the Daylight. That was on the San Francisco train, because the

110

San Francisco train used to leave at eight o'clock in the morning and arrive in San Francisco at six o'clock. Well, we would start out serving breakfast, and then we would serve a lunch. Breakfast would go right into lunch. There wouldn't be no cut-off time at all, because if a person came in at ten o'clock and wanted a breakfast, he could get it, see. So there wasn't no split time. And gettin' into San Francisco around six o'clock, there wasn't no dinner at all. The dining room would stay open until we pull into the station and the passengers started getting off the train. The crew would fix up and get off before the switch engine pull the train out.

A lot of times we worked long hours from five o'clock—call the crew at five o'clock in the morning—and lot of times the cooks would be the last ones out after we got through serving passengers. There's five to six waiters out there—each waiter got a station, he'd take care of his station. They work together and get through quick. But four cooks in the kitchen—we got to scrub the slats, scrub this, scrub pots, put the pans away, and got to take care of the food. Put everything away after we finish feeding, and gotta be sure nobody's coming in to eat after we put the stuff away, because you can't turn nobody down. You can't refuse nobody, if you got it. If you don't have it, you can suggest something else to 'em.

I have worked as many as 16 hours. In other words, be on watch. Being on watch means this. You gotta make Parker House rolls. Before you leave the kitchen, you set a sponge to make Parker House rolls. That's just like making loaves of bread, only you know what a Parker House roll is. You set that sponge, and then before you go outta the kitchen, that sponge is rose up, see. Then you knock it back down. The next morning you get up three o'clock, go into the kitchen, and knock that sponge down. Then you knead it and start cutting off pieces, rolling it out and cutting off these rolls like that. Then fold 'em up, put butter in 'em, and put 20 to a pan. We had to make as many as a 125 of them rolls. That's why you had to get up at three o'clock, 'cause at five o'clock you call the crew. And by the time the crew is all set—dining room set up, six-thirty—Pullman porters come in for coffee and rolls, see? So when you put in from three o'clock in the morning till ten, eleven o'clock at night, that's a long day. And the second cook and the chef cook used to make those watches. That was the longest day you would have, see. And if you was running from Los Angeles to Chicago, we'd have maybe two watches apiece going and two watches apiece coming back.

We have seen some pretty tough times. We've had some men fall out in the kitchen during the summertime crossing the desert, it'd be so hot. This is one thing that I learned from the elders. Don't drink a lot of water, especially cold water, in that kitchen while you're working. This is what they used to do. They used to take oatmeal, raw oatmeal, and put it in a big glass jar, and water on it, and sit it down in the bottom of the dresser box, where it was cool but not cold. And whenever you want a drink of water, just drink off that oatmeal, because we had fellas that fall out—absolutely fall out. They had to take 'em out to the vestibule and put a towel or something on their face. After a while they'd come around, but they'd be so darn weak they wouldn't be able to finish a day's work. I don't know what was in that oatmeal that would prevent falling out, but the water wouldn't be cold. See, these that would fall out would usually be drinkin' a lot of cold water, see, put ice in the water or put it right on top of the ice where it would be cold around the milk can. The milk can was a ten-gallon can with ice all around it, and a lot of 'em would put jars down in there. Crossing the desert, that kitchen, I bet it has got as much as a hundred and ten, fifteen in that kitchen. We didn't know nothin' about no air conditioning. The dining room had fans. They had fans in the dining room in the corner, each corner, to keep the dining room cool.

You had steam from the engine. See, the engine used to furnish steam for the whole entire train. And I remember one time we got snowbound. We were snowbound between—it was up in Missouri, and we got snowbound. Wasn't but two places on the whole train that had any heat. That was the engine and the diner, in the kitchen in the dining car. Naturally, the engine froze up, and pretty soon we didn't have no steam, and the whole train was cold. We were stuck there for about 18 hours before we got some relief, you know, and got us some steam furnished to the train. That was back in the early thirties.

When we used to go on these specials, a lot of times we'd have two diners. If we had, say, 250 passengers on a special, they'd put on two diners, because they wouldn't want the passengers to be waiting too long to get into the diner. They put each diner kitchen to kitchen in the event that this diner needs something, see, go get it from that diner. You wouldn't have to go through the diner and into another car or nothin' like that.

On these special trips we'd have maybe six, seven thousand dollars' worth of foodstuff. The run is over 15 days. We couldn't get a lot of stuff in Mexico that we could get in El Paso or Tucson or Chicago, so we'd have to have supplies ahead in the baggage cars, with these big boxes loaded with ice, and put our meat and stuff on top with the canvas so that it wouldn't get wet but at the same time stay cold.

I had a special with Mary Pickford and Douglas Fairbanks. It was a party of about 15. They were going to San Luis Obispo, then they'd have to take automobiles up to the Hearst Castle. They came in, they were lovely. They chartered this diner and three cars, I believe, and a baggage car, of course. We went up there on this special with them, and they was in the diner. I was second cook then. The chef was one of the instructing chefs that Mr. Kendall chose to take out this special—Tom Harrison. And Fairbanks put on a waiter's jacket like he's gonna wait tables, and he come in the pantry, you know, and hollered to the kitchen, said he was puttin' in an order. He told the waiter, says, "I'm gonna wait on these over here."

They had a lovely time, and they gave every man a check. I think it was $25. That's what the kitchen got. Oh, they had something special on there. One thing I remember, they had broiled lobster. I remember that because that was something that we very seldom carried on the menu.

I had another actor when I had the Shriners' convention to Chicago. He was a comedian. He wore glasses. Oh, that was way back in the twenties. Harold Lloyd. That's it! That's it! He gave me a pair of glasses, just the frame. I had them over there [on the TV] for years and years. I guess some of my friends saw 'em and . . . but Harold Lloyd, that's the man, he came back in the diner and the kitchen. They had a whole train to themselves. And there was a lovely group of people.

The biggest difference [in Jimmy's experience] was between the wooden diners and the steel diners—until, of course, the Daylight streamliner came out. Now that was a big difference. That was all the difference, the whole entire train. Quite a difference.

I went to East St. Louis and brought the first streamlined Daylight to Los Angeles. Yeah, me and there was two cooks, two waiters, and a steward. We deadheaded all the way to East St. Louis, and we brought the first streamliner. I think it was 1937. On our way back we stopped at Pine Bluff, Arkansas, to display the train. And there wasn't no school that day. All the people in town come aboard the train. They showed them, and the steward explained everything, just how everything worked, just like as if they were coming in to eat. And the kitchen, showed 'em the kitchen, just like going through a museum, because it was something different, you know. It had a fancy bar and a fancy dining room. Beautiful thing! And all the main cities we come to, we spent so many hours for the people to view the train and go through it and look it over good: Shreveport, Louisiana; Houston, Texas; Del Rio, Texas; El Paso, Texas. All them divisions and cities of any size. Yes, sir, just like when the big circus come to town; everybody come down to see the circus.

And passenger business really picked up. Oh, man, we'd got outta here top and bottom—loaded! They had a cafeteria car and a regular dining car, and I was chef on the cafeteria car—horseshoe coffee shop. And next to it was the tavern car.

And the second streamlined Daylight—same crew went back to East St. Louis and brought it back. But what we did was this. When we got to El Paso, we put on a supply, and we served passengers on that particular trip. Yeah, we served the press and whatever passengers came in. But the first one was strictly a show train.

Oh, it was a beautiful train! It had so many conveniences on it, too, you see, and it was just a pleasure to work on the train. It had a great big beautiful diner. Had things in it that would attract your attention, you know, as you go in. Just like going into a museum. It had many conveniences in the kitchen that we didn't have in the old diners. The refrigerator for one thing, and the range, it had the propane gas, and that was wonderful, too. That eventually got around to the other diners in later years.

They had technicians in the event anything went wrong while the train was en route to California. Those technicians was on there to check it out. I think there was about five or six of 'em, and they had to be fed, you see, so we had to feed them. That was the real point, to take care of the technicians, feed them, then to be on the train so that the people who come on the diner in the kitchen, they could see the crew.

In 1943 Jimmy Clark joined the merchant marines and exchanged a dining car kitchen for a ship's galley.

I was working in the galley—I was chef. 1943. As I say, when we were kids, we used to sell papers on board the ship and go aboard the ship and sell 'em to the mates and skipper and all. And we used to say, the kids used to say, "When I grow up, I'm gonna be a seaman, I'm gonna go on a ship."

Then this foster son that we practically raised, when he was 18, he wanted to go in the merchant marines. So I took him to San Francisco; I was running to San Francisco, and I knew a retired seaman. I took him over and introduced him and told him that my foster son here say he'd like to join the merchant marine and become a seaman. Pretty soon he got a ship, and he shipped out, and I said I'll get a leave of absence, since I can get a leave of absence without losing seniority or anything. Then I'll get some experience, too, see, and I'll fill up that desire about when I was a kid—going aboard a ship and working on a ship.

Yeah, we sailed outta Long Beach on this ship November 15, 1943. When we got to Bombay, the ship sometime wouldn't make but four knots an hour because the submarines, you know? And the skipper had his orders, and naturally he knew what to do to protect the ship. Then we had planes trailing us—our planes. Bombay was our first port. We crossed the equator on Christmas night '43. I remember that very well.

The rest of the fellas on board the ship, the old-timers, they said, "We gonna have an initiation. We gonna initiate all the new men aboard the ship." Anyway, they say you're gonna join the Neptune Society. So I said, "Well, I tell you, fellas. I hope you don't include me, because I'm not too very well." Which I wasn't too very well, but I was well enough to do my work in the galley.

So they said, "Okay, chief, we'll let you go. We won't bother you." But the other guys, new guys, they initiated them. They said they took 'em down below the deck and made 'em take off their clothes. Made 'em think they gonna drown them, you know, put 'em in a sack or something and dropped them overboard and brought 'em back up again.

When the boys told me what had happened, I say, "Well, I'm sure glad I didn't go through that, because I don't know what had've happened to me."

There was quite a bit of difference, because you're cooking for a crew, see, you're not cooking for paid passengers. All those fellas want is a whole lot of food. They don't care what it is, just give 'em enough of it. That's the way we stocked those ships up. When we put on them supplies, we had storerooms and refrigerators, and we had food galore. And naturally, when I started puttin' that dining car–style cooking on 'em, they went for that, you know. They went into the mess hall to eat and kept telling me, all that good food, "What ship did you come off of?"

I say, "I didn't come off no ship. This is the first ship I've been on. I coming off the dining car."

Only money I got was overtime money. You got overtime when you're in a zone like in the Mediterranean and in the South Pacific, in the war zone. You got an extra pay—so much extra every hour you spent in that part of the zone. So that's all the money I drew when we got into New York and got paid off, 'cause I had my money sent home so my wife could have money to supply herself and keep the house going. I had $600 in overtime money alone.

When I come home off that first trip, I decided that I'd go back to New York and ship out of New York. My foster son was shipping out of New York then. 'Course, you didn't have no choice, you know. When you go up to sign on a ship, you go where they send you. You don't know where you're going. Wartime. I went up to see my superintendent [railroad dining car department]. Went down to the commissary, and they, all of them, saw me in my uniform. I bought me a uniform, and they all saw me and praised me. They say, "Jimmy, we just hope you make it back on the road."

I went to New York, and I made three more trips. I made two trips to England on a tanker. We were hauling high octane gasoline and oil to supply the airplanes that was operating out of England, fighting over Germany. Oh yeah, prime target. A tanker's a dangerous thing because a tanker's subject to break in two, see. On the stern is where the quarters are, you know, and on the aft of the ship is where the skipper is and the mates stay. Then, between, there's nothin' but tanks of gasoline. It's a long ship. We had thousands and thousands of barrels of gasoline and oil on there. It was terrifying. One of the messmen say to me, "Say, chief, are you praying?"

I say, "Well, I tell ya. I don't know whether prayers would help us or not, but I guess we're all praying. Just pray that we don't go down and we make it."

On our second trip loaded with this gasoline, one of our tankers was

115

torpedoed up in the Irish Sea. This is about three or four o'clock in the afternoon, and at that time the sun was almost like midday here. We got the signal. Right away we knew it was a danger signal, something had happened, 'cause we heard the vibration on our ship, and we all made it to our stations. We all knew where our stations was, with our life jackets on. We could see this tanker, nothin' but blazing smoke. Eighty-something men aboard, not a man got off. Planes going around thinking that somebody might've got overboard, they might rescue them. Men didn't have a chance, because loaded with gasoline, and one of those German torpedoes hit it—went off just like that.

On our way back [to New York Harbor], we were one night outta New York and we run into a hurricane. Skipper came back to the galley about six o'clock, still daylight, he says, "We're headed into a storm, and we got orders to break up our convoy."

They was traveling in convoy, about 40 ships in convoy. All the skippers got orders to break the convoy, and every ship for himself so there wouldn't be no chance of a ship running into one another, sinking one another. But this little skipper that we had, a Texas skipper, he says, "I'm gonna head right into this storm."

Other ships started turning around, going different directions. And man, about eleven o'clock, that ship was doing everything but capsize. Everybody had their life jackets on up at the lifeboats. I don't know what you'd be doing at a lifeboat, 'cause you couldn't man a lifeboat. The skipper ordered everybody out on deck. We couldn't do nothin' but slide, slip and slide, passing one another like this. So finally, he ordered us all back into the mess hall again, 'cause he thought maybe somebody might accidentally slip over the side. If the ship capsized, we would go down for sure—which we did lose five ships in that storm. About two o'clock the whole commenced to easin' off like that. All the fellas was still in the mess hall, see. They wouldn't go back down to go to bed, they wouldn't think about going down there. Stay up in the mess hall with their life jackets on.

So I went down in daylight to get something, and my second cook, he say, "Say, chief, look through the port hole there." I looked through the porthole. He say, "What do you see?" Well, I saw a buoy bouncin' up and down in the harbor, New York Harbor. He say, "Now, look over to your right and look up, and see what you see?" I stuck my head out and looked over to the right, and it was the Statue of Liberty.

He say, "You see that pretty gal over there?"

I say, "I sure in the hell do." Statue of Liberty. We made it. See, that skipper, he made it right on through that storm. After we got in port and got settled down, that's when we heard about these five ships that we lost in the storm. I stayed in 17 months. I came out in '45.

After I came back to the railroad, the boys told me, "Jimmy, get on the rip track [working military specials]." That was hauling soldiers all over. You don't know where you're goin', see, almost just like goin' to sea, but you're hauling military, 'cause we still was in war. So that's what I went for. When I went in to sign out, the man, he asked me which way or where I wanted to go. He knew I had seniority. I could choose if I wanted to. So I told him, "Mr. Peterson, I believe I'll try the rip track."

He said, "Okay, it's up to you. As soon as we get us something out on the rip track, I'll let you know." He say, "You got different crews, you know. You got new men just come to work. A lot of fellas joined the army or were drafted in the army. We got a lot of new men, and most of them are on the rip track because they can't hold no regular line."

So I took the rip track, and I liked it, because you're going different places, and I was meetin' new fellas, you know, and breakin' them in and training them. We'd stock up the special, and sometimes we'd be gone a week, eight days. They brought out some old stuff [cars] that they had to use because they didn't have enough to keep the regular trains going and supply the government.

My last run, I think, was on the rip track, because I got sick. I come in off a special—we call 'em specials—and my wife was down to the station to meet me. I could hardly make it off the train out to the car where she was parked, and I told her the condition I was in. I told her, "I think I'm gonna have to get off, retire on disability."

So she encouraged me. She says, "Well, you do that, because the condition you're in, you've got no business tryin' to work. You can hardly get in the car, let alone get to the car. I'll get a job, and we'll make it. You put in for disability and pension." So I did. November 1950.

The Southern Pacific really didn't want to retire me. I had told the company, my manager of the dining car, that I was planning this disability pension. I'm not braggin', but I'm only telling the truth—that I was a worker that was up to par with everybody. I think they just wanted to keep me working because I was concerned with the Southern Pacific affairs and the way they operated their dining car department just like I was about the way my wife operated our home.

I must say that the Southern Pacific was like a father—just like a wonderful home and all the employees that I worked with and worked under, coming up from dishwasher to chef. I've seen over the years blacks become traveling instructors, traveling waiters, traveling chefs—catch the train and instruct 'em, review their service, see if their service is up to the standard. That was something that they didn't have when I started to work. Those are the improvements.

I didn't know anything about discrimination, although there was discrimination. But for some reason or another, I didn't even think about it. It just didn't seem like it applied to me, because the whites liked me as well as the blacks. They did as much for me as the blacks. In fact more, in a way, because if they said something to the superintendent or the manager of the dining car concerning me, it was recorded and kept. Then I got the results through promotion and through getting these good trips, you know, these special trips and things, being a young chef.

Naturally, being in the kitchen, we could never see or hear what's going on, because the pantry was between the kitchen and the dining room. That would cut off a lot of what we might hear. We couldn't see nothin' in the dining room from the kitchen. Sometimes a waiter'd come into the pantry, might be complaining about something, but it didn't concern us, 'cause we wasn't putting in an order or asking about an order. We wasn't concerned about what they were talkin' about. Only thing that I could see pertaining to the service is, naturally, you know the black man is gonna be courteous at all times, even if he's insulted. He's gonna take it with a smile and go in the pantry and say, "Old so-and-so said so-and-so to me, but I ain't gonna let him beat me outta my tip!" You see what I mean? He's thinkin', "If I get angry, he won't have to tip me, but I'm gonna go out there and smile to him anyhow and make him drop down." And I think they used a little diplomacy there because, you know, they depended on their tips. If you're nice, you can expect a tip. If you're not nice, you don't.

At that time, you see, when I was running on the road, I didn't mingle with other races. The limited time that we had on the layover time in Chicago or New Orleans, we were with the crew, and we had a place where we'd go and eat, you know, a black restaurant, if it's in the South. Even Chicago was the same way. We went to a restaurant where it was a black settlement, 35th and State Street in Chicago. That was a black community, see, and naturally the blacks was there, and that's where I would be. I never did have a problem out there.

The only time I can remember being in a position of segregation was right here in Los Angeles in the year that I came here in 1917, me and my mother. I went to a theater up on Main Street, and I noticed when I went in. I went to the center of the theater and got me a seat where I could see straight. And [the usher] came to me, and she says, "I'd like to have you come over here and take a seat," and she pointed. When I looked where she pointed, there was a group of blacks. So I just simply said, "Oh, this is fine. I can see wonderful here." So she says okay, and she went away. She didn't say anything to me, so evidently it wasn't compulsory segregation.

There was another theater on Main Street, a burlesque show where the girls used to do striptease. Why, a black couldn't even buy a ticket there.

No. They wouldn't even sell a black a ticket because naturally they didn't want a black man looking at a white woman striptease, you know. But in San Francisco it was different. Now, I went to one of those theaters once in San Francisco, and black and white were sitting there together. That was in the early twenties. But there was a little part of this and that everywhere, see.

In the theaters in the South—there's only one theater that I can remember in Mobile where blacks could go, and they'd have to go up in the balcony. They couldn't go on the main floor. The Lyric Theater. It was a movie theater and a theater for stage shows, likewise. It didn't bother me in the least, because I never had any friction, you know. I never came into any scramble or harsh words about it, anything like that.

I must say that I had a wonderful experience, when I went to work on the railroad, of coming in contact with so many people of different races. It's the greatest experience I could've ever had coming up from the bottom like I did under the different circumstances and conditions and make it to '86 with only this blood condition and this arthritis when so many of the wonderful men I worked with have gone on, passed away, so many of 'em, white and black.

When I sit down and meditate alone sometimes, it looks like it's been a long time, especially when I think about some of my coworkers that have passed on. And I look at them, and I think about the years that we worked together. Just like me, for instance, now it's been 36 years since I worked. And then again, to me it don't seem like it's been that long. I don't miss it, but I did for a while. For a while I really missed it. I used to even dream about gettin' up and going out. I think about it a whole lot—'course, that could have something to do with missing it.

And I want to say this, too. Over these 86 years that I've lived, I've seen some wonderful improvements between black and whites. Not only in the West, the North, and the East, but in the South likewise. Some wonderful changes between the two races.

My greatest philosophy in life, number one, is love, respect, and peace. Now, those three things go together. Now, when you have those, you know happiness got to be there, happiness gonna fall in line. And, of course, there are other things. As far as earning a living, making a living, or whatever you're doing, regardless of what it is, do it your very best at all times. One of the greatest aims in life with me is to try to help those who are helpless and need help and feel sorry when you can't help. I even feel sorry for the criminals. I can't help 'em, but I can feel sorry for 'em. I won't hate 'em, because behind every condition there is a cause or a reason. It may not be seen. It may not be heard of by us human beings, but behind it is a reason, there's a cause somewhere.

And I often say what a wonderful world this would be if man was as successful with peace as he is with developing many wonderful things in life to make life so happy and so pleasant and so convenient. If he could just turn that book over, and peace would be just the thing. That's the way I look at life. I wanna see the bright side all the time of life.

I don't know if you ever heard about the three Ls, because L stands for so many things. But one of the grandest things that L stands for more than anything in the world, is "love." But these three Ls was "look," "listen," and "learn." And those things inbedded into my mind to the point where I lived with it, and it helped me all through this world, and it's helping me to this day.

George McLain

7

GEORGE McLAIN
Southern Pacific Cook and Instructing Chef
1920–1962

The August 1964 issue of Southern Pacific's employee magazine, The Bulletin, featured an article in their ongoing series "S.P. Chefs' Favorite Recipes." That month's chef, George McClain, had been with the company for over 40 years, starting as a dining car cook in 1920 and working his way up to instructing chef by 1941. In addition to serving the usual celebrities and dignitaries, George McLain supervised all meal preparations for the 1959 rail journey by Soviet Premier Nikita Khrushchev over Southern Pacific lines.

Born in 1904, the son of a Mississippi slave, McLain learned cooking in his mother's kitchen while growing up in San Antonio, Texas. He advanced swiftly through the Southern Pacific dining car department and was made chef within two years of his arrival in Los Angeles in 1920. By 1931 Southern Pacific appointed him head dietician in its new sanitarium in Tucson, Arizona. While there, he furthered his education at the University of Arizona. After five years in Tucson, he asked to be assigned back on the road, where he most enjoyed his work. George McLain retired in 1960.

My father was a slave. He was freed—he was 12 years old when freedom cried out. Yes, sir! And he knew all about it, but he was no baby. See, the man that owned him in Mississippi had a daughter, and his daughter married a man in Canada, and that's where I got my name from—I got my name from his daughter that married. She was a Crenshaw; she married McLain. That's a Canadian name. And then he give my daddy to her for a wedding present, and that's why he got the name McLain. Twelve years old. Yeah, that's right. The Crenshaws had the plantation, but the guys in Canada didn't have. You know, they were just regular people, but they were glad to get a little boy that'd do all that handy work, I guess, and that's my daddy. So after my daddy grew up, they give him an education, they sent him to school.

Well, he didn't have too much of a education, but he could read and write and things like that. Then when he got up grown, why, he come back to the States, see, because he wanted to find his relatives, wanted to find his dad and his sisters and his mother, so he come back after he got grown. Well, that was about ten years 'fore he got back.

Yeah, there's a big history behind the racism in this country. Where I went to school, they had to change the time lettin' school out because the white had to pass the colored school and the colored had to pass the white to get to the Negro neighborhood, and they got to fightin'. They raised so much hell they had to change the time; they let the white out at three o'clock and wouldn't let the black out until three-thirty. That'd give the white time to get home. Oh, they had to battle that all their life.

See, when I started workin' the railroad, why, all through the South they had a Jim Crow car on the train, and you had to ride in that Jim Crow car. And when they got to El Paso comin' here, why, then they'd pull that Jim Crow car off and you had to get in the car with the white people, and the white people didn't like that. People leavin' outta here, they load 'em on there, and there is nothin' said. But when they get to El Paso, then they had to segregate 'em, see? All that stuff you went through and different things like that.

In Texas and Louisiana they had separate dining rooms for ya. Yeah, in there you had to go in a place for colored and had to go to a place for white. You couldn't go in a white dining room or couldn't go in a white station, and you had a room off in the station for colored, room over here for white. But you see, when you travel around, you get used to all that, goin' different places, and whenever "the man" tell you you're goin' south, why, you know what you gotta put up with.

I seen a time in San Francisco, you'd walk the streets all day, you never see a colored person. Oh, indeed! Those were all Chinamens and Orientals and the whites, but you never see no Negroes. I remember when there wasn't but one place in San Francisco [African Americans] could get a place to stay. That was over in the Fillmore District over there. You couldn't stay in none of these white hotels. I mean, I don't care how big a Negro was, if they brought him out here, he couldn't stay there in those days. He had to go to the colored neighborhood.

I started to work for the Southern Pacific when I was 19 years old. I got outta school, and I wanted a job, and there wasn't many colored people in California, you know, and they were hirin' 'em, bring 'em out here to work on the diners and clean the cars and different things. Well, they was importing all the help outta Texas and Louisiana and Mississippi, and they had a travelin' waiter. They would send him down there, and he'd select people to work on the train and different things.

See, my home is San Antone, Texas. After school was out, I heard about this, and I come down there, and the guy give me a job. He says, "Well, we got a train comin' through here from Houston, and he's short of a cook." At that time the Sunset Limited diners didn't come through to Los Angeles; they cut out at El Paso, then the western diners come as far as El Paso, see. So the man says, "We need a cook in the kitchen. You ever work in a kitchen?"

I say, "Yeah, I worked in a kitchen." That was my job at home. See, I had three brothers. One of 'em cleaned the yard, one of 'em did the housework. I did the cookin'. My mother taught me a whole lot about cookin'. I started from that, and that's all I ever did in my life. So I went in the kitchen, and I worked to El Paso; that's where they cut our diners out there to go back to New Orleans. And when I got to El Paso—I never been that far away from home in my life—why, the crew, the cooks and the waiters, they's all goin' over in Mexico where those Spanish girls were, you know? And my mother had warned me, "Be careful," when I got away from home, you know, and don't be followin' around, go in bad places. Well, I said, "I'll sit here in the station and get me something to read until they come back."

They had two trains on the Sunset Route, Argonaut and the Sunset Limited. Sunset was a special all-room car train, and the Argonaut had the chair cars and tourist cars and Pullmans. One was first-class [Sunset], the other was second—but you had to be a big shot to ride that Sunset then, and I mean they didn't play around with it. So I was sitting there in the station, the guy come and ask me, did I want a job. I say, "I already got a job. I just come in here on the Sunset."

He say, "All those boys done gone to Mexico."

I say, "Yeah, they all over in Mexico. I couldn't go over there 'cause I didn't know my way around, and I didn't want nothin' to happen."

He say, "Well, we got to have a cook." Old man Styles was superintendent of the commissary in El Paso. He say, "Well, you come on and make this trip for me to Los Angeles, and they'll give you a pass and send you back, but I've got to have a cook, and I don't know where I can get one."

So I got on there and come on to Los Angeles. When I got to Los Angeles, they told me where I could get a room there; that's the old Lincoln Hotel, a Chinese place right across from Fifth and Central. That's where the station used to be, and I went over there and got me a room, and they told me where the commissary was, to get up and go down there, and they'll give me a pass back home, see. I got down there, why, they need a cook to go to Portland, Oregon, on the West Coast. Asked me, do I want to make the trip. I say, "Well, I'm out here to make money, but I was expecting to be going back home." He say, "Well, we'll send you back home when you get back from this trip."

So I went to Portland and come back, and I go down the hotel, and I clean all up and everything. I decided to go down and get my transportation so I could go home. And I say, "Look, my money's running low." They say,

"You should have a check upstairs in the office." So I went down there. They had a check for me. At that time old man Luss was superintendent of the Los Angeles commissary. He was one of the oldest ones that I knew. And D. H. Luss asked me, would I like to make a trip before I go home. I say, "I just made a trip." He say, "Well, we got another one. We need a cook on the Golden State Limited to Chicago." I say, "Well, I'll make that trip." So I made that trip.

We hit that Rock Island, we had to spread sheets in the kitchen to keep those cinders from gettin' in the food. Yeah. And you couldn't raise the windows. If you raise the windows, why, you got all the dust come in the windows, see. But the Southern Pacific, they poured oil down along their track to keep that dust from flyin', see, but these other railroads didn't have it, and you had to work on that when you hit those other foreign roads. Yeah.

By the time I made that trip and come back, I had a couple checks, and I wasn't thinkin' about goin' back to Texas. Everything is so different out here, see. And I stayed there from then on.

At that time help in that part of the country was scarce; you couldn't find it everyday. There wasn't a whole lotta people in El Paso—mostly Spanish people—they knew nothin' about cookin' or nothin' like that. But this guy Styles in El Paso, why, he see any colored person, he'd ask 'em if he wanted a job 'cause he had a hard time gettin' help to go on those dining cars. But they could find 'em in Houston, New Orleans, and Jackson, Mississippi—they find plenty of 'em down there. I'll say a third of the people that immigrated out here in California, the railroad immigrated 'em. Yeah, they brought 'em out here. They need help. Wasn't no help out here. In fact, you couldn't talk none of these [white] guys to get into one of them hot kitchens working at one of those kinda jobs. They lookin' for a better job. Oh, yeah. We had one white crew run on the Lark, and they quit. But it's hot in those kitchens. No air conditioning. Long as they could get other work—and there was plenty of work then, people gatherin' fruit and all that kinda stuff—they didn't have to do it.

Well, that was the status of using black help in the dining car, and 'course, they got plenty of waiters. They immigrated waiters and things out here. The white people didn't want none of their own people waitin' on 'em; they wanted the black waiters. Yeah! Sure! That's what they liked. They used to it. Yeah, from slavery days. You take outta the South—all those hotels and different things got black waiters. Very seldom you find a hotel got white waiters in it. May have a white lieutenant or somethin' like that, but all the help is black. And they'd tell ya, "This is a white man's job," or, "This is a black man's job." And they tell you that, and that's it. And they had certain jobs for Negroes, certain jobs for white. It'd burn 'em up to see they got a white man on a Negro's job.

George McLain with family in Southern Pacific yards, Los Angeles, California, 1940s.

The waiters was plentiful, but the cooks wasn't. The cooks was the ones to get. The waiters would stay on there because they got good tips, see, and the cooks didn't get no tips. Hell, I started workin' for the company, $30 a month, and when I retired I was gettin' a thousand. So that's the difference. 'Course, I was there 42 years, and out of 42 years, I went on up to chef, then to supervisor, instructor, and I played a big part with the Southern Pacific while I was working there.

To think I put 42 years—I went from an old coal burner to a diesel engine. I was on the train when the Southern Pacific had their first diesel engine on the Golden State to Chicago. Oh, yeah. I worked the diners when they was coal burners, and I was on one special and they cut us out, 'cause this railroad didn't pull no diners that didn't have steel underframes. Let's see, what railroad was that where they cut us out and we couldn't go any further? Someplace we go there, they didn't pull no wooden cars on their passenger trains. I remember that just well, 'cause we didn't go any further. Union Pacific! As far as we got on that train was Omaha.

I started as a second cook, and I didn't know much. I didn't even know how to cut up a fish, but the old chef taught me. I learned all that stuff. See,

I'm a self-made man, and I was one of the greatest decorators they had in the company. I used to take mashed potatoes and color 'em pink and take that pastry bag and make roses on the plate around a steak. Oh, I made so many different pretty things. Take potatoes and peel 'em and make a round ball and cut 'em and lay 'em around a dish or something like that. Well, that was my specialty. That's why I was promoted so fast, and everybody would just rave about it.

Oh, gee, I remember one time we had Mary Pickford and Douglas Fairbanks on a train there. Mary told the waiter, say, "This darn food is too pretty to cut into. I just hate to break it up, it looks so pretty." But I had that name of being one of the greatest decorators they had in the company. I taught a whole lotta cooks how to decorate and how to make their dishes look attractive, you know? 'Cause a person eats with his eyes: if it looks good, he'll eat it, but if it don't look good, he's not gonna eat it. So that's one reason why I advanced this far.

Then in '33 I went to the sanitarium. They sent me down there as a dietician. Well, when I was workin' on the railroad and everything, I went to school, too. I go to school, I take up dietetics, and finally I got a place where I could get a correspondence course, and I finished that. Southern Pacific took over that El Paso and Southwestern Railroad, and they taking the station and made a sanitarium out of it, and they need a dietician down there, so they sent me down there. I stayed down there five years.

I liked that part of the country down there, but I had the same trouble that Southern Pacific had in Los Angeles—I couldn't get no good help. And you can't work a job unless you have good help. I'd bring those guys down there, and they'd work a few months or something, and they'd get pretty wealthy and they're gone—I had to hire somebody else. Sure, I run all around. I used to go down to New Orleans, but it was hard for me to be away from my business, because you couldn't trust those cooks with those diabetics and things like that where all the food had to be weighed. They're on a special diet, and their doctors insist on that I take care of that myself, and I did. My days off, I did go down there and see about those diabetics' dishes and their special diets. But finally, why, I got a man in there and I trained him, Howard Bates. Then I told them I wanted to go back on the road, so they put me back on there and left him in charge. And he stayed, I think, about five years after I was gone.

When I was supervisor, I rode one train to the other train. I got on, and I inspect the meat, the food, watch 'em serve some dishes, and rode to the next station, got off, and caught another train. A lot of times I'd ride to Yuma and get off, and I'd wait and catch another train and probably ride to Tucson, or sometime I'd catch a train outta Tucson and rode to El Paso. See, every time I catch one of those trains, I had a different crew. It wasn't like catchin' the same person all the time. Very seldom I'd grab one crew 'lessin I found something bad on there, then I'd double back and catch 'em, see if they correct it, tell 'em 'bout it—and they liked me for that, because I didn't have 'em all the way on the carpet [in the superintendent's office]. I don't always start writin' 'em up, but I tell 'em what I want, and they'd do it.

I had to make out an itinerary where I would ride during the week. They never told me where to go, but I would get the complaints where people complain about the food or something like that, and then I'd cover those trains and cover those crews. Oh, so many different complaints: food being served cold, food untasty—that was my complaint about the food not being hot—or they had to wait so long for their meals, the cooks are slow or people come in the dining room after they did and got served before they did, and those kind of complaints. Or somebody would order food that had taken longer to cook, but you couldn't explain that to the public. I go in and sit down there, and then you come in after I do, and you get your food before I get mine, and I say, "Well, what they doin'? They playin' favorites," or something like that. So those are a lot of complaints we got.

And then I had the big job of sanitary conditions: see that the glasses was washed properly, dishes were sterilized and washed, 'cause you could spread a disease. But that was a time in those days, why, you had to have all those dishes and things thoroughly cleaned, and you had to see that the men clean 'em and wash 'em properly. Dishes, had to have 'em in scaldin' hot water, and all those things was a job. And then there's the sanitary condition of it: that silver had to be polished. That's all my job, to see those things was did and catch the crews that wasn't doin' it. Some of 'em, I had to send 'em to the big boss or the carpet, and some of 'em, why, I got results, I didn't have to. But I tried not to do that, but some of 'em I'd 've had to turn 'em over to the big boss, and then he'd call 'em on the carpet to come in town, and if he don't get any satisfaction—he call 'em on once or twice—we had to pull 'em off. Yeah.

I've got on many trains and found meat in their box and throwed it out. Yes sir, it's no good. "You ain't serving this to nobody. Throw it in the garbage can." That was part of my job. I had to inspect that meat 'cause many got sick, just like this trip where that woman got poisoned on those oysters. She claimed the oysters. Wasn't nothin' wrong with the oysters, 'cause I had checked 'em and everything. But it was something she had that she got ptomaine poisoning on those oysters. I don't know. A lot of time people eat stuff or drink different things cause ptomaine poisoning. Same with spoiled food. Any spoiled food'll cause ptomaine poisoning. That's why my job was so important.

But now everything comes in a package. In other words, now is the Life of Riley for those cooks and things on the diner. They get all that stuff cut and packaged and different things, all they got to do is warm it up. Shoot, we used to throw a half a damn beef on there, and you had to cut that beef up. If you didn't know how, you was in bad shape, and you got to know what to do with all parts of it.

I ran across one of my old cookbooks in there among my things that I rewrote. That was during Prohibition time, when the country was dry. You couldn't get wine and alcohol to go in dishes that required it, and we had to make up a new cookbook and eliminate that wine and stuff. You had some wine with salt in it for cooking, but you could only use that on meat and so forth like that. You couldn't use nothin' sweet and no drinks. So it was a tough time.

Yeah, that Prohibition went a long, long time. I made some good money during that Prohibition time. Shoot, I used to bootleg that . . . we get that darned alcohol in Chicago. You get a jug for about two or three dollars and put it in some half-pint bottles or pint bottles. Then every time you had a trainload of soldiers, you could sell it to 'em, see. Yeah, we hauled all those soldiers out from Lake Michigan out to the coast, and every trip or so we had a carload of sailors. And if you had any liquor, they sure would buy it. I sell those pints for a dollar, half a pint for 50¢. I made good money off of that stuff. But you couldn't carry too much, 'cause you wouldn't want the commissary man see you packin' a whole lotta stuff down there. But what's in your grip you could take. Well, I'd always take a gallon. That was plenty of money in those days.

Just think: $30 a month, that's all the money I made! I had to pay room and rent, keep my clothes clean, and take care of your family out of $30. You know you had to hustle to make some money somewhere. Cooks don't get no tips. Sometimes the waiters give you fifteen or twenty-five cents after they done got tips all the way across. And people wasn't tipping that much, no way. Waiter'd go from here to Chicago, but he wasn't getting but $19 a month [salary], plus you guarantee you couldn't get that because when they got through taking hospitalization and insurance out of it, you wouldn't get that much.

And you had to pay for broken dishes. Yeah! They had to take so much out for broken dishes. The railroad company didn't go for none of that stuff; it was all on the help. You better be careful with those dishes and don't break 'em, 'cause if you do, why, they're gonna take it outta your salary. Yeah. And I wish I had the money now that them poor waiters and cooks have paid for people that take that stuff for souvenirs. Yes, sir! And they catch one of 'em, they don't say nothin', they didn't make no holler about it. They takin' silver coffeepots, silver spoons and knives—kept 'em just for souvenirs—all the napkins and things like that, they take 'em. Then at the end of the month, when they short, why, so much they short, they deduct it from all the employees' salaries. Yeah, that went on for many a year.

See, well, there used to be around $19,000 worth of silver on every car; that's the way they come out equipped. And shucks, that stuff wouldn't last no time. Yeah. Them damn silver pots is worth about $10 apiece. They had one for your coffee; then you had a creamer on there. Oh, they tried different things to stop it. They had sugar cruets they made where you couldn't take them and different things like that, but they takin' everything that wasn't nailed down. And those linen napkins? Very seldom that a crew make a round trip and come back, there wouldn't be 10 or 15 of those linen napkins short; people done take them. And naturally, a waiter ain't gonna say nothin' to nobody about takin' 'em, 'cause he's lookin' for a tip, and then he wanna hold his job. If he go to hollerin' about that, and they hear that he's snitchin' to the office, why, he wouldn't be on there long, you know. Oh, those was terrible days.

And for so many years the railroads charged 'em room and board on the train. You ate on there, didn't you? You had to pay for it, see? But you know, the railroad had to pay those men back pay for the money that they'd been taking away for room and board? The government stopped it. Yeah, they told the railroad they couldn't take that money out of those people's salary—it was wrong. It *was* wrong!

It used to be that in the dining car those men had to get up early enough to put away their beds, roll up their beds, and put 'em down the hole in the possum belly and clean up and set up the dining room, 'cause the railroad wasn't thinkin' 'bout gettin' no dormitory for those men. They wasn't gonna pull no extra car there for that dining car help. So they made 'em sleep in the diner, and I just tell ya, that was something awful, but they did it—sleep on them chairs and those slats and different things. And then they get up in the morning, they have to raise the windows to air out that car where eight or ten men been sleepin' in there before they could set it up for breakfast.

The steward got a cot to sleep on; he slept in the corner on a cot, and a waiter had to make his bed down for him. And he make his bed down for him, and he slept in one corner, and then a lot of stewards kicked up on that—"Ah, you got a white man sleepin' there with them niggers." They raised Cain 'bout it. They didn't get nowhere with it, though. But they did away with that. The government required 'em to put on dormitories to stop them from sleepin' in the diner. But how many years did they sleep in 'em?

The railroad abused the black man for a while. They did at the beginning. It got outta hand, but they come to find out that a black man was one of their great securities. He did more work and things like that and did work that nobody else would do. They found out the black man was somethin' that they needed. See, the thing about a corporation like that, they hire a man (and you be president of this company) well, you got two things in mind—that is to make more money for the company, and build your job up. But the other men under you, they the ones that got to do the work.

So if anything happen, you'd try to squash it and different things like that, but you ain't goin' out there to try to change the thing around. No! The railroad company is a group of men, and everybody's trying to make a livin'. And this group of men—most of the intelligent ones are gonna try to do it intelligent, and the ignorant, belligerent one, he's gonna do anything to get it.

Just think of all those men that was caught stealin' from the company. A waiter'd steal fifteen or thirty cents, they fire him; a steward would steal hundreds of dollars, and they never catch him! I know plenty of 'em stole a lot of money from the company. Oh, yeah! They used to take that company's money—they had blank checks, they'd use 'em and put the money in their pocket. The steward would ask you when you get on a car, "Who you workin' for—yourself or the company?" You say, for yourself, why, then he gonna send meal orders in there with no checks and they put that money and split it. If a waiter says, workin' for the company, why shoot, he'd get rid of him. But if he's workin' for himself, why then he'd go throw some money his way. Yeah, I know a whole lotta these guys here got nice beautiful homes and everything, and that son of a gun done stole the company blind.

You think a Negro could be a steward on a diner? No, indeed! If you wasn't white, you wouldn't get that job. They had men on those dining cars so much superior to some of those white stewards, but they didn't get the job because they were black. Then they started puttin' 'em in charge on those coffee-shop cars and different things like that. They didn't have many, but it wasn't long before they put 'em on all the trains. They erased that prejudice on those stewards, because they couldn't get a white man. The company wouldn't pay a white man enough to keep that job, and he could get a better job, so they were always over a barrel on it. I know two or three of these youngsters that I broke in that were stewards when Amtrak takin' over.

The thing you couldn't live down is the name that they call you and things like that. Like one time I told 'em—you're puttin' those turkeys on the Morning Daylight for roast turkeys, they's roastin' 'em in the commissary kitchen and puttin' 'em on there for the cooks to make sandwiches out of. And I told 'em 'bout the legs, I said they can't make no sandwiches out of those turkey legs, and the cook is throwin' 'em in the garbage can. We're losing money—we've got to get some money out of it. So I stepped out, and this guy was one of the white guys talkin' like that, "Hey, you think that nigger know what he's talkin' about?" [laughs]. I ignored it. See, you had to ignore those things. All through life you have to ignore an ignorant person. If you get mad—let him make you mad and you get upset—why, you ain't no better off than he is. But you had to ignore those kind of statements.

You know the setup. You see, the average Negro that's got any kind of education or anything like that, he know from whence he come, and he know where he's tryin' to go, and so he's got to use the best psychology to get there, and if he don't use it, why, he ain't gettin' nowhere. Right now, just like I say, right here in Los Angeles, I know when they wouldn't let a Negro drive a streetcar, wouldn't let him touch a streetcar. But they got that— they're drivin'. They was drivin' those streetcars before they pulled 'em off. Yeah, but they come a long ways. They wouldn't give a black man one of those jobs. They wouldn't let a black man be a teller in a bank, but they got there. But they got that through intelligence, education, and honesty, and that's the way that the times have changed.

That's the way I got advanced on the dining car, by studyin' and figurin' out people, you know, learn how to treat people. That's one of the most important things. The average person don't know how to treat you; they'll insult you in a minute. A lot of these here belligerent Negroes will insult you, and they're ready for a fight and all that stuff. But what you gonna accomplish out of a fight? You're not gonna accomplish anything out of it, but they're ready to fight or they're ready to insult you. But that's from a belligerent and ignorant person, and they're the only people that do that.

See, I worked with the top men. Whenever I went out with those men on the railroad, my voice was law. Whatever I told 'em, if they didn't—all I had to do was use my pencil. He'd have to go see the boss before he got out. I've had guys threaten to hit me and different things. I walk away from 'em, 'cause I know if he hit me it'd have been his job. You speak to 'em about doin' certain things wrong, and they get all horse-tied with you and tell you what they'll do to ya. I said to myself, say, "I know what I'll do— I'll put the pencil on him," and when he get back in town, he'll have to explain why he did this to me. And when I meet him again, he'll meet me grinnin', say, "I'm sorry we had that little mix-up the other day."

"That's all right," I say, "you just do your job. We can still be friends." But you can't resent those kind of things. Those are things in life that so many people—even a lot of people who's educated—they don't figure that way. Some of 'em figure 'cause they got an education they can rule the world; some of 'em ain't got no education and think they know everything. So that's the way life goes.

I met a lot of belligerent white people, too. I had a steward tell me—old man Bell, he was a steward on the Lark—he say, "Listen, ain't no nigger come tell me how to run my diner." And "the man" had sent me out there and told me what to tell him and what to tell the crew, see? Well, now, if I'd been the person to get upset, I could have dealt him a whole lotta misery. But I said to myself, "Those people need help." And so the next time I saw him, why, he apologized, told me he was sorry. Yeah. Well then, if I'd of raised up and went and put all of that stuff that he give me—and all the insult he give me—on paper and put it in that office, why, he'd of went to the big man in the office up there, and he take action, see? But I didn't. You see, there's more ways to handle a person who's uncouth than to try and fight him.

When they brought that first Sunset streamliner [1950], they sent me down to Houston to show the men how to equip it and different things. And one of the superintendents down there say, "You tell me, with this brand-new train, they send a nigger down here to tell us how to run it?" I didn't say nothin'. I just ignored him like I didn't see him, you know, 'cause I knew what I was doin', and I knew how they feel down there. If I hadn't of been born and raised in the South, it'd of been different.

It's just like you can train a animal, that you can pet him and different things, but if you don't train him right, he'll bite ya. So you've got to know how to handle those people. And that's why I got along with the railroad— I knew how to handle the men and always make the men realize that whatever they doin' is important as my job. And you tell 'em that, why, and they find it out, then they wanna do better. But if they think, " 'Cause he's a big shot he got that white-collar job, and look how he talk to us," and different things like that. . . .

I never call one of those fellas by their [first] name on the job. I may call 'em when I get off, but if I get on the train, it's "Mr. So-and-So, thank you. I appreciate you doin' certain things for me"—that's it. But that's more than tellin' a guy, "Well, you've got to do so-and-so. The office is hollerin' about so-and-so. You doin' this wrong; you doin' that wrong." That guy gonna learn to hate you. So you can't do those things. You've got to use psychology among men, especially when they got a lower IQ. But if you know people and know 'em well enough, why, you'll find out when you meet somebody that is intelligent, why, you'll always know it; he'll let you know. And if you meet somebody that ain't intelligent, you'll soon find that out, 'cause he's gonna be ignorant, and he's gonna show you that he's ignorant, and that's what I have went through many years in my life. As I say, I'm in my eighties, and I went through all that stuff in my young life. Yes, sir! I met intelligent people, and I met ignorant and belligerent people, and then I met people who was fair and wanna see the whole world live right. So I have had all that.

An accident occurred on the Southern Pacific Railroad during World War II that has not been well documented. A missile fired from neighboring Camp Cooke, along which the SP main line ran for some distance on the coast line, scored a direct hit on the Daylight's kitchen car, killing a female cook. The mere fact that a civilian train was hit by "friendly fire" on American soil is unusual enough, but that a woman was working in the kitchen of the Daylight is a story unto itself. George McLain was a key figure in getting women working in Southern Pacific kitchens during the war.

I had a heck of a time. I had to go before the governor of the state of California to get permission to work those women on the train because at that time a woman could only work so many hours, and that woman had to work long hours. They said, "Well, if they leave home, they're still on the job, even if you stop them from working." But I had to explain to 'em, told 'em, I couldn't get the men. I tried. I had an employment office over here on Central Avenue where I was trying to get help—didn't have no luck. So I finally got them on there 'cause I would split their shifts. I had to put special seats on there where they could come out and sit down, and then they could go back and work during the meal. But I had a hard time getting those women in there.

All of them was colored. I had 'em dishwashers and third cooks. I had two women was second cooks, but then all the men was chefs. They got along fine, they didn't have no trouble. I had special quarters for 'em and everything like that. The men got along better with the women than they did with each other, because they wouldn't do nothin' to help those men but everybody was tryin' to help those women, you know. And all those guys tryin' to make love to those women and help them and wash dishes for 'em. You put a guy on there, and he's second cook, and I get on there, the woman's up on the range cookin', and he's down there washin' dishes, done changed jobs [laughs]. Yeah, that was a job all right. But it worked out. Finally, after the war was over, why then I got the men back on there. Some of the women stayed quite a while after the war was over, but they finally drifted away.

Yeah, that war was a big job! I had to see about supplies, getting something for 'em to eat and figure on dishes they could use without meat. We got many a different dish. We always got plenty fish and plenty fowl, but we had to figure out the menu. You couldn't give them people just fish and chicken. You had to figure something out. Shucks, and I seen the time that you put some meat on one of those menus, it wouldn't last no time. Why, everybody that'd come in there would eat that meat, 'cause meat was hard to get. It was pretty tough, but we made it through that.

You couldn't get no French dressing, no mayonnaise. No, we had to make all that. I had a chef in the bakery shop there at the commissary where I had all that stuff made—made my French dressing, made my mayonnaise, made my pie crusts. I had to put all that on the car already made up. Sometimes we didn't get but two beefs a week, or sometimes three. And that Lark never did get out of steaks, but there was no other train you get a steak on unless you get on the Lark. Then you take that cheap meat, and you'd put it on that tramp train—on one of the Coasters, West Coast or on the Argonaut—on one of those trains where everybody rides. But you take all that good meat, and you put it on the fine trains.

As McLain gained stature within the SP dining car department, he was able to implement new features into the diners that considerably aided the crews' duties and saved money for the railroad.

One SP innovation was triple-unit dining car units: three cars were permanently joined together. On some trains, such as the Daylight, the kitchen was the center car and serviced a diner on one end and a coffee shop on the other. On some trains, like the Lark, the kitchen was placed at one end, with the dining room adjacent and a lounge coupled to it. The triple units were the zenith of American dining car design, and many features of the new diners were pioneered by George McLain and the Southern Pacific.

Well, they were hell, I'll tell you that much—seat too many people. See, that triple unit—kitchen in the middle and the dining room on each end—used to have two different meals. It had a coffee-shop meal in one, and they have select dining car meals in the other, and you had to prepare all that food. We carried as many as eight cooks in the kitchen. On this end of the kitchen unit is steam tables, and all the food goes this way, and on the other end, in the dining car, it was a pantry.

I brought over one of the first units to Los Angeles, round about '41 or '42. It was one of the units that they have on the Lark. The Lark had a triple unit, but they only had one dining room. [The other car, besides the kitchen, was a lounge.] I just had gas stoves put on the train, and these new units was gas ranges—propane. A long time they fought me on that. They didn't want to put 'em on there, said that with the train running the wind would blow out the pilot light on there. Finally, I got hold of a big boss in San Francisco, he say, "Well, we're gonna try it out. You say you can do it. We'll take one of those café cars and put it in there first, and if it works all right, then we'll do the diner."

So we got together and figured out how to harness those pilot lights so the wind wouldn't blow them out. Oh yeah, that was my idea. I fought with 'em for a long time over that. I stayed there with that mechanic until he got that thing connected up and got it fixed and watched it, lit it up and burned. Then I went to Tucumcari, New Mexico—that's halfway to Chicago. I burned it all the way down there and all the way back. I didn't have a bit of trouble. So when I got back, I said, "Well, it's okay."

So they looked it over, and they started pulling the old diners off with the coal burners and the wood burners and puttin' in gas stoves. After I got 'em to goin' and everything, why, the cooks didn't wanna ride a train less it had a gas stove on it. And then after they got those gas ranges on there, then I had 'em put on the carbo freezers, you understand? Use dry ice. And those iceboxes—where they used to have to get on top and ice those cars every so often—why, they put those carbo freezers on there and put probably 100 pounds of dry ice in there, and they go to Chicago, see? And then they let all that help along the line off; they didn't have to bother with it. They'd probably have two men to water the train, but they used to have a bunch every time a train pull in the station.

The first air conditioning they put on there they had—down under the train—they had a place they called the possum belly, and they made that into a icebox, and they put ice in there, and they would get the refrigeration off of the ice to cool the diner. And that's the only way they got refrigeration in the diner till they finally got the machinery in there that keep that refrigeration.

They used to have little screens. They had to raise those windows and put those screens in there 'cause it'd be too hot in that diner to eat. But see, then they throwed those screens away after they got that air conditioning in there. Ah, those was the tough days, when they didn't have no air conditioning. Then something I never did get—I tried to get 'em to make those kitchens air conditioned, but they just couldn't make it. They said the heat was too severe in there and it wouldn't work. They never did do it, and I don't know if any railroad had air conditioning in the kitchen.

Yeah, they put that electrical equipment in that dining room, and that dining room was so cold sometime you feel like you catch a cold workin' in there, but that kitchen was still just hot. And the thing about it, that kitchen, if you open your windows, you get all that dirt and stuff'll come in there, that trash that they pick up along the way, and if you kept 'em closed, it was hot—and that was the bad part about 'em.

We had to make our own menus. The chef and the steward used to make 'em up. When I started on there, they had a typewriter on the car, and the steward would type up these special menus.

Your standard menu, you got that on the car, see. They had them printed by the thousands. Say, we got french fries on there. If they're 25¢ why, it'd be on every menu you get. If you have coffee, tea, and so on, that'd be on there. But now, where you have your special meal, you may have—say, over here I got some grated veal cutlets Milanese, I got some broiled salmon with butter sauce, I got some chicken fricassee, I got ox tongue with spinach. When they got ready to make the menus out, the steward'd pull out his typewriter and type that special menu up. Then they'd put it on that hectograph. It made copies. You could make as many copies as you want off of that because it had a heavy ink on there. You just print it off, and then they would paste it in the menu, and that was your special. But that's the way we made menus for years. Finally they stopped and started to make 'em in the general office.

As a supervisor and instructing chef, George McLain was responsible for overseeing any special movements or parties, for which the dining car standards had to be first-rate. He crossed paths with presidents, dignitaries, politicians, and actors during his lengthy career, and he talked about some of the more noteworthy personalities. By special request, he made his own Strawberry Space Pie for President and Mrs. Truman on numerous occasions.

Oh yeah, that's my own pie dough. I made a crust like you're makin' a lemon meringue pie, then you take your strawberries, and you shook 'em down, let 'em sit a while in that sugar, and you put it on top of that cooked crust. Then you take whipped cream and put it on with a bag. I got one of my old bags up there now. Then you put your roses and things on the top of those strawberries, then you keep a few whole ones out, and you put 'em around over there. And, oh, [Mrs. Truman] thought that pie was great. In fact, when he got out of office and they went to Honolulu, they wired for me to come up and make her one, and I had to go up to Ogden, Utah, to meet that train and make her another one of those pies.

You know, when Truman was campaigning for president, he come through the Northwest, and I had to go all the way up to Seattle and meet that train, and then I rode with him all the way down as far as Douglas, Arizona. They had a special train, but he got off that train, and he flew from Douglas, Arizona, on down south, where he was campaigning.

Every time they had some big shot on there, I had to be on the train. That's where my trouble come in. They used to call me nine, ten o'clock at night and tell me to catch a train the next morning—so-and-so's gonna be on there. D. J. Russell, president of the Southern Pacific Railroad, I've been on his private car many a time. I went up there on his private car to bring President Harding to Los Angeles, but [Harding] never did make it—he died. But [Russell] was gonna let us use his private car. He had one of the finest private cars that anybody ever had on the railroad. [S. P. 150, named *Sunset*] See, all those presidents had a private car, and you can live on 'em, you know. It was beautiful! It was the first silver car come out when Southern Pacific bought those silver cars. I believe it did have the Sunset [insignia] on it.

Russell was a tough man, though. Oh, he was tough, and rough. He didn't play with 'em. He'd fire anybody, kick 'em out if they wasn't right. I know he kicked out the general manager of the dining car, Tommy Lockhead, and brought in Butler. I never did know what his trouble was, but he didn't like [Lockhead's] operation. But mostly, though, [Russell] worked on those guys workin' those shops and preparin' those locomotives and fixin' those trains. That's what he was tough on, and takin' care of that track. Yeah, everybody knew him. He was a big man.

See, when you are associating with professional people, you have to be professional yourself, you have to act in that category. You can't just go to work and, like the guy say, go there and Uncle Tom with 'em. They don't want that. They want people that know what they're talkin' about, and I had that to realize.

On 3 February 1945 the Yalta Conference began in Crimea, Russia, with President Roosevelt, Joseph Stalin, and Winston Churchill in attendance. The conference continued until February. Upon his return to the United States, an ailing President Roosevelt made his way from the West Coast to Warm Springs, Georgia, where he died on 12 April 1945, a victim of poliomyelitis. It was to be his last train trip through California on Southern Pacific rails.

Roosevelt died down in Georgia. I fixed his last meal to eat in California. I went down to San Diego, and them son of a guns didn't tell me nothing. They just told me to get my tools and my bag and go down to San Diego, and they wanted me to prepare the best meal I ever prepared in my life. Well, I couldn't imagine what it was. So I got on the train—nobody told me a word. I didn't know who I was gonna cook for or nothing.

And when I got to San Diego, a guy met me in gray. He looked like an Englishman, and he had him two soldiers with tommy guns. At that time, why, they were putting them Germans on the pole. They catch 'em, they think that they were performing in this country, why, they'd put 'em on a plank and pack 'em in the air, and anybody that wasn't patriotic, they were in trouble. And I said I know I hadn't did anything. So I said to the soldiers, "What's wrong? Why you taking me?"

They didn't say nothing. And that man in gray, I asked him, he says that, "You're going to fix a meal for the president of the United States."

So then, when I got down there, then they explained it to me. Told me that the chef on this train, he'd been working for the B&O for 36 years, and he never saw abalone. At that time they didn't fly no fish from one city to the other. If they couldn't ship it, you didn't see it. So a lot of this southern fish and western fish didn't get nowhere, 'cause it'd spoil or it was too expensive to pack it in ice to get it on some three-or four-day trip on the train. So when they told the president of Southern Pacific Railroad about it, he told 'em, "I got a man that'll cook anything that'll swim, crawl, or fly!" [*laughs*]. He was talking about that when he sent me down there. I never will forget that.

But it was pitiful that they kept that man [Roosevelt] in office, 'cause he couldn't get around. They had a wheelchair, they rode him along, and they had artificial steps made on the rear of the train where they could put the wheelchair on it and raise him up to go on the car. He was practically an invalid. They handled him like a baby. Oh, his mind wasn't bad or nothing like that. He's nice—talk and everything, ask questions—but he wasn't able to get around.

He gave me a $50 bill, and I asked him to initial it. He initialed it, and I kept it for about 20 years [*laughs*]. I finally spent it. I said, "What's the use of me keeping this hanging around here just to show people? Fifty dollars is fifty dollars. I'll just go spend it." I went to the bank, and all of 'em want to look at that bill.

Perhaps the most unusual passenger George McLain prepared a meal for was Soviet Premier Nikita Khrushchev, on 20 September 1959. The premier was in Los Angeles, having added that city to his itinerary in hopes of visting a Holly-wood movie studio and Disneyland. He was not allowed into Disneyland, for security reasons. 20th Century–Fox Studios hosted a special party in his honor that was attended by many stars and dignitaries. The event was a fiasco. Khrush-chev was not amused by Shirley McLaine's can-can number, and Los Angeles Mayor Norris Poulson delivered an unfriendly speech that pointedly criticized the international guest and his homeland.

By the time Premier Khrushchev boarded the Daylight train, his mood was not happy. It was up to the Southern Pacific Railroad—and for his part, George McLain—to make Khrushchev's only American train ride a pleasanter memory than Los Angeles had provided. Khrushchev boarded the special 18 car train at 8:30 A.M. at Union Station in Los Angeles. His party of 100 was cloistered in the rear portion of the train, with nearly 300 newsmen occupying the rest of the train. Southern Pacific had set up a dining car to serve as the rolling press room, equipped with typewriters and a Western Union filing desk.

While going over his schedule with official U.S. host Henry Cabot Lodge in the dome-lounge car, Khrushchev interrupted their conversation to remark, "I'm glad I took the train. This is a fine train and a nice route." Later he strolled through the train, meeting newsmen and answering questions through his inter-preter. He got off the train at both Santa Barbara and San Luis Obispo for a few minutes to greet the crowds that had lined up to catch a glimpse of him. The train finally pulled into San Francisco at 6:15 P.M. in the evening.

Well, they sent me a wire—I was out on the road—they sent me a wire to come in and said that Khrushchev was going out on the Daylight. They run a second section. The regular Daylight carried 14–16 cars, and they went ahead and acted as a pilot, see, so that nobody would damage the track or nothing. And his section followed it. Oh, they were particular about that guy. I never will forget it. That's the only train ride he had in America, and he boarded the train at the Union Station, and everybody was screened that rode that train. Oh, they had plenty of FBI and special railroad bulls and everything else on there. They had that train guarded. They even had some on the first section to see if anything happened. Everybody that was on that train, they had to have a permit and they had to show it to the FBI before

140

Nikita Khrushchev stretches his legs in San Luis Obispo, California, while traveling from Los Angeles to San Francisco by special Southern Pacific Train in 1959. George McLain was supervisory chef in charge of meals aboard the train.

they got on the train. If anything had've happened to him, why, it'd've been war with Russia, you know, so they were very particular about it.

I didn't pick my own crew, but I did pick a couple of cooks I wanted on there. It was under my supervision. See, I was the supervisor, the instructor. Very little cooking I did, but I supervised the cooking, and they had to fix it the way I wanted. We had a new menu every meal. One was Russian, but they had another menu for the detectives and the bodyguards and the train crew. But Khrushchev ate off of the American menu, while we had roast beef. He was wanting some of that roast beef, and we give it to him. But all the rest of those people with him, why, they ate off Khrushchev's menu.

After breakfast—they had breakfast on there that morning—and when I come through the diner, why, he got up outta his seat and shook hands with us. He didn't speak English, he said it in Russian, but I understood what he was saying. Yeah, and every time the train stopped, he hit the ground, he wanted to get out and walk, went around and shook hands.

The biggest experience I had was delivering a baby on the Imperial. A woman got on there, and they wasn't supposed to let those women on there when they were pregnant, you know, so far gone pregnant. But that woman got on there, and she'd gone into labor, and they took her in the Pullman car there. So they come to me—I was chef then—told me that a woman was up there about to have a baby, said was no doctor on the train. I say, "Oh, well, I'll deliver it. Get out my butcher knife."

I take my butcher knife, I went up there, pump that woman's stomach, and tied that cord and cut it. The reason why I knew how to do it, my mother was a midwife, see, and she used to have all her books and things and sit down and talk, and I'm taking everything in. So I delivered that baby. And years after that baby was growed up, his mother would write. She never got through thanking me for it. But they had no business lettin' her on the train.

Oh, I was glad to get off. It got to the place where it kept me nervous. Then, if you deal with a whole lotta people that are belligerent and ignorant and different things, you get tired of that stuff.

Right now, at my age and things, I've got nothin' to do but—which I ain't thinkin' about it—but I gotta sit here and wait to die. I *could* live to be 100! [*laughs*]. But you never know!

Ralph Carrington

8

RALPH CARRINGTON
Amtrak Attendant, Onboard Supervisor
1973–

Born in 1955 in Charleston, South Carolina, Ralph Carrington came to California with his family as a child. By the time he went to work for Amtrak in 1973, the "golden era" of rail travel was just coming to a close. The old porters and waiters who taught Carrington how to railroad, the last of a rapidly dwindling breed, were working out their remaining years in a new style of service that bore little resemblance to what they were used to.

Much has changed on Amtrak as well since Ralph hired out in 1973. At that time Amtrak was in the midst of a turnover of management and personnel that resulted in the need to hire many new employees fairly quickly. Today the company hires older, more mature individuals; it would be nearly impossible to find an 18-year-old working in the kitchen of an Amtrak train today.

At the time of his interview, Ralph was working as a sleeping car attendant and hoped to become an on-board service superintendent, or "chief," as they are commonly called. He has since been promoted to chief and works Amtrak trains running out of Los Angeles. His authority on the train is second only to that of the train conductor. Such opportunities were very rare for an African American man in the Pullman era.

I was born a poor black child [*laughs*]. I'm 32, so I was born in 1955, Charleston, South Carolina. When I was five years old, the family moved out to California, so basically I'm a Californian, you know, raised out here. I grew up in the Compton area, still reside in the Compton area. I was one of them running-wild teenagers with no direction. My mother and father divorced when I was in the fifth grade, and [that] put a lot of burden on her. She was working those three jobs, so, of course, she didn't have that kind of opportunity to keep a good eye on me.

Gangs were getting quite prevalent in Compton at that time. I wasn't no part of that, but we were a couple guys in the neighborhood who were friends but didn't claim no allegiance to any gangs. We did some kind of wild things. In the early days I was able to maintain my academics, so on the outside it appeared like everything was fine. I wasn't really that terrible, but I'd hate for my son to be like I was. Being 18 scared me out of crime the most. Being a little guy, I heard so many stories about "the pen," and I thought I was too little to go through the pen, 'cause I was just gonna be muscled around. And that kind of made me straighten up my act more than anything.

The reason I even went on into Amtrak was because I was not allowed to participate in my senior-year graduating ceremonies. That was the disciplinarian assessment. Well, that's what they did to me for being the class clown kind of guy. But anyway, that day they were graduating I went down there looking for a job on the freight trains. I heard SP was hiring. So I went down there, and it so happens that the guy who was over personnel happened to know my mother, and he told me, "No, we're not hiring, but Amtrak is."

So I asked him, "Well, what's an Amtrak?" And he told me, you know, passenger train service. I had never seen a passenger train. I thought they were extinct. I didn't think they had 'em anymore.

So he says, "Yeah, they're hiring. Call this number." So I called the number, filled out an application. They gave me a physical ten days later, and then ten or eleven days later they called me and told me I'm hired as a fourth cook.

My first trip they called me on the phone and said, "You're going to New Orleans. Report to work at eight or nine something in the evening on June 16. Goodbye." I didn't know what I was to do. I had asked a few people— my family, my mother and them. I said, "What'd you think I do, fourth cook?" We came up with I must be the salad maker.

So 1973 was also the time of platform shoes, right? [laughs]. I bought me 15 knives for $10 at a swap meet or something like that, a real raggedy set, but they looked pretty. Bought myself some new white pants, some platform shoes. They said they'd give me a jacket. So I get to work and, you know, fourth cook was a dishwasher. This old chef—I forget his name—he says, "You my new cook, youngblood?"

And I said, "Yes, sir."

And he says, "You ever been out here before?"

"No sir, first trip."

And he says, "Your job is easy." And I just started smiling. He says, "All you gotta do is put your head down and your ass up." And I didn't know what that meant. He went over to the dish tub and demonstrated. And that's how you be, your head in the dish tub and your ass up here. And it was a hell of a trip.

These old men kind of adopted me, took me under their wing. Half of 'em were alcoholics. I didn't know it then, but they drank a lot. I thought they were just partying. We got to New Orleans, and the legal age of drinking is 18 in Louisiana, at least at that time. I wasn't much of a drinker, and these guys took me out, and we drank scotch. Never had I drank a scotch. Needless to say, I was drunk. They helped carry me back to the hotel.

Also part of my job then—they had wood-burning stoves, and the fourth cook was to light the stove, you know, put the logs in and get the fire going. So I get to work, and the chef says, "Okay, youngblood, fire up that stove." And I've got a hangover—I'm not feeling good. I'm pumping this wood in here and lighting it up, and it's getting cherry red like he want it. All that metal, you know, hot! And I passed out. The heat hit me, and all I can remember is my knees wavering, and then I woke up in the sleepers a couple hours later.

So I was ready to quit. I said, "I'm sorry, this job just ain't for me. This is no way." You know, this is my resignation speech I'm trying to prepare when I get back. And when I do get back, my girlfriend's there to meet me, and just the joy of being home on ground, I just forgot about it immediately. Went home and made one more trip.

When I went there, I was only gonna work the summer, 'cause I had these occupational goals, these dreams of being a veterinarian. Animals were my forte at the time. I really was not a communicator of people at all. I had my little select group of individuals who I dealt with, and they came from my sheltered neighborhood as well. I didn't have no idea of other cultures and people from other neighborhoods, let alone other countries. I just dealt with my little friends and my animals.

I went there to work the summer and never looked back! A lot of those old-timers told me—they kind of kept me there, being young and naive— they were telling me things like, "Hey, youngblood, college don't guarantee you nothing. And I've put x amount of children through school with this job. It's a good job. You better stay here." That was kind of influencing on a young mind, especially since I really looked up to these fellas, and I thought they were telling me what they really meant from their heart, which they probably were.

And my friends kept me there. They're the ones who thought it was glamorous, 'cause I'd come back and tell 'em stories. Granted, I would tell 'em all the things that were positive—the couple good things that I enjoyed. I wouldn't tell 'em about the behind-the-scenes negatives. So they were saying, "Man, that's great. You get to go, you get to do this, you get to do that." And I'm like, "Ah, you guys are here partying, and I'm missing out on that." And by them saying it looked good, I thought, "Well, maybe it ain't so bad."

Then, of course, when I got my first few paychecks of my life, I thought that was fantastic—$450 every two weeks. I made at least two and a half trips to New Orleans. For a young man, it was very impressive. That's the first time someone just handed me four hundred and something dollars. And then, also, I had gotten myself a car, and I got a little apartment. I started establishing a lifestyle. So I thought, "Well, school can wait a year or so. Let me just give it a break, and then I'll go back into school." I now have no ideas of those goals or those dreams no more. That's nothing I want to do anymore. I sometimes wonder what would have happened if I had, but it is no longer a goal of mine. Time pretty much eroded those desires, just pure time.

I came in at the tail end of the dying of the old service. They still had china on the table and fresh flowers—the silver bowls. The "railroad," I never saw, so I can't even compare to it really. I understand through vivid description and seeing some artifacts from it and things like that. I understand some of it. But even when I heard the older guys say, "This ain't no railroad, it's Amtrak," I didn't see it as they did at that time. I thought it was a railroad but just different. "This is the new-fangled railroad."

I listened, that's all I did was listen to the older guys. And I was picking up railroad history in a trip. They told me, "It's easy now. We don't have to do what we used to have to do." Actually, I thought it was fantastic. When they compared how it used to be and how dogmatic it seemed to me, you know, I couldn't fathom working for 20¢ an hour or something like that. I thought I was riding on the new wave of transportation—"this is what's happening now."

But whenever they talked about, "Man, we used to have this diner looking good," and when they got into that feeling and compared it to Amtrak, it's like, "This is bullshit. This ain't real service. Service is . . .," and they'd explain what service is. So they had that kind of dissension. Still, overall I knew, especially for an old man, it was much easier doing it Amtrak's way than the way they used to have to do it. In the early days [of Amtrak], I think they liked it 'cause it was still freer than when they used to be. You take home hams, you party, you gambled, and they didn't have to give service. They just had to pick up plates and put 'em down. So those kind of things they liked.

Let me tell you about a trip I had. I went to Seattle—I was a waiter. And there's an old fella—he's retired now—and we get to the hotel in Seattle, and everybody knows everybody well. I'm the newcomer. So they're all having their camaraderie, and this fella is asking different people, "How many you want?" People are answering, "One." "Two." I don't know what he's talking about. So he comes to me kinda laughing, "Hey, youngblood, how many you want?" I said, "Two." He said, "Okay," and he goes back to somebody else. And I go in my room, and I'm kinda unpacking, sitting on the bed. And I hadn't been there maybe less than 30 minutes, and I hear a knock at the door. I think it's him again. And these two women are at my door, and they're kind of snickering, you know, looking at this boy. He's standing there with 'em, and he's laughing. He said, "You said you wanted two."

Now I'd only made love to one person, and that was only a few times. And I was scared out of my wits then about it, and with these two women I was frightened. I was like, "No, man, I thought you meant hamburgers or something," and I slammed the door on 'em, and I didn't come out of my room anymore that day 'cause I was very embarrassed. I didn't know what to do. But they told me, and they explained things to me. A couple of 'em couldn't believe it. They made fun of it. But that's what they did.

I learned how to play poker. I'm a good poker player today, too. Poker and women and drink. That was the thing—on the train and off!

This crew was a family, but each crew seemed to be its own family. Once one person went from one crew to another, then he became part of that family. But there was a sense of family. Today, definitely not. Definitely not! There's not as much soul there. Really, that doesn't mean on color. There are even white employees who have been there ten, twelve years who will say the same thing. Again, mostly any job way back when was a service-oriented job for a black. When I came to the railroad, all the employees were black except for a few of the bosses. So the emergence of white people brought division partly in fact because some of the blacks just didn't like whites, some of the whites just didn't like blacks. And this didn't even start to happen until 1980. When anyone new came in, it was like, "You guys don't know. You don't know what we've been through."

And then management, they were coming in with ideas like, "If you see somebody out there messing up, report them. They're giving all of us a bad name. Don't have no bad apples. Let's get 'em out." And they're coming in there with this idea like, "Yeah, we're gonna make this company great. We're gonna get rid of these bad apples." And whenever a white person did it—and here's a guy who's been out there 27 years gets turned in—animosity started to build up. So then it became a division—it became a big division right there. I think the plan kind of worked from a corporate point of view, bringin' in that fresh blood. Got rid of a lot of partying, alcoholism, and bad apples. But when you saw a friend go—a working associate anyway—you felt kinda bad, especially when I had this young moldable mind.

They were telling me stuff like, "Yeah, the white folks are messing it up," and I'm looking and I'm saying, "Yep, they sure are, aren't they?" I really didn't know much better. I learned it wasn't quite so. There were changes that happened, and I was able to look at it realistically and adapt to it accordingly.

Looking at the overall picture, I think being black in America does have its obstacles or hindrances. One reason I don't think it affects me—because in what I do I have no problem. But I have never tried to do anything different to find those kind of obstacles, so personally, they don't really bother me. I never looked at things in black and white too much. I didn't see that, being odd or different.

There would be some people who might come up there and say,"Hey, George!" which was what all black people were called back at one time. Some people would say, "George," or, "Hey, boy," to me, and a lot of times I would swallow that up and say, "Yeah, what can I do for you?" because to me it was a game of he thinks he's getting over on me, but my thought was, "I'm getting your money," you know? That's how I dealt with those kind of people with that kind of mentality. They're a dying breed. Those are 70- or 80-year-old folks now.

I'm no more conscious of it on the road or at home. There are incidents that come up that can make it come to the forefront of your mind, you know, but normally I don't dwell on it at all. Maybe, now that I think about it, it has something to do with me just seeing myself as a man of God, and any other man who feels the way I do as a man of God, truly then, there'll be no difference between us.

When the train comes out, it's like a bell going off, "showtime." When the train leaves, it's automatic. It is a groove. I don't pump it up and maintain a high. I know where I can get my little swings in. There are little tricks. I've been out there sick, and you don't feel good, but I do what I can, you know. There are times of the day where you know things are going normally, and there are times when you have no control. So sometimes you've just got to grin and bear it and hope that other customers help you.

I run my game. People run games in offices, people run games in politics, in churches—I run mine on the train within [Amtrak's] guidelines. It's very much an act. A guy once asked me about my marketable skills. He said, "If you got off here, what would you do?" And I thought about it, and all I could tell him was, you know, I think everybody fantasizes being an actor. But when I told him that I meant it seriously, because I put on quite an act out there. I have quite a railroad personality that's completely different than my home personality.

People are always writing Amtrak letters how good I am. Everybody's room has a little thing to fill out, "What do you think?" People will say, "There's mice on the car." "The air conditioning was too cold." "Ralph was excellent." When people got gripes, they'll send them in more often, and I get most of my compliments out of gripes, since it's part of the format anyway. So they [Amtrak] recognize it. I believe I have mastered what I do out there. I spend a whole lot of time getting everybody how I want them to be, and that might take the first third of the trip.

I run my car. If it's an old conductor, he knows me long enough to know I run it. You know how they say, "If you make any changes, go to the conductor, get it okayed with him?" I make my changes and then go to the conductor, "This is what I did." He says, "Cool." I don't think everybody has that right. But I do feel like the captain of my ship. I'm good at what I do. I'm confident. I used to want a pat on the back for being that way. Again, it's the only thing I've ever done, so I think any other lifestyle would be an adjustment for me. How would a person be able to do it another way, I would need to know. I've given myself a Ph.D. in human behavior, especially things that pertain to what I need to know. I might not know if you're a mass murderer in disguise, but I can tell if you're a drug courier, if you're happily married. I can tell.

It's a service job. At first I used to feel bad because I was a servant. There's no other way of saying it, you're a servant, and that has a derogatory sound about it. You know, "I carry somebody's bags. I help people on the train. I gotta clean bathrooms." Ugh—sounds terrible! But I learned how to deal with that, and it's okay, man. But I didn't feel entrapped by a culture, like I'm doing what they did and, "Wow, can't a black man ever get out of this kinda rut?" especially when I got into the gratuity part of the job.

I first started making tips because I was a waiter. You know, when I was a cook, I was behind the scenes, young and a-learnin'. I came out the kitchen and became a waiter. There, I just accepted whatever monies people left. But I learned if I can, not clown, but make 'em smile a little more, enjoy their meals, I'd get a little more money.

I'll never forget the time—in the wintertime, we're on the Starlight, and people are coming into the dining car, and there's absolutely no heat at all. We're in the Cascade Mountains—snow everywhere—and people are coming into the dining car with overcoats on, eating their food. Everybody's talking, and there's that frost coming out of everybody's mouth, and you gotta eat your food real fast. And it was a very funny scene to see, you know, people in overcoats huddled over their food trying to get it down because it's so cold. And they really got no choice, 'cause if you wanna eat, you gotta go in the dining car and eat.

If it would've happened to me today, I think my tips would not be affected too badly, because I know how to make them say, "Well, yeah, Amtrak sure is bad, but Ralph, you're making the best of it for us." I know how to make a bad situation into a better situation, at least in the mind. Then, I didn't know how to handle it, so tips went down a little bit.

Though women worked as registered nurses and maids on the better trains during the heyday of rail travel, those positions were phased out to reduce operating costs as ridership dwindled in the fifties and sixties. On Amtrak, however, women were no longer relegated to special service categories but were hired to perform the same tasks as men had traditionally handled. For the first

time in history women worked side by side with men on the trains, even bunking
with the men in the dormitory car.

It's a good job for a woman to make some money, you know, some in-between stuff, but I can't envision a woman being out there years and years. A couple of reasons. It's stereotypically a male-dominated occupation. They don't even make as many tips, 'cause a lot of guys—she'll say, "I'll get your bags." "No, honey, I'll get it," you know, so since they're doing less, they're getting less.

They're under constant flirtation remarks. If they have any attractiveness about 'em, the crew, the passengers, someone's always bombarding them with some kind of "Yo, baby."

And again, it's a special kind of man that deals with a woman out there. I mean, he's gotta be a real special kind of guy to trust his woman on the railroad. And most men have too many insecurities for that. I've watched all the ones who've failed or the ones who lasted out there this long, but their relationships continually fail.

And then I was stereotypical. When the women first came out there, I was like the old guys—"Women don't belong out here"—so I had to kind of beat that down, 'cause that was my immediate reaction, before giving them a chance. It's just tough. It's tough for a woman out there. And again, I look at it through my eyes. I would not have mine out there.

My funnest days were running this car—it was called a sleeper-lounge. It had a dome bar, and that was everybody's favorite place to be. Everybody liked sitting up in the dome, 'cause it gives you the best view. I was the bartender and the porter. That's the most duties I ever had, 'cause not only do you have to be the electrician, the maid, and the porter, you're the bartender, too.

And that's another thing. When you're a regular porter, you know, between stops, you go to your room, you sit down and sleep if you want to. But when you're bartender, too, the bar is always open, so you gotta keep the bar open. You don't get no sleep unless you sit in your seat. But if you want to show some professionalism, you didn't want to do that. And if you had a good group who wanted professionals—you know, they tip well if you're more professional.

Anyway, I was running that sleeper-lounge, and there was this little girl off the coaches who would wander back there, very friendly little girl, and I was bored, wasn't nothing happening. So we talked and everything. Later on that evening, I was putting some dry ice in the boxes, and she saw it hit some water and how it was foaming up, and she was intrigued by that. And

I had seen her mother, too, so I said, "Oh, let me put it in a cup." I gave her the cup with some water in it, with an olive and a stirrer on it, faking like it was a drink, and I told her, "Take this to your mama and show her."

So the mother comes back, and she just went, "You could of killed my baby. What if she'd of drank this. I should shoot your ass," talking crazy like this. Then she pulled a pistol out of her pocketbook and points it at me.

For a hard second I was just scared. I backed up, and I tried to—"Please put the gun away, please. Let's talk a little quieter." This was a black woman, and it also embarrassed me 'cause she was black, you know, "Hey, you're making us look bad here, girl. Ain't too many of us here."

Then she said, "Well, what do you mean talk quieter?" She did calm down a little bit. And I guess she might of had a bit of a leg to stand on, but she took it extreme. She was talking about the hot ice in the water bubbling up. That's what she was afraid of. So we get into L.A., and they calmed her down. Anyway, I'm brought up on charges behind this, which was really easy to rectify. I just told 'em it was a sincere gesture, and I guess they understood I wasn't trying to do nothing. They gave me this speech on safety, "You could of harmed her," and blah-blah-blah. That was a pretty rough one.

I've had carry-bys—not waking people up. I guess the most comical one of those happened maybe two or three years ago. And it wasn't completely my fault, because the conductor had sold a friend a room, and room movement had taken place. The manifest wasn't correct, 'cause about four people had been placed in different rooms. And I was going by my manifest.

I had gotten up late in the first place. I was waking up these people who were getting off at Kansas City. Fortunately, we were about 45 minutes late, so I was able to get all those up. There's one guy who was downstairs, and I'd forgotten about him. We were in Kansas City late—we were there quite a while—raining like hell that day. So we're leaving Kansas City, and a friend of mine, he and I were talking at the bottom of the stairwell, and this guy pops out of room 12 and was tucking his shirt in his pants, talking about, are we in Kansas City yet. And my friend looked at me like, "Man, you done carried this guy by." And I looked at my friend, and I looked at him, and I said, "We just left Kansas City," and I shot up the stairs. I just left the two of them standing there. I thought, "Shit, let me go get the conductor and find out what to do."

And I know this guy's gonna be pissed off anyway, 'cause he's mad when we got late and he had a meeting to get to and all this stuff. I really didn't want to confront him. Thought I'd give it to the conductor, just let him handle it, and I'd just suffer the consequences later. So anyway, the conductor was one of those guys that I'm really pally-wally with, and the conductor goes back there, and the guy's blowing up. So the conductor

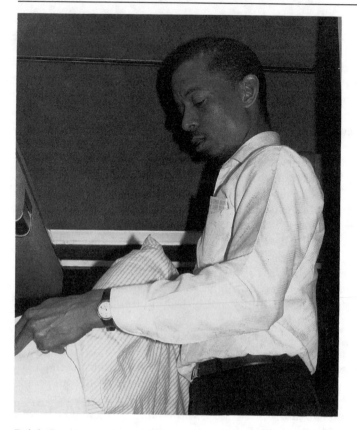

Ralph Carrington placing slips on pillows in Amtrak Superliner sleeper.

says, "Well, look, tell you what we'll do," and he didn't like the guy's attitude, you know!

"We'll just stop right here at this next little town," which was some little unscheduled town, "you get off right there, and you go down here to this café, and you call a taxi or something, and they'll take you back to Kansas City. That's all we can do for you." And the guy had to be somewhere, so that's what he did. But I was nervous, I was really nervous.

Well, you know, anytime any part of the train comes off the track, it constitutes a train derailment. People think of tumbling down a ravine or something.

The first one—a very uncanny accident—the train hits a car trying to beat it across the track, just outside of Eugene. The signs were down, and I guess she was gonna beat it. The train hits the car, a little Mustang 2 + 2, knocks it into a little drainage ditch that runs along the track. The engine's separated from the rest of the train. They kind of went off into a field by themselves. The dormitory on back was tilted, every car up to the diner. I was a cook at this time. The diner on back was on the track and straight. The diner came closest to where this car was. You know our little door there? We could see the car and everything right there. So me and this cook named Charlie Morris jumped out. There were three people in the car, a pregnant woman who was pinned under the wheel and two children. And the children were in the backseat crying. They were okay.

He grabbed one, I grabbed one. The lady was pregnant—you could see her breathing—she was heaving real hard. But she was pinned. Couldn't move her, and she wasn't responding like, "Ma'm, are you okay?" An ambulance was dispatched and everything. The ambulance driver comes, and it was his family! So he becomes unnerved, you know, he just falls to pieces, and another ambulance comes and takes him away. I understand the woman eventually died.

I was the littlest guy on the crew, too, so I was made to go into the dormitory, and it was the most tilted of 'em. It was all the way on the side. So I crawled in and got everybody's stuff out. And myself, one cook, the bartender, and one waiter stayed with the equipment, and we went to Eugene. The rest of the crew and the passengers went on to Seattle. We stayed overnight in Eugene, then took the whole train back to L.A., which was a fun trip.

Coming into Albuquerque westbound one trip, I'm in the last car, the sleeper, and the engine's constantly blowing at every intersection. The engineer says he's blowing his whistle through this intersection, and all of a sudden this guy's laying between the track. He never saw him until he blew his whistle, and the guy just raised up, you know. We just plowed right through him. We were rolling pretty good, about 80, we're a little late. So the train stops almost two miles down, we back up, and we're on an Indian reservation. And they have their own law, so we have to wait for their tribal police or however it works to come out to the scene.

So while we're there, the conductor's keeping everybody on the train, you know, telling everybody to stay on. But I jumped off. And the police were there, and I guess part of their report is that they take pictures of identifiable parts of the body. "Here's the head, here's the torso, here's a piece of midsection," you know. He's taking these Polaroids, and I'm holding 'em [body parts] while he snaps 'em, you know.

I kind of did it to see if I could stomach that. Before I joined the railroad, I wanted to go to Vietnam. I tried to go to Vietnam at 17. I had pent-up frustrations. I wanted to be army infantry frontline, and so I was wondering could I've stomached that had I seen it anyway, and this was one kind of way for me to find out. That was an incredible sight to me.

I got left by a train once. That was pretty bad. The reason I even got left was I left my wallet in the crew base. I had a little clutch bag—a wallet and other little stuff inside this little bag—and I left it on the desk in the crew base. So by the time we got to San Bernardino, I knew it was gone. I told [the train crew] that I'm gonna have to run in and call them and tell them to either wire me my stuff or at least give me some money from the steward, and I'll pay you back. I'm out here with no money or nothing, working the coach.

So I called that night, and so-and-so was there, and she wasn't a supervisor. She told me to call back in the morning so she could find out what to do. So we get to Winslow, and at that time Winslow was a ten-minute service stop, and we were a little late, and I told the conductor my situation. I was working the ten car up there with him, and he said, "No problem. I'll watch your door while you go make your call."

Well, he said he forgot, you know, and he highballed the train without me. And here I am in Winslow, Arizona, wearing all this red uniform stuff, no money, no ID, on a Sunday, the train station's closed, everybody's shut down—don't know what to do. I called the crew base and told 'em my predicament, and they were like, "Well, catch the train coming back that night—jump on it and come home."

And I said, "You think they're gonna write me up?"

She said, "Yeah, they'll probably write you up."

I thought about it, and, you know, I didn't want to lose money. I thought, "What am I gonna do?" And I remember this fella that works on the railroad said he was from Winslow. So I got out the phone book, looked up his last name, called his parents, told 'em my situation. They said they'd pick me up. I called the crew base and told 'em I'll stay the night, catch the train the next day, and just double back. And they said okay.

Anyway, I stayed in Winslow and had a great time there. I really did. Caught the train the next day, jumped off in Chicago. I jumped off one train and back on the other and came on home.

It's not an eight-to-five. It is thoroughly different. To me, now, I carry a lot of luggage because I gotta have books, I've gotta have music, I've gotta make myself as comfortable as possible out there. It's my home for the next several thousand miles, and a lot of people like to conduct themselves as if they are at home. That's how the partying and such came to be, 'cause if you're out there and you're miserable-like—"I wish I was at home, this is terrible"— well, you're there for a short time. But if you think you're gonna be there for any length of time, you've got to get comfortable and make the adjustments, and hopefully you'll make proper adjustments.

As far as my family life, I do what almost any family man would do to make sure the family's fine. My hobbies are in my home: my fish, cutting the grass, just being at home. And then the days I take off to myself, which aren't many, most of those are skiing. If I go off myself, it's always 'cause I'm going skiing for a day or two. I take them with me sometimes, sometimes I don't.

When I met my wife, I was into the schedule already, so I think it does take a special woman to deal with a man in this occupation, or vice versa. But my woman is that. She is able to deal with it. And the children, again, have kind of grown up with it. So it's not hard on the family. As a matter of fact, they almost see it as a plus, because they reap some of the benefits. They get free travel. They go places. My children have been places where other kids haven't.

You know, when they're young, they would say, "I wanna do this. I wanna be like my dad and work on the railroad." The older ones now say, "An airline pilot," or something else, which is cool, but where I thought I was a servant, they thought, "Dad works on the train." So that, too, was kind of good for me.

I miss my children, especially when I see other kids on the train, some of 'em who are bad. I say, "Boy, if my children were here, they'd shine," 'cause their train manners are great. They aren't wild like other kids. Or I might see someone whose child is pretty bright, and I'd think, "Mine are bright, too. I wish they were together." The other day we were coming into Flagstaff—a big, bright, beautiful morning. The moon is pretty high up on the horizon, the sun's up, it was a fantastic view, and I remember saying to myself, "I wish my wife was here to see this."

I was a "que sera, que sera" attitude in the beginning. Off the train it was out of sight, out of mind. I was never analytical. I just dealt with it as it came and had fun. Now I look at these days very analytical, things that happen to me or things that I want to happen, comparing how it was last year to now. I don't think I would enjoy the railroad coming into it now. No, partly because of seniority. There's all kinds of fringe benefits. Seniority means you've been there a long time, so, you know, you're supposed to know by now, how to do everything, know the angle to everything. I've got my angles down. I'd hate to come in trying to learn 'em.

I was under the presumption that someone was gonna discover me on there, someone was gonna recognize Ralph as being better than this and take me away. I used to hope that. But that's a fantasy. So I do no longer hope. I fear—it may be a form of regret—that I have no marketable skill on paper. I think I'd have to trained at anything almost, you'd have to show me, if this rug is pulled from under me.

I can imagine—here you come to a new job, here comes this young kid, 20, 21, "Naw, Ralph, you ain't got it, man." I imagine that would be a little

157

damaging to the ego or pride. There would be some uncomfortableness in that, and then I would hopefully conquer it.

I'm not dissatisfied with my life as it is, so I can't say anything else would've been better. So I have no regret. If Amtrak is still here and I want to be here, I could be doing that. In occupation, it's very easy to see me doing this. Anything else I could say, I'm not sure.

Epilogue

The 1960s were the final years of railroad-owned and -operated passenger service in the United States. The airlines, the bus industry, and the private automobile had cut so deeply into rail travel by 1960 that only 10 percent of the population were choosing commercial rail carriers. The cost of riding a Pullman car was double that of an airline ticket. Railroads had been pulling out of the Pullman Company since the late fifties, leaving the company heavily in debt. The corporation limped along until 1 January 1969, when it ceased operations after posting over $22 million in losses. A century after it had begun, the Pullman Company was history.[1]

The railroads survived no better and continued to cut back on trains and service until they, too, were relieved of the financially draining passenger train by the passage of the Rail Passenger Service Act of 1970. In accordance with this legislation, the National Railroad Passenger Corporation was formed as the official carrier of the nation's passenger trains. With its corporate title shortened to Amtrak, service began on 1 May 1971.

With the passing of the Pullman Company and the railroad passenger trains, the tradition of the African American rail service employee drew to a close.

Amtrak was the beginning of the end for the all-black passenger train. The title "porter" was dropped and the word "attendant" substituted for it—a clear indication that white workers were ready to accept what had become decent-paying jobs on the train but did not want to be confused with the porter of days gone by.

Today, all nationalities are represented aboard Amtrak trains, and women are working alongside men in occupations that were formerly all-black and all-male. Racial discrimination has eased, and working conditions are much improved. Ralph Carrington's promotion to train supervisor would not have been possible 40 years ago. But there is something missing—the historic transformation of those "cold pieces of steel" by not only the warmth but the dignity and pride in workmanship of the African American passenger train worker.

Dining car chef on the Baltimore & Ohio receives a load of fresh turkeys from a commissary worker. B & O Historical Society.

Chesapeake and Ohio ad featuring a waiter.

Black dining car steward on the Santa Fe Railway in the 1960s. Santa Fe Railway.

Waiters on the Broadway Limited dining car toast Marjorie Woodworth, star of the Hal Roach comedy *Broadway Limited*, during her trip on the Pennsylvania Railroad's famous 16-hour all-room streamliner from Chicago to New York and back.

A Pullman ad from the 1930s. The white plantation overseer and his slaves had now been replaced by the white Pullman conductor and his porters.

Santa Fe's El Capitan as it looked when Sam Turner worked its dining car. Santa Fe Railway.

The Super Chief. Santa Fe Railway.

Postscript

David Perata has provided an important bit of American history in the compilation of these materials. By regarding the recollections of African Americans who worked the railroads, he has given us an insight into many facets of American life. This is appropriate in that railroads played a determinative role in the expansion and social development of our nation.

The role of the African American in this process of expansion, as it relates specifically to the railroad, is also important. As they had done in building the South, African Americans were called upon to bear a disproportionate burden of the economic development of the nation. I say disproportionate because the economic theory that drives our nation is that work is to be rewarded, and rewarded fairly. As with the slave who owned little and was indeed owned by another person—a reprehensible arrangement for which we continue to pay—the railroad worker was a servant who allowed others not of the same race to live a higher quality of life and to accumulate further capital for their own purposes.

As African Americans continued to fight for their full liberation and complete enfranchisement, their relationship to the railroad grew in importance. Despite the hardships, railroad workers began to spawn a middle class in the African American community. They were an important and regular means of communication between major communities scattered around the country, spreading political and social news.

Finally, with the advent of the movement to organize railroad workers into the Brotherhood of Sleeping Car Porters, great American leaders such as A. Philip Randolph and my uncle, C. L. Dellums, who sprang forth from the African American community, brought the civil rights and social justice movement of the community squarely into the economy.

So it is important that we hear from those who traveled the rails for their livelihood, to hear of their hardships and experiences. They tell a tale as much of America as of the railroad, a tale that bears witness to the distance we have traveled towards equality and the length of the journey yet before us.

—Ronald V. Dellums
Member of Congress, California

The Interviews

In June 1986 my friend Michael, who had done some air-conditioning work at a house near Pasadena, California, mentioned that the homeowner had worked for the Pullman Company. My interest was immediately piqued because only three years before I had attempted to interview former Pullman porters while working from Oakland to Chicago on Amtrak's San Francisco Zephyr, armed with only a pen and notepad. These early meetings inside an empty drawing room on the Zephyr made me realize that I could never capture these rich stories without recording them on tape. By the time Michael stumbled across this Pullman employee in 1986, I had quit Amtrak and so had most of the older black men with whom I had worked. Somewhat discouraged by the results, owing to my lack of preparation, and distracted by other pursuits, I shelved the idea. Michael and his wife, however, later convinced me to once again take up the oral history project. The Pasadena homeowner, Stanley Spiers, turned out to be white. He had worked in the Pullman upholstery department for 40 years in Richmond and Los Angeles, California. Because I had no other leads, I set up an interview with him—and thus began the project that has evolved into this book.

Stanley Spiers turned out to be the only white Pullman employee I interviewed. I ultimately excluded his story because the information did not pertain to the onboard African American service employees. Mr. Spiers did, however, give me the name of a Pullman porter he knew who lived in the Los Angeles area. That man was Virgil Smock.

An oral historian couldn't ask for a better stroke of luck! From Virgil I naturally went on to interview his brothers George and Babe, and from them I learned of James Steele. After that I tracked down leads like a detective—some were dead ends, others turned out to be gold mines. From Jimmy Clark, for example, I got the name of George McLain, whom I had read about in an article in the SP Bulletin. Mr. McLain was a close friend of Jimmy Clark's and had worked with him for many years on the Southern Pacific.

I had found a small cluster of retired black railroad men who met regularly at Jimmy Clark's each Saturday. Not all of them wished to be interviewed, but I spoke with those who seemed interested in the project. Some slipped away. One Los Angeles–area resident had been a key Brotherhood of Sleeping Car Porters official, and his wife was very supportive about setting up an interview. But his age and poor health made the interview too risky to pursue.

Each taped session lasted from one to two hours. A list of prepared questions guided me through each interview, beginning with family history and moving into the interviewee's years on the railroad. I found that by working from a set of generic questions based on what I knew about their occupations, the interviewees led me into areas I never would have been able to foresee.

Each interview was transcribed "as told," with very little change of syntax or dialect. Some topics have been combined for the sake of continuity, but no sentences have been rearranged in a manner that would alter the meaning. I photographed all of the men as I interviewed them, though in some cases I returned to take more photos for variation.

Many lasting friendships were gained from this project. The Smock brothers became good friends, as did Jimmy Clark and Stanley Spiers. But time has already taken George Smock and George McLain, and Jimmy Clark and James Steele are very ill as of this writing. It is an intensely intimate experience to listen to the tapes of those men who have passed on. By the end of each interview, a special bond had been formed that I feel to this day.

Interviewees

Stanley Spiers, 28 June 1986, Arcadia, California

W. A. Wilson, 6 July 1986, Monrovia, California

Virgil Orite Smock, 15 July 1986, Mira Loma, California

George Henry Smock, 22 July 1986, Mira Loma, California

Sam Turner, 23 July 1986, Los Angeles, California

James T. Steele, 7 October 1986, Los Angeles, California

Cleveland Jacobs, 14 October 1985, Los Angeles, California

Norman Brookman, 21 October 1986, Los Angeles, California

Garrard Wilson "Babe" Smock, 19 November 1986, Lynwood, California

Julius Payne, 14 January 1987, Oakland, California

C. "Mac" McDowell, 14 January 1987, Oakland, California

Alex Ashley, 18 January 1987, Oakland, California

Jewel Brown, 16 January 1987, Oakland, California

Jimmy Clark, 22 January 1987, Los Angeles, California

George McLain, 6 March 1987, Los Angeles, California

Ralph Carrington, 9 November 1987, Compton, California

Notes and References

Preface

   1. Jewel Brown, 16 January 1987, Oakland, California.

Introduction

   1. John H. White, *The American Railroad Passenger Car* (Baltimore: Johns Hopkins University Press, 1978), 246.

   2. Jervis Anderson, *A. Philip Randolph: A Biographical Portrait* (New York: Harcourt Brace Jovanovich, 1972), 156.

   3. White, *American Passenger Car*, 246.

   4. Ibid., 248.

   5. Arthur Dubin, *Some Classic Trains* (Milwaukee: Kalmbach Books, 1964), 16.

   6. White, *American Passenger Car*, 248.

   7. Ibid.

   8. Ibid.

   9. Ibid.

   10. Arthur Dubin, *More Classic Trains* (Milwaukee: Kalmbach Books, 1974), 95.

   11. Ibid.

   12. White, *American Passenger Car*, 261.

   13. Robert J. Wayner, *The Pullman Scrapbook* (New York: Wayner Publications, 1971), 6; Dubin, *More Classic Trains*, 104.

   14. Anderson, *Randolph*, 158–59.

   15. Julius Payne, 14 January 1987, Oakland, California.

   16. Norman Bookman, 21 October 1986, Los Angeles.

17. Alex Ashley, 18 January 1987, Oakland, California.

18. Bookman interview.

19. Bookman interview.

20. Virgil Orite Smock, 15 July 1986, Mira Loma, California.

21. Brown interview.

22. Interview with C. L. Dellums (Bancroft Library, University of California at Berkeley, 1973).

23. Ibid.

24. A. Philip Randolph, "The Truth about the Brotherhood of Sleeping Car Porters," *The Messenger* (February 1926).

25. Brotherhood of Sleeping Car Porters files (Bancroft Library, University of California at Berkeley).

26. Milton P. Webster, "Organization among Pullman Porters," *The Black Worker* (August 1936).

27. A. Philip Randolph, "The Case of the Pullman Porter," *The Messenger* (July 1925).

28. Malcolm X, with Alex Haley, *The Autobiography of Malcolm X* (New York: Grove Press, 1964).

29. Anderson, *Randolph*, 165.

30. F. Boyd, "Previous Struggles of the Pullman Porters to Organize," *The Messenger* (September 1926).

31. Anderson, *Randolph*, 165.

32. A. Philip Randolph, "Pullman Porters Need Their Own Union," *The Messenger* (August 1925).

33. Anderson, *Randolph*, 165–67.

34. Ashley Totten, "Why the Plan Is a Fraud," *The Black Worker* (part 1, 1 March 1930; part 2, 15 March 1930; part 3, 1 April 1930).

35. Ibid.

36. Anderson, *Randolph*, 85–96.

37. Ibid., 83.

38. Ibid., 168.

39. A. Philip Randolph, "Report to the Fourth Annual Convention in Cincinnati, Ohio," *The Black Worker* (November 1936).

40. Milton P. Webster, "Report of Proceedings: BSCP Meeting," 1948 (Bancroft Library, University of California at Berkeley).

41. Randolph, "Report to Fourth Annual Convention."

42. Anderson, *Randolph*, 178–86, 206.

43. Ibid., 178–79.

44. A Philip Randolph, "The Brotherhood and the Filipinos," *The Black Worker* (February 1930).

45. Randolph, "Report to the Fourth Annual Convention."

46. William Green, "Message to the Pullman Porters," *The Black Worker* (August 1936).

Epilogue

1. White, *American Passenger Car*, 266.

Bibliography

Anderson, Jervis. *A. Philip Randolph: A Biographical Portrait.* New York: Harcourt Brace Jovanovich, 1972.

Bergman, Peter M. *The Chronological History of the Negro in America.* New York: Harper & Row, 1969.

Dubin, Arthur. *Some Classic Trains.* Milwaukee: Kalmbach Books, 1964.

———. *More Classic Trains.* Milwaukee: Kalmbach Books, 1974.

Johnston, Bob. "Showdown for Amtrak." *Trains* (January 1995): 40.

Ritchie, Donald A. *Doing Oral History.* New York: Twayne Publishers, 1995.

Roberts, Myron. "The Day the Big Bear Came to Town." *Los Angeles* (October 1981): 199.

Ryan, Dennis and Joseph Shine. *Southern Pacific Passenger Trains*, vol. 1, *Night Trains of the Coast Route.* La Mirada, Calif.: Four Ways West Publications, 1986.

Santino, Jack. *Miles of Smiles, Years of Struggle: Stories of Black Pullman Porters.* Chicago: University of Illinois Press, 1991.

Wayner, Robert J. *The Pullman Scrapbook.* New York: Wayner Publications, 1971.

———. *Car Names, Numbers and Consists.* New York: Wayner Publications, 1972.

White, John H. *The American Railroad Passenger Car.* Baltimore: Johns Hopkins University Press, 1978.

Wright, Richard K. *Southern Pacific Daylight.* Thousand Oaks, Calif.: Wright Enterprises, 1970.

Resources

Bancroft Library, University of California at Berkeley: Extensive and valuable resource for history of events surrounding the Brotherhood of Sleeping Car Porters (BSCP) and numerous other black railway unions. Houses *The Messenger* and *The Black Worker* on microfilm, as well as BSCP Pacific Coast Division Papers (Manuscripts Division).

Chicago Historical Society: Houses BSCP papers covering 1925–69 (Manuscripts Department) and personal material on George M. Pullman.

Library of Congress, Washington, D.C.: Houses BSCP records and a collection of A. Philip Randolph papers (Manuscripts Division).

Newberry Library, Chicago: Houses Pullman Archives, including employment (porter) records, management records, company policies, and various issues of the *Pullman News* (the company magazine).

A. Philip Randolph Institute, New York City: Extensive collection of Randolph's personal files.

Schomburg Center, New York Public Library: Contains photographic resources on black labor, including the Pullman porters, and bound volumes and microfilm of *The Messenger*, which, with *The Black Worker*, are perhaps the best sources for firsthand accounts of the history of the Brotherhood of Sleeping Car Porters and other black unions emerging at that time.

Index

The Author

David D. Perata is a freelance writer and photographer who worked for Amtrak as a train attendant for three years in the early 1980s. His articles and photos have appeared in a variety of regional and national publications and his photographic work has been used in political and industrial advertising. Prior to his writing career, he studied music and songwriting at UCLA and photography at Sierra College in northern California.